Microsoft®
PUBLISHER 2002
BASICS

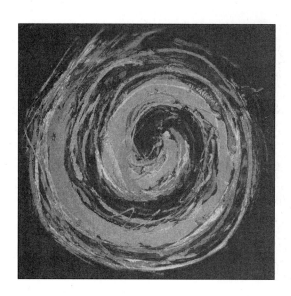

Mary Alice Eisch and
Kathleen Krueger

THOMSON

COURSE TECHNOLOGY™

Australia • Canada • Mexico • Singapore • Spain • United Kingdom • United States

THOMSON
COURSE TECHNOLOGY

Microsoft® Publisher 2002 BASICS
by Mary Alice Eisch and Kathleen Krueger

Senior Vice President, School SMG
Chris Elkhill

Managing Editor
Chris Katsaropoulos

Senior Product Manager
Dave Lafferty

Product Manager
Robert Gaggin

Product Marketing Manager
Kim Ryttel

Associate Product Manager
Jodi Dreissig

Development Editor
David George

Director of Production
Patty Stephan

Print Buyer
Laura Burns

Production Editor
Custom Editorial Productions Inc.

Compositor
GEX Publishing Services

Disclaimer
Course Technology reserves the right to revise this publication and make changes from time to time in its content without notice.

ISBN 0-619-05559-6

Get Back to the Basics...
With these *exciting new products*

This new edition from our BASICS series provides a step-by-step introduction to Microsoft's popular desktop publishing software, Publisher 2002.

Other books include:

NEW! Internet BASICS by Barksdale, Rutter, & Teeter
35+ hours of instruction for beginning through intermediate features

0-619-05905-2	Textbook, Soft Spiral Bound Cover
0-619-05906-0	Instructor Resource Kit
0-619-05907-9	Review Pack (Data CD)

NEW! Microsoft OfficeXP BASICS by Morrison
35+ hours of instruction for beginning through intermediate features

0-619-05908-7	Textbook, Hard Spiral Bound Cover
0-619-05906-0	Instructor Resource Kit
0-619-05909-5	Activities Workbook
0-619-05911-7	Review Pack (Data CD)

NEW! Microsoft Office 2001 Macintosh BASICS by Melton & Walls
35+ hours of instruction for beginning through intermediate features

0-619-05912-5	Textbook, Hard Spiral Bound Cover
0-619-05914-1	Instructor Resource Kit
0-619-05913-3	Workbook
0-619-05915-X	Review Pack (Data CD)

Microsoft Works 2000 BASICS by Pasewark & Pasewark
35+ hours of instruction for beginning through intermediate features

0-538-72340-8	Text, Hard Spiral Bound Cover
0-538-72411-0	Text, Perfect Bound, packaged with Data CD-ROM
0-538-72342-4	Activities Workbook
0-538-72341-6	Electronic Instructor's Manual Package
0-538-72343-2	Testing CD Package

Computer Concepts BASICS by Pusins and Ambrose
35+ hours of instruction for beginning through intermediate features

0-538-69501-3	Text, Hard Spiral Bound
0-538-69502-1	Activities Workbook
0-538-69503-X	Electronic Instructor's Manual Package
0-538-69504-8	Testing CD Package

How to Use This Book

What makes a good computer instructional text? Sound pedagogy and the most current, complete materials. Not only will you find an inviting layout, but also many features to enhance learning.

Objectives— Objectives are listed at the beginning of each lesson, along with a suggested time for completion of the lesson. This allows you to look ahead to what you will be learning and to pace your work.

Step-by-Step Exercises—Preceded by a short topic discussion, these exercises are the "hands-on practice" part of the lesson. Simply follow the steps, either using a data file or creating a file from scratch. Each lesson is a series of these step-by-step exercises.

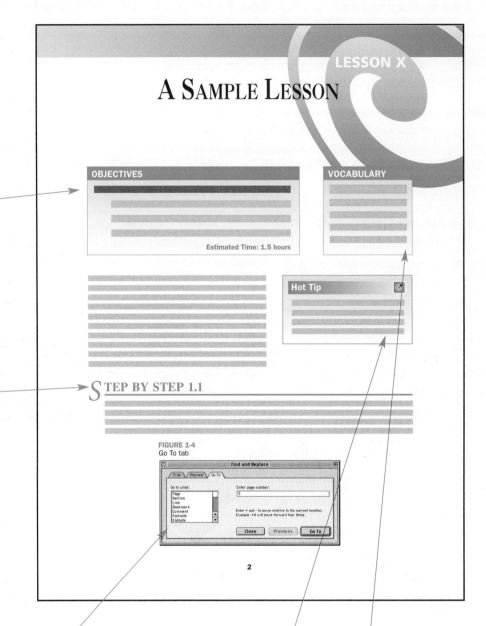

LESSON X

A SAMPLE LESSON

OBJECTIVES

Estimated Time: 1.5 hours

VOCABULARY

Hot Tip

STEP BY STEP 1.1

FIGURE 1-4
Go To tab

Find and Replace

Find / Replace / Go To

Go to what:
Page
Section
Line
Bookmark
Comment
Footnote
Endnote

Enter page number:
5

Enter + and – to move relative to the current location.
Example: +4 will move forward four items.

Close   Previous   Go To

2

Enhanced Screen Shots—Screen shots now come to life on the pages with color and depth.

Marginal Boxes— These boxes provide additional information about the topic of the lesson.

Vocabulary—Terms identified in boldface and italic throughout the lesson and summarized at the end.

How to Use This Book

Summary—At the end of each lesson, you will find a summary to prepare you to complete the end-of-lesson activities.

Vocabulary/Review Questions—Review material at the end of each lesson enables you to prepare for assessment of the content presented.

Lesson Projects—End-of-lesson hands-on application of what has been learned in the lesson allows you to actually apply the techniques covered.

Critical Thinking Activities—Each lesson gives you an opportunity to apply creative analysis and use the Help system to solve problems.

Appendices—Appendices will vary, but focus on topics such as certification, concepts, operating systems, and other additional information.

Lesson X   **1**

SUMMARY

VOCABULARY *Review*

REVIEW *Questions*

PROJECTS

CRITICAL *Thinking*

PREFACE

Congratulations on choosing to learn how to create publications using Microsoft Publisher 2002. *Microsoft Publisher 2002 BASICS* is designed to be a self-teaching guide. While the text may be used in the classroom, it is also a good resource for office or home computing.

Organization of the Text

Take a few minutes to page through this text. Begin by looking at the materials at the front of the text. In addition to this Preface and the Table of Contents, you should find a section telling you how to use this book, a list of features new to Publisher 2002, and a Start-Up Checklist that lists the hardware requirements necessary to run Publisher.

Take a look at the lessons. The nine lessons are product-based—each introducing a different type of publication. Useful information is provided about the use and design of each type of publication as well as an introduction to the Publisher tools you'll need to prepare that publication. Step-by-step exercises take you through sample publications, with hands-on projects at the end of the lesson to reinforce the skills acquired. The end-of-lesson material also includes review questions and a critical thinking activity.

At the back of the text are the following appendices:

■ Appendix A provides information about preparing a publication with spot and/or process color and preparing a publication for duplication at a printing service.

■ Appendix B provides a comprehensive list of keyboard shortcuts to help you use Publisher 2002.

It is important to proceed through the lessons in order, reading the information provided in the paragraphs carefully. The step-by-step exercises that provide practice in the use of the tools are printed in a different font face and have numbered steps leading through the use of the feature. It is helpful to read completely through an exercise before beginning it to get a general idea of the purpose of the exercise and then work through the steps methodically.

A tenth lesson has been provided on the CD-ROM accompanying this book. This lesson uses a scenario about Parker Animal Clinic and allows you to further practice what you have learned.

A suggested time for completion is provided at the beginning of each lesson. The actual completion time may vary depending on your previous experience with computers and Windows, your previous experience with Publisher, and the learning setting—an independent or instructor-led classroom.

Other Resources

A set of prerecorded documents saves keying time in the exercises. These documents are referred to as the "data files." These files are available on the accompanying CD-ROM. With your instructor, determine the location to store the prerecorded files before beginning the lessons.

Another CD-ROM accompanying this book provides support for the instructor. It contains a variety of instructional materials including the following:

- Lesson plans for the instructor
- Learner lesson plans
- Progress record (for keeping track of work submitted by the student)
- Hands-on exams
- Prerecorded data files
- Lesson figure files that may be made into transparencies
- PowerPoint presentations
- Scheduling charts
- SCANS materials

The Scenario

Welcome to Otter Creek! Otter Creek is the name of a fictitious city in Wisconsin. The publications that you will create in the nine lessons of this book will be for various governmental and non-profit organizations within this city. In Lesson 10, provided on the CD-ROM, you will be employed by Parker Animal Clinic of Otter Creek. We hope you enjoy your employment and the variety of publications you will be creating as you work through the lessons.

Acknowledgments

We wish to thank our families for their love and support as we have worked on this project. Thanks also to our learners who continue to teach us and challenge us. We are also grateful for our opportunity to teach at the Appleton and Oshkosh campuses of Fox Valley Technical College, which is one of the sixteen colleges that make up the greatest technical college system in the country. That's where our true learning takes place.

Kathleen Krueger
Winneconne, Wisconsin

Mary Alice Eisch
Larsen, Wisconsin

WHAT'S NEW

Microsoft Publisher 2002 includes the following new features:

- Multiple Publisher documents can be opened at one time.

- An Ask a Question text box appears in the upper right corner of the Publisher screen for keying a question regarding how to use Publisher.

- Smart Tags appear in a document where there are options relating to pasting from the Clipboard and AutoCorrect.

- Various task panes appear on the left side of the screen listing features that are relevant to the task you are performing. Some of the Task Panes are listed below.

  - New Publications Task Pane—This task pane combines the Publisher Catalog and the wizard tool in one task pane rather than three separate tabs.

  - Clipboard—Up to 24 objects can be stored in the Clipboard, and the related task pane shows a picture of each object for easy insertion.

  - Search task pane—Search for text within a document as well as other files on your computer.

  - Publication options, designs, color schemes, and font schemes are all listed in one task pane. Font schemes are new and are based on built-in styles.

  - Styles and Formatting Task Pane—See what the styles look like in an easy-access list.

  - Mail Merge Task Pane—Use the easy four-step wizard from this task pane to create mail merge documents.

  - Insert Clip Art Task Pane—Insert clip art from the task pane and search for clip art related to a specific topic.

- The Language bar that is part of the Office suite allows users to dictate text and commands into Publisher as well as upload handwritten notes created on handheld devices.

- The same OfficeArt tools that are available in the other Office programs are now available in Publisher, which includes additional AutoShapes and other drawing elements.

- A header/footer feature is now available that looks much like the same feature in Word.

- Print Preview is now available.

- Toolbars can be customized.

- AutoRecovery is now available. Depending on how the option is set up under Tools and Save, a file will be saved automatically on a regular basis when the file is open.

- The Thesaurus tool for checking synonyms and antonyms is available.

- Publisher files can be sent through the Send as E-mail command.

- A Picture toolbar is available to adjust an inserted picture.

- Save As Picture is a great tool for saving objects or groups of objects created in Publisher as graphic files.

- The Word Import Wizard allows the user to open a Word file in Publisher with automatic formatting.

- Horizontal rules can be added above or below paragraphs.

- Just like the *big boys* in the publishing software currently available, Publisher will now prompt you when you open a file that contains a font that is not on your computer nor embedded in the publication. Publisher will substitute a similar font and give you the option of choosing a different font.

- New features relating to Web design include the ability to save, open, and edit HTML files within Publisher, insert a hyperlink in a Publisher file, use VBA tools, choose a certain level of Web browser when creating a Web site in Publisher, and save Publisher files to a team Web site.

Start-Up Checklist

HARDWARE

✓ Processor
  ✓ Pentium III or higher
✓ Speed
  ✓ 133 MHz or higher
✓ Memory (RAM)
  ✓ 8 MB available for Publisher 2002
✓ Hard Disk Space
  ✓ 180 MB available free disk space for Publisher, plus 100 MB for Microsoft Office XP Media Content CD
✓ Display
  ✓ Super VGA (800x600) or higher resolution with 256 colors

✓ Input Devices
  ✓ Mouse (required), scanner, digital camera, microphone (all optional)
✓ CD-ROM drive

SOFTWARE

✓ Microsoft Publisher 2002
✓ Operating System
  ✓ Windows 98, Windows 98 Second Edition, Windows Millennium Edition (Windows ME), Windows NT 4.0 with Service Pack 6 (SP6) or later, Windows 2000, or Windows XP or later

TABLE OF CONTENTS

ADVERTISEMENTS

What Is an Advertisement?

An *advertisement* (ad) is a message designed to promote a product, service, event, or idea. It should be simple and to the point, and it should spark your interest with a catchy phrase or logo.

Design Considerations for Advertisements

There are many design considerations when creating an advertisement. Following are some things that must be taken into account when the ad is being designed:

■ Size—The ad size will depend on the publication in which it will appear. It may be in a newsletter, magazine, or newspaper. Although ads are designed somewhat differently for the three types of publications, you need to find out the requirements for the ad size because it will have to fit into a predetermined layout. Some ads cover a full page, while others cover one-half page, one-quarter page, or less. Small ads have to stand out because they must compete with all the other information on a page.

■ Headlines—Avoid all capital letters (all caps). All caps are hard to read because of the uniform height of the letters.

■ Font Design—Use no more than two typefaces in a publication. (You'll learn about font design, or typefaces, later in this lesson.)

■ Placement of Objects—Place the most important objects in the upper third of the ad. People will not spend a lot of time reading an ad and may never get to the bottom portion.

■ Business Name—Make sure the business name is big and bold. Avoid all caps.

■ White Space—Make sure the objects are not too crowded within an ad and that there is empty or "white" space surrounding objects.

■ Cost—Make sure you find out the cost of the ad you wish to run so you keep within your budget.

The Lesson Project

In this lesson you will be creating an advertisement to be placed in a newsletter for the Otter Creek Seniors Center. The ad will inform senior citizens of their bus riding privileges. The completed publication will look much like Figure 1-1.

FIGURE 1-1
Completed Lesson 1 Project

What Is Microsoft Publisher?

Microsoft Publisher is a page layout or desktop publishing program. By definition, ***desktop publishing*** is a system or set of tools used to combine text and/or graphics into a full-page layout. All businesses publish documents of various types and sizes.

You will find this software to be very user friendly while providing you with all the necessary tools to create publications ranging from simple to complex. All publications are made up of objects, such as text or graphics. In Publisher, all objects are inside frames. These frames can be moved around on the page and they can be resized.

Starting a New Publication

When you start Microsoft Publisher, the window will be divided into two panes. The left pane is the *task pane*. The task pane offers three choices: create a publication from a design (*Start from a design*), create a blank publication (*New*), or open an existing publication (*Open a publication*).

■ **Start from a design.** The drop-down list offers three choices—Publication Type, Design Sets, and Blank publications. When a choice is made from the list, the right pane of the window shows the Publication Gallery for that choice. Depending on what choice is made, the Publication Gallery may offer more than 100 templates from which to choose.

■ **New.** Here you may choose to create a new publication using a blank document, a new publication based on an existing publication, or from a personalized template created by you or someone else.

■ **Open a publication.** This section lists the last three publications on which you worked. In addition, an Open button allows you to access other existing files.

> **Computer Concepts**
>
> The options in your Microsoft Publisher program may be set to automatically start a new blank publication. If so, you would not see the New Publication windows as shown in Figure 1-2.

S TEP-BY-STEP 1.1

1. With the Windows desktop showing on your screen, click the **Start** button on the Taskbar.

2. Click **Programs** (**All Programs** in Windows XP) and choose **Microsoft Publisher.**

3. If the New Publication window illustrated in Figure 1-2 appears, click **Blank Publication** under the **New** section of the task pane.

4. Keep the file open for the next exercise.

FIGURE 1-2
New Publication Window

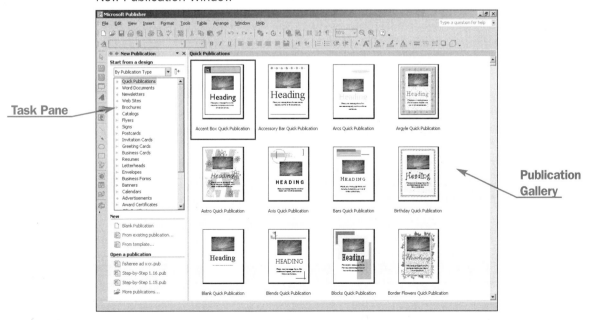

The Microsoft Publisher Window

If you have not seen Microsoft Publisher before, you may be surprised to see all of the toolbars and rulers. It is a busy window! Following are descriptions of the various items in the Publisher window. These items are shown in Figure 1-3.

FIGURE 1-3
Microsoft Publisher Window

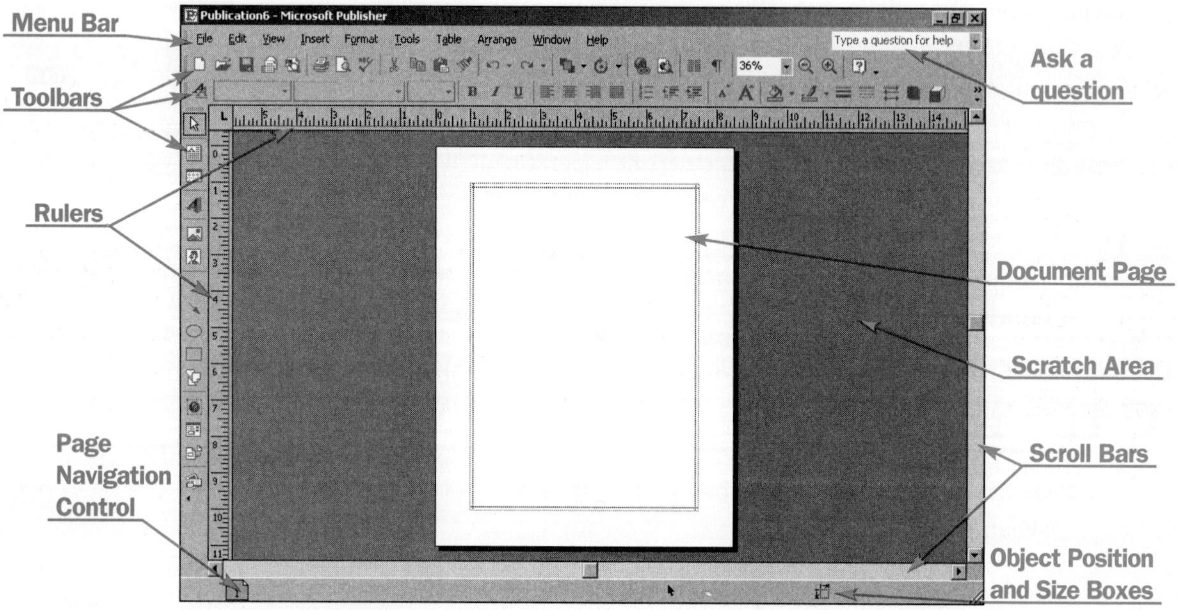

Menu Bar

At the top of the window below the title bar is the menu bar. These menu items open drop-down menus that list all the commands available in Publisher.

Toolbars

Below the menu bar are various toolbars. The toolbars that are active will be determined by what object you are working on in your window. Toolbars offer shortcuts to tools that are in the menus on the menu bar.

Rulers

You should see two rulers. One is a vertical ruler that runs along the left edge of the window and the other is the horizontal ruler that shows below the toolbars. These rulers are very useful when placing and sizing objects.

Document Page

The document is represented by the picture of an 8½ x 11-inch page in the middle of the window. Inside the document page are light pink and blue dotted lines for the margins and the columns.

Scratch Area

A gray area that is referred to as the Scratch Area surrounds the document page. Objects waiting to be placed in the publication can be placed temporarily in the Scratch Area.

Scroll Bars

Along the bottom and the right side of the window are the scroll bars that are used to move the document left and right as well as up and down in the window. When you are working in a close-up of your document, you may need to scroll horizontally to see the beginning of a line or vertically to see the top of a page.

Ask a Question

In the window's upper-right you will see an **Ask a Question** box on the menu bar. You can key questions in this box to quickly find help with the software.

Page Navigation Control

In the window's lower-left is a Page Navigation control showing you how many pages are in the publication and what page is currently showing in the window.

Object Position and Size Boxes

At the bottom of the window and toward the right are the Object Position and Object Size Boxes. The Object Position box gives the location of a selected object in relationship to the zero marks on the horizontal and vertical rulers. The position is determined using the coordinates of the object's upper-left corner. If no object is selected, only the X and Y coordinates of the mouse pointer will be shown. In the Object Size box, the first measurement is the width and the second is the height. You will become quite familiar with these features as you use the program.

STEP-BY-STEP 1.2

1. Move your mouse so the pointer moves around on the window. Notice the hairline markers that appear on the vertical and horizontal rulers to identify your exact location on the page. Also notice how the values in the object position box change.

2. Carefully position the tip of your pointer in the upper-left corner of the document area. Notice that the hairline markers on both rulers will be at zero.

3. Note that the gray box on the vertical scroll bar is about halfway between the top and the bottom. Drag it all the way to the bottom of the scroll bar.

4. Now drag it all the way to the top. Your document will move down. Finally, position it at the center again and try moving the horizontal scroll bar at the bottom of the window.

5. Finish by centering the page in your window. Keep the document open.

Viewing the Task Pane

When you choose New Blank Document, the Task Pane disappears. You can redisplay the Task Pane by opening the View menu and choosing Task Pane. The Task Pane offers some options: changing the type of publication if the new publication task pane is showing, or choosing a different task completely. In Figure 1-3, no Task Pane is showing. This allows more space for the document pane. Figure 1-4 shows the Publisher window with the Task Pane showing. The current task appears in the title bar of the Task Pane. You can change the task by clicking the triangle for the drop-down list. You can hide the Task Pane by clicking the small X in the upper-right corner of the Task Pane.

FIGURE 1-4
Publisher Window with Task Pane

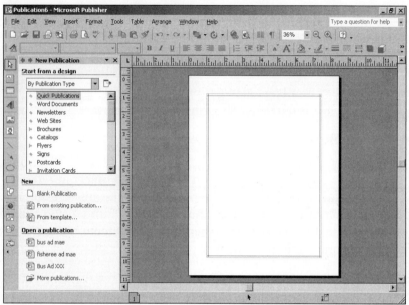

STEP-BY-STEP 1.3

1. Click the **View** menu and choose **Task Pane**.

2. Click the triangle on the **New** Publication bar for the drop-down list and look at the choices.

3. Choose **Quick Publication Options** and look at the styles.

4. Close the Task Pane by clicking the **X** in the upper-right corner of the Task Pane.

Viewing the Page

Publisher provides different levels of magnification of the page currently being displayed. The levels range from full page, where the entire outline of the page shows but the objects are small, to 400 percent, where very little of the page shows, and the print is four times as big as it will be when the document is printed.

The advantage of all of these choices is that it allows you to zoom in on a detail for close work or to back out to the full page to see the overall layout of the element. You can change magnification in three places:

■   View menu, Zoom submenu

- Zoom box (see Figure 1-5)
- Any part of the document page by right-clicking and choosing Zoom

FIGURE 1-5
Zoom Box

STEP-BY-STEP 1.4

1. Click the drop-down arrow beside the Zoom box (see Figure 1-5) to see the list. Try several of the sizes and watch as your page size changes.

2. Use the **+** and **–** buttons to the right of the Zoom box (see Figure 1-5) to change the view. Then return to the **Whole Page** option.

3. Right-click on any part of the document page and point to **Zoom** to display a submenu of magnification choices. Choose **100%**. (The Selected Objects choice is not available because you did not click on an object.)

4. You can toggle between views with the **F9** key. Change the magnification to 50% and press **F9** again. It should change to 100%. Press **F9** again. It should change back to 50%.

5. Keep the file open for the next exercise.

> **Note**
>
> Publisher has dozens of keyboard commands like F9 in Step 4. Most of these commands are listed in Appendix B. Check this list frequently to see how you can work more efficiently.

Page Layout

Before objects are added to a publication, changes may need to be made to the layout of the document. The default setting for a publication is 8½ x 11 inches in portrait orientation (short edge at the top). If a different size paper is needed or if landscape orientation (long edge at the top) is required, these changes can be made in the Page Setup dialog box, which can be accessed from the File menu.

The Page Setup dialog box contains two pages.

■ In the Layout page you can choose Orientation. In addition, you can choose a different publication layout from a list of typical publications. You can also set your own size with the Custom choice. In this publication, you will create a custom size (see Figure 1-6).

■ The Printer & Paper page contains printer and orientation choices. If you have more than one printer from which to choose, click the drop-down list to the right of Name and choose a printer. For example, you may want to print a draft on a laser printer and a final copy on a color ink jet printer. The choice between portrait and landscape can also be made on this page along with the paper size and location of the paper in your printer.

FIGURE 1-6
Page Setup Dialog Box

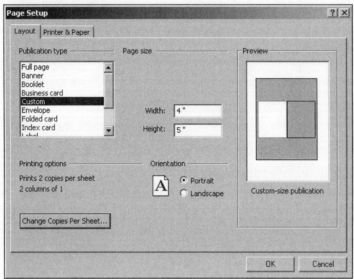

STEP-BY-STEP 1.5

1. Open the **File** menu and choose **Page Setup**.

2. In the **Layout** page, click **Custom** under the Publication type.

3. Drag across the 8.5 in the Width box to select it and key **4**.

4. Make sure **Portrait** is selected under Orientation. Click **OK**.

Layout Guides

The light pink and blue lines that show on the document page are called *layout guides*. Layout guides do not print, but they play an important role in the design of the document. They provide a visual "reference" for the margins of the document. Pink layout guides show the margins for your document.

In later lessons you will work with columns. Blue layout guides show column and row margins. All three kinds of layout guides (margins, columns, and rows) help you with the placement of the elements in the publication—text as well as graphics.

Setting Layout Guides

You can change the location of the layout guides when you change the page margins or when you set up columns and rows within those margins. Page margins include top, bottom, left, and right margins. The left and right margins may be used for inside and outside margins for facing pages.

The number of columns you'll use depends on the type of publication you're preparing. Columns are used in many publications because a shorter line length is easier to read. Rows are used in publications that must be divided horizontally into equal parts. Examples of documents with rows include labels, catalogs, and price lists. Margins, columns, and rows do not restrict how text flows or where your graphics may be placed on the page. The guides only act as a reference for the white space that surrounds each page and the division of each page into columns and/or rows.

Let's practice setting page margins. You will be working with the Layout Guides dialog box (Figure 1-7) in this Step-by-Step exercise. Whenever you are working in a dialog box and press Enter, the dialog box is closed. If you have several changes to make in a dialog box, move from text box to text box (the places where you key the information) with the Tab key or use the mouse to click the insertion point into the desired text box for the change. Press **Shift+Tab** to move to the previous box. If you accidentally press Enter, you can reopen the dialog box to make the remaining changes.

FIGURE 1-7
Layout Guides Dialog Box

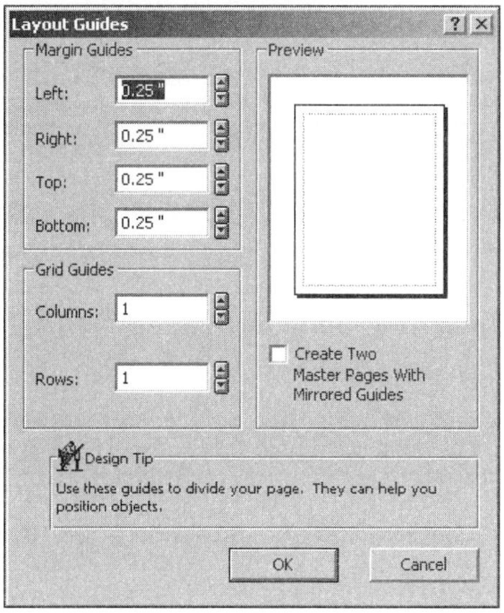

STEP-BY-STEP 1.6

1. Open the **Arrange** menu and choose **Layout Guides**.

2. Key the value **0.25** and press **Tab**. Notice the left margin in the dialog box preview window reflects the change you made.

3. Change each of the other three margins to **0.25** and watch the preview window change.

4. Leave the Columns and Rows at **1** each. Click **OK**. Keep the file open.

Layout Guide Options

Snap to Guides

You can use the layout guides to line up objects exactly. This is done by turning on an option called *To Guides* from the Snap choice in the Arrange menu.

While the Snap To Guides feature is useful for views of all sizes, it is especially valuable when you are working in Full Page view because the layout guides become "sticky." The mouse pointer catches slightly when it passes over a sticky guide. The pointer will also tend to jump to the next guide as it is being moved across the window.

When the To Guides option has been chosen, a check mark ($\checkmark$) will appear at the left of the option, as illustrated in Figure 1-8. To turn the option off, you must again choose it from the Arrange menu.

FIGURE 1-8
Arrange Menu/Snap Submenu

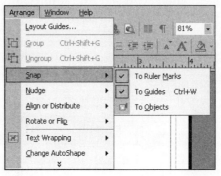

Hide Layout Guides

You can hide the layout guides to make more display area available on the document page. The option to show or hide Boundaries and Guides is found in the View menu.

S TEP-BY-STEP 1.7

1. Open the **Arrange** menu and point to **Snap**. The menu should look like Figure 1-8.

2. Click on **To Guides**. This will turn off the guides.

3. Open the **Arrange** menu again and point to **Snap**. Notice the check mark ($\checkmark$) is not there. Click **To Guides** to turn it back on.

4. Open the **View** menu and choose **Boundaries and Guides**. The menu will disappear, and you will see your document page without the margin guides.

5. Return to the **View** menu. Notice that now the check mark is missing at the left of Boundaries and Guides. Click **Boundaries and Guides** to display your layout guides.

6. Keep the file open for the next exercise.

Creating an Object

To create an object on the document page, you must first create a frame for the object. A *frame* is a container for an object. You must choose a tool from the Objects Toolbar (Figure 1-9) to create a frame. We'll begin at the top of the toolbar and discuss each button.

FIGURE 1-9
Objects Toolbar

Objects Toolbar

The Objects toolbar illustrated in Figure 1-9 is the row of buttons at the left of the window. Each tool performs a specific action. Notice that the tools appear to be grouped.

- **Select Objects**—The first tool on the top is known as the Selection tool. That button should be enclosed in a blue box because the pointer is chosen by default. When you choose one of the other buttons, the tool you choose will be enclosed in a box.

- **Text Box**—The second tool bears the text box frame icon. This tool is used to create a frame into which you'll place text.

- **Insert Table**—The Insert Table tool is used to create a table consisting of rows and columns into which text can be entered. You can plan a table and perform your own formatting or you can choose from more than 20 preformatted tables.

- **Insert WordArt**—The Insert WordArt tool is used to draw a frame into which you can place fancy text of some kind such as a title.

- **Picture Frame**—The Picture Frame tool is used to draw picture frames into which you can import a picture or some kind of graphic.

- **Clip Organizer Frame**—This tool is used to insert images from the Publisher Clip Gallery.

- **Line**—The Line tool is used for adding rules (lines) to your document. Those lines can be any length or any width and can be vertical, horizontal, or at an angle.

- **Arrow**—The Arrow tool is used for adding arrows that typically point to another object in the publication.

- **Oval**—The Oval tool is used to draw ovals or circles.

- **Rectangle**—The Rectangle tool is used to draw rectangles or squares.

- **AutoShapes**—The AutoShapes tool is used to create a variety of other geometric shapes.

- **Hot Spot**—The Hot Spot tool is used for creating hyperlinks on a Web page.

- **Form Control**—The Form Control button is used for boxes and buttons when asking for information from a Web site visitor.

- **HTML Code Fragment**—This button enables you to enter HTML Code when designing a Web page.

- **Design Gallery Object**—This tool is used to enter Publisher-designed objects such as banners, or coupons, and also to pull quotes into your publications.

Using the Text Box Tool

If you use word processing software, you generally just start keying on the page where you want the text to appear. This procedure is possible in some desktop publishing programs as well. In Microsoft Publisher, however, you must first create a frame into which the text will either be keyed or imported from a text file.

It is simple to create a text box. Begin by clicking the Text Box tool. Your pointer becomes a *crosshair* instead of an arrow. Position the mouse pointer in the document page at one of the corners where you want your text box frame to begin (usually the upper-left corner). Depress the left mouse button and drag the crosshair pointer (usually toward the lower-right corner) until your frame is approximately the size you'd like it to be. At that point, release the mouse button. When your frame has been created, it will have white circles on all sides and corners. These circles are called *handles* and are used for resizing the frame. If you don't like the size of the frame or the current position of the frame, you will be able to resize it and move it. You will learn that later.

There is also a green circle that is attached to the top of the frame by a line. This is a tool that may be used to rotate a frame.

S TEP-BY-STEP 1.8

1. Click the **Text Box** tool on the Objects Toolbar, then move the pointer so that it is somewhere on the canvas. Look at the pointer. Its new shape is called a crosshair.

STEP-BY-STEP 1.8 Continued

2. Point with the mouse pointer at the upper-left corner of the layout guide (pink line) and depress the left mouse button. Drag to create a frame that measures about **3.5** inches wide and **3.0** inches high. (Watch the Object Size Box in the lower-right corner for the measurements as you draw the box.) Release the mouse button when you are done. The frame should look somewhat like the one in Figure 1-10.

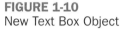

FIGURE 1-10
New Text Box Object

3. Look at the sizing handles surrounding the frame. Find the green rotate tool. Keep the publication open as you read on.

Sizing and moving a Text Box

Drag one of the handles of an object to make the object smaller or larger. To use this method of sizing an object, make the object active by pointing to it with the mouse pointer and clicking once. Then move your pointer over one of the handles until you see a double-headed arrow labeled Resize. When the arrow appears, hold down your left mouse pointer and drag. Watch the Object Size Box in the lower-left corner of the window as you adjust the size. The first value is width and the second value is height.

You can use the Measurements toolbar to take the guessing out of sizing. Simply key in the width and height or use the spinner buttons to the right of the width and height text boxes to increase or decrease the size. The Measurement toolbar can be chosen from the Toolbars choice in the View menu. You can move it around in the window by pointing to the bar at the top and dragging it to the desired position. The Measurement toolbar looks like Figure 1-11. The Measurement toolbar can also be used to format text in a text box frame. This will be covered in Lesson 2.

FIGURE 1-11
Measurement Toolbar

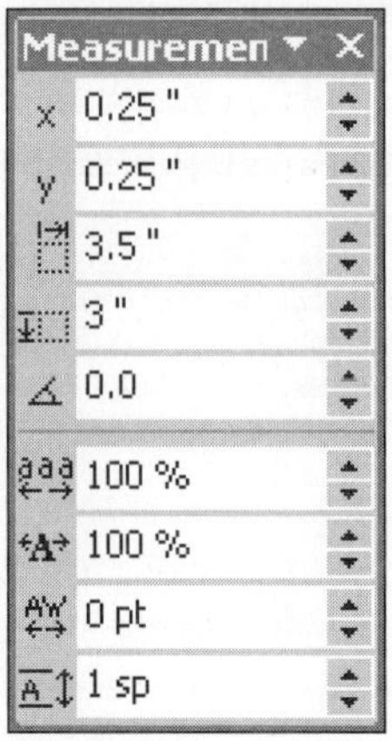

Measuremen ▼ ✕		
x	0.25 "	▲ ▼
y	0.25 "	▲ ▼
⟶	3.5 "	▲ ▼
⬇	3 "	▲ ▼
∠	0.0	▲ ▼
⟷	100 %	▲ ▼
←A→	100 %	▲ ▼
AW	0 pt	▲ ▼
A↕	1 sp	▲ ▼

Moving an object can also be done in two different ways. You can drag the object around the page using the Move icon (looks like a little truck) and release the mouse button when the object is in the desired position. You can use the Object Position Box in the lower-right corner of the window if you have a specific position in mind. The x value is horizontal and the y value is vertical. These positions are measured from the upper-left corner of the document where the horizontal and vertical rulers begin at zero. The Measurement toolbar can also be used to specify a position by keying a value in the x and y boxes.

STEP-BY-STEP 1.9

1. Click the Text Box frame you created in the previous exercise, if necessary, to select it.

2. Point to the handle in the lower-right corner. When you see a Resize icon, hold down your left mouse button and drag toward the lower-right corner of the document page.

3. Release the mouse button when you see the Object Size Box show approximately **3.5** inches x **4.5** inches. This takes lots of practice, so don't be concerned if it is not exact.

4. From the **View** menu, choose **Toolbars** and then **Measurement** to display the toolbar.

5. Key **3.5** in the width box and **3** in the height box as shown in Figure 1-11. Keep your document displayed as you read on.

Keying Text

Adding text to a text box frame is easy. When the text box is active (it has handles around it), you should see an insertion point blinking in the frame. This is where the letters will appear as you key them. You will probably want to increase the magnification of the screen so you can read the letters you are keying.

When you reach the right side of the frame as you are keying text, you should let the text wrap around to the next line unless you want to start a new paragraph. Press Enter once or twice to start a new paragraph.

In the next Step-by-Step, you are going to key only part of what will be the final text (see Figure 1-12). The rest will be in a separate text box frame.

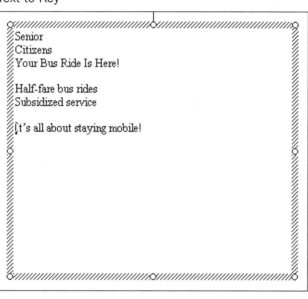

FIGURE 1-12
Text to Key

STEP-BY-STEP 1.10

1. Activate the text box frame by clicking in it.

2. Increase the magnification by pressing **F9** or using **Zoom** so you can see the text you are keying.

3. Key the text in Figure 1-12. (If you make any keying errors, you will learn how to correct them soon.) Keep the publication open as you read on.

Editing and Formatting Text

Here are some techniques for editing text:

■ If you catch yourself making an error as you are keying text, use your Backspace key to delete the characters to the left of the cursor.

■ Use your Delete key to delete characters to the right of the cursor.

■ If you see a word(s) underlined in red, point to the word(s) with the mouse pointer and right-click to see what spelling suggestions are available for the underlined word(s). If you see the correct spelling in the list, click to insert it.

■ If you see a word(s) underlined in green, point to the word(s) with the mouse pointer and right-click to read the suggested grammar correction. If you like the suggestion, click to insert it.

■ To insert a word, click to position the insertion point where you want to add the word. Then key the new word.

■ To delete a word, double-click it to select it and press Delete.

STEP-BY-STEP 1.11

1. Check for any words underlined in red. Right-click the words and select the correctly spelled words.

2. Check for any words underlined in green. Right-click the words and select the grammatically correct words.

3. Delete the word **Bus** in the third line.

4. Add the word **taxi** in the second-to-last line after the word **Subsidized**. Keep the publication open as you read on.

When you create a text box, the Formatting toolbar becomes active. Note that your Formatting toolbar may appear in a single line across the top of the window. You may choose some formats before you begin keying. If the text is already keyed, you must select the text that is to be formatted and select the desired formatting (see Figure 1-13).

FIGURE 1-13
Formatting Toolbar

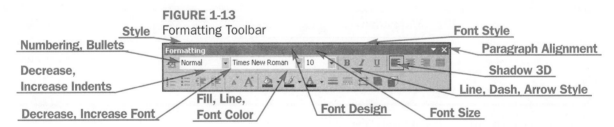

Four types of text formatting will be used in this lesson. They are font design, font size, font style (bold, italics, and underline), and paragraph alignment.

■ Font Design—The design of the type refers to the typeface. Examples of typeface are Times New Roman and Arial. If a font has feet on the letters, it is referred to as a *serif* font and looks like what you are currently reading. Times New Roman is an example of a serif font. Serif fonts are good for body text such as paragraphs. If a font has no feet, it is referred to as a *sans serif* font and looks like the steps in the Step-by-Step exercises. Arial is an example of a sans serif font. Sans serif fonts are best used for display text such as titles and headings. Font design can make a difference in the *tone* of the publication. One font design may be best for a conservative publication and another may be best for a more creative publication. Choose a font that helps convey the message.

■ Font Size—Fonts are measured in points. One point equals approximately 1/72 of a vertical inch. So 72-point text would be one inch tall. Type is measured in points ranging from 6 points (6 pt.) on the small end to several hundred points on the large end. Font size for paragraphs is generally 10 or 12 points. Titles typically have a larger font size than the paragraph font size so that they stand out.

■ Font Style—Font Style is a variation within a font design such as bold, italics, and underline. Italics and bold work well for making words stand out. Underline is rarely used.

■ Paragraph Alignment—Alignment refers to the left and right sides of a paragraph. Typically, paragraphs are formatted with left alignment and titles are formatted with center alignment.

   ■ Left—ragged right, even left

   ■ Center—ragged left and right

   ■ Right—ragged left, even right

   ■ Justify—even left and right

STEP-BY-STEP 1.12

1. Select the text box frame you edited in the previous Step-by-Step. Use the tools on the Formatting toolbar to format the text as directed in the next steps.

2. Select the first three lines and format them as follows: Impact, 26 pt. bold, and center alignment.

3. Select the next two lines and format them as follows: Arial, 16 pt. bold, and center alignment.

4. With the same two lines selected, click the Bullets button. (Your bullets may not be the same size as those in Figure 1-14.)

FIGURE 1-14
Formatted Text

STEP-BY-STEP 1.12 Continued

5. Select the slogan and format it as follows: Arial, 20 pt. italics, and center alignment.

6. Grab the sizing handle at the bottom of the text box frame and drag it up a little below the text in the frame. (If you go so far that you lose some text, readjust it.)

7. Keep the publication open as you read on.

Saving a File

When working with Microsoft Publisher, you should save your work often so that nothing is lost if your computer power is interrupted. You have enough completed now to warrant saving. Check with your instructor as to where you should save your files. For these materials, it will be assumed that you are saving your work on a disk in Drive A. Although you will be told in these materials what to name each of your publications, filenames may be up to 255 characters, including spaces. You will be instructed at the end of future lessons to delete certain completed files from your floppy disk so that you will have room for your work. Do not save work from any other classes on your disk. Publisher files can be large in size depending on the objects. Graphics, WordArt, and large-sized fonts add to the size of a publication.

STEP-BY-STEP 1.13

1. Display the **File** menu and choose **Save As**.

2. Ask your instructor for the location where this file should be stored. Name the file **bus ad *xxx***, substituting your initials for *xxx*. Publisher will automatically append the extension *.pub* to your file name. (See Figure 1-15.)

FIGURE 1-15
Save As Dialog Box

STEP-BY-STEP 1.13 Continued

3. Click **Save**. Keep the publication open as you read on.

Creating Another Text Box Frame

In the next Step-by-Step you will create another text box frame using the same procedure you used in Step-by-Step 1.8. You will draw and format the frame much like you did in the earlier exercises.

STEP-BY-STEP 1.14

1. With **bus ad *xxx*** showing in the window, choose the Text Box tool on the Objects toolbar.

2. Draw a text box frame below the first text box frame that begins at **3.25** inches on the vertical ruler and at the left margin. Make it **3.5** inches wide and **1.25** inches high.

3. Key the text shown in Figure 1-16.

FIGURE 1-16
A Second Text Box Frame

4. Select and format the first line in Arial, 14 pt. bold, and center alignment.

5. Select and format the second line using Arial, 18 pt. bold, and center alignment.

6. Select and format the address and city using Arial, 10 pt., and center alignment.

7. Select and format the last line using Arial, 18 pt., bold, and center alignment. Save the publication and keep it open.

Filling a Frame With Color

A common formatting technique is adding background color to a frame to make it stand out. This is known as a *screen*. The color you choose depends on what is in the frame. If the frame contains text, the color should not be so dark that it makes the text hard to read. Often the text should be bold to make it stand out within the formatted text box frame.

Use the Fill Color button to add color to a frame. This button displays a palette of colors (see Figure 1-17). Publisher bases the available colors on the *color scheme*, which is determined when a publication is created. A color scheme contains five colors that complement each other. These colors are assigned to various text objects. The default color scheme is Bluebird. Color schemes will be covered in a later lesson.

FIGURE 1-17
Filling a Frame with Color

STEP-BY-STEP 1.15

1. With **bus ad *xxx*** showing in the window, select the new text box frame.

2. Click the arrow beside the **Fill Color** button on the Formatting toolbar.

3. Choose a gray or similar color that is not too dark.

4. Click the **Save** button on the Toolbar (the one that looks like a disk) to do an interim save of your publication.

Adding a Picture

Depending on the size of the ad, a picture may be added that will help attract attention to the ad or help clarify the message.

A picture can be added from a picture file stored on your computer system or a removable disk such as a floppy disk or a CD-ROM. It can also be added from the Microsoft Clip Organizer. In this lesson, we will add it as a picture file. It is necessary to use only those graphic formats that are compatible with Microsoft Publisher. Those formats include the following:

- Encapsulated PostScript (.eps)

- Graphics Interchange Format, CompuServe format (.gif)

- Joint Photographics Expert Group (.jpeg or .jpg)

- Microsoft PhotoDraw or PictureIt! (.mix)

- Microsoft Windows Bitmap (.bmp)

- Portable Network Graphics (.png)

- TIFF, Tagged Image File Format (.tif)

- Windows Enhanced Metafile (.emf)

- Windows Metafile (.wmf)

Other graphic formats may be added, but special graphic filters need to be installed in order for these types of files to be added. These graphic files include the following:

- CGM

- graphics (.cgm)

- CorelDRAW! (.cdr)

- FlashPix (.fpx)

- Hanako format (.jsh, .jah, and .jbh)

- Kodak Photo CD and Pro Photo CD (.pcd)

- Macintosh Picture (.pict)

- Microsoft Picture It! (.mix)

- PC Paintbrush (.pcx)

- WordPerfect Graphics (.wpg)

A picture frame can be placed by itself on a document page or it can be layered with other frames. In this lesson, you will be layering the picture frame on top of the text box frame because we need to keep the ad to a certain size. When objects are layered, it may be necessary to tell Publisher what object should be at the top and what object should be at the bottom. Since the text box frame was created first, it should not be a problem to add the picture frame on top of the text box frame.

To insert a picture, click the Picture Frame button on the Object toolbar and then draw the frame in your publication. When you do this, the Insert Picture dialog box will appear as shown in Figure 1-18.

FIGURE 1-18
Insert Picture Dialog Box

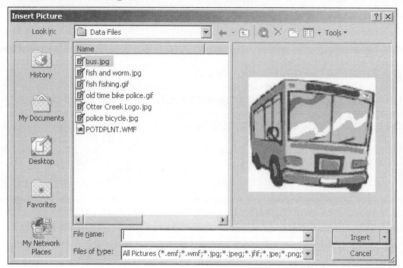

Data Files

A number of prerecorded files (both text and images) are provided for you to use as you prepare your publications in this course. One of those files is needed for the next Step-by-Step. You will need to check with your instructor to find out where the prerecorded data files are located.

S TEP-BY-STEP 1.16

1. With **bus ad *xxx*** open in the window, click **Picture Frame** on the Objects toolbar.

2. With your mouse, point to the upper-left corner where the top and left margin guides meet. Press and hold the mouse button as you drag down and to the right until the Size Box measures approximately **1.5** inches wide and **1.5** inches tall.

3. When the Insert Picture dialog box opens, locate the folder that contains the prerecorded data files and locate **bus.jpg**.

4. If you do not see a preview of the picture file, choose **Views** on the Insert Picture dialog box toolbar and change to **Preview**.

5. Double-click the bus to insert the **bus** picture, or click once to select the file and then click **Insert**. Click the **Save** button on the Standard toolbar.

Sizing and Moving a Picture Frame

With the picture frame in the ad, select it so that the handles appear. You need to make it bigger. You could use the same method you used for the text box frame, which would be to move your mouse pointer over a handle until a Resize icon appears and then hold down the left mouse button and drag in or out. This works fine when you are not too concerned with an exact size. In this case, you need to make it an exact size, so you are going to use the Format Picture dialog box (Figure 1-19) to specify a size.

FIGURE 1-19
Format Picture Dialog Box

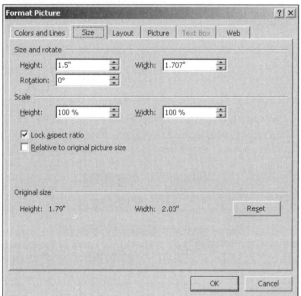

The Format Picture dialog box can be opened by right-clicking on the picture frame and choosing Format Picture or by choosing Picture from the Format menu. In the latter case, you have to make sure the picture frame is selected first. With the Format Picture dialog box open, you will choose the Size tab and key in the desired height and width.

Once a picture is inserted in a publication, the Picture toolbar tools become available.

Computer Concepts

If you do not want the picture to be sized proportionately, make sure the Lock aspect ratio option is off. The problem with turning this option off is that you risk resizing the picture disproportionately and it could change the look entirely.

Overflow

If a text box frame is not large enough to hold all the text as a result of resizing, a box with an *A* will appear in the lower-right corner of the frame. This is referred to as the Text in Overflow indicator. When there is too much text for the frame, it is stored in a special memory called the *overflow area*. It stays there even if the file is closed. When the frame is made large enough to show all the text, the Text in Overflow indicator will disappear. (Sometimes a text file has extra blank lines at the end. These blank lines are considered text and make the text file seem larger than it really is.)

STEP-BY-STEP 1.17

1. Your **bus ad** *xxx* document should still be open in the window. Right-click on the bus picture.

2. Choose **Format Picture**.

3. Choose the **Size** tab.

4. Make sure the **Lock aspect ratio** is not selected (no check mark).

5. Key **1.5** in the Height text box in the Size and Rotate section. The size should automatically appear in the Width text box. Click **OK**.

6. Notice in Figure 1-20 that the slogan has disappeared. With the text box selected, an *A…* in a box appears at the bottom of the top text frame. This means that there is more text than what is showing and that the excess is in the overflow area.

FIGURE 1-20
Ad With Inserted Picture

7. Click on the bottom middle handle of the top text box frame and drag the handle down until the missing text reappears. The top text box frame should now measure approximately **3.0** inches in height.

8. Save the publication and keep it open as you read on.

Adding a Border

To add emphasis to an ad, a border can be added to any kind of frame. This border can be of various thicknesses and colors. To add a border, select the frame and choose a border style using the Line/Border Style button on the Formatting toolbar. The line styles (Figure 1-21) are listed by point measurement. There are 72 points in an inch. The default color is black. In this lesson we will not change the color of the border.

FIGURE 1-21
Adding a Border

S TEP-BY-STEP 1.18

1. Select the text box frame at the bottom of the ad. Click the **Line-Border Style** button.

2. Select the ¾ **pt** style.

3. Check your work to make sure everything shows and looks good. Then click the **Save** button on the Toolbar to save your work again as **bus ad xxx**.

The Completed Publication

Congratulations! You have finished your first publication.

Your publication should look like Figure 1-1. The Boundaries and Guides were turned off in the View menu for a more finished appearance in the figure.

Printing a File

Up until now you have been working with a soft copy, which means you have been viewing it only on the screen. To see a hard copy, you need to print it. To print, click the Print button on the Standard toolbar or open the Print dialog box from the File menu.

The Print dialog box (Figure 1-22) offers a choice of printers when you click the drop-down list to the right of Name. Also, if you have a multiple page document, the print range can be selected. You may want to print certain pages or just the current page. Depending on your printer, publications that contain graphics, color, WordArt, and large-sized font objects may print slowly. In that case, printing one page at a time can help speed things along. While you are checking the printed page, you can print another page. You can also select the number of copies in this dialog box. The default is one copy.

FIGURE 1-22
Print Dialog Box

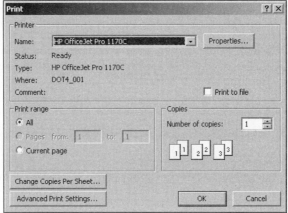

Because you are working with a publication that is smaller than 8½ x 11, you may be able to print more than one copy on a page. When you see a button at the bottom of the Print dialog box labeled Change Copies Per Sheet, you may choose how many copies per sheet you wish to print. In the next Step-by-Step, you will designate one copy per sheet in the Small Publication Print Options dialog box.

STEP-BY-STEP 1.19

1. Open the **File** menu and choose **Print**. Select your printer, if necessary. Leave the Print range at **All** and the Number of copies at **1**.

2. Click **Change Copies Per Sheet** to display the dialog box shown in Figure 1-23.

3. Select **Print one copy per sheet**. Click **OK**.

4. Press **Enter** or click **OK** in the Print dialog box.

FIGURE 1-23
Small Publication Print Options

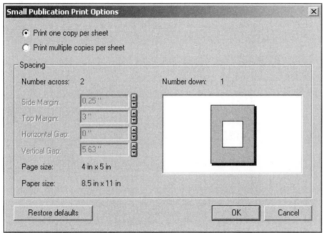

5. Open the **File** menu and choose **Close**. Click **Yes** if you are prompted to save the changes made to this publication. Your **bus ad xxx** document should be closed and you will see a blank document page.

6. Open the **File** menu and choose **Exit** to exit Microsoft Publisher.

SUMMARY

In this lesson, you learned:

- The purpose of a desktop publishing program is to create publications containing text and graphics that require more layout decisions than publications created with a word processing program.

- Microsoft Publisher has an Object toolbar that is used to create frames for various objects.

- A text box frame is an object into which text is either keyed or imported.

- Text in a text box frame can be edited and formatted.

- Graphic files stored in a computer can be inserted using the Picture Frame tool.

- Picture frames can be moved, and resized.

- Microsoft Publisher is compatible with many graphic file formats.

- Page size and orientation can be changed in the Page Layout dialog box.

- Borders can be added to make a frame stand out.

- Publications can be saved and printed.

VOCABULARY *Review*

Define the following terms:

Advertisement	Handles	Screen
Color scheme	Layout guides	Serif
Crosshair	Overflow area	Task pane
Desktop publishing	Sans serif	Tone
Frame		

REVIEW *Questions*

WRITTEN QUESTIONS

Write a brief answer to the following questions.

1. Explain the purpose of frames in Publisher.

2. Explain the purpose of the Scratch Area.

3. Explain the purpose of the position and size indicators in the lower-right corner of the screen.

4. Explain the purpose of the layout guides.

5. Explain the purpose of the Measurements toolbar.

6. Explain how to add a border to a frame.

TRUE / FALSE

Circle T if the statement is true or F if the statement is false.

T   F   1. Picture frames can be moved and resized.

T   F   2. Only Microsoft Publisher graphics can be used in publications.

T   F   3. The Arrange menu is used to change the page size.

T   F   4. No text editing can take place in a Publisher text box frame.

T   F   5. Use the Formatting toolbar to create new picture and text frames.

T   F   6. Advertisements are messages designed to promote a product, service, event, or idea.

T   F   7. The pane that appears at the left of the window when you begin a publication is known as the Scratch Area pane.

T   F   8. The more fonts you use in an advertisement, the more appealing the advertisement will be.

MULTIPLE CHOICE

Select the best response for the following statements.

1. What is the box at the top of the window that allows you to look at the document using a larger or smaller view?
   A. Zoom
   B. Snap to
   C. Page Setup
   D. Print

2. When using the mouse to draw a text box frame in the Document Page, what icon does the mouse pointer become?
    A. Arrow
    B. Moving
    C. Resize
    D. Crosshair

3. When moving a text box frame around in the Document Page, what icon does the mouse pointer become?
    A. Arrow
    B. Moving
    C. Resize
    D. Crosshair

4. When resizing a text box frame, what icon does the mouse pointer become?
    A. Arrow
    B. Moving
    C. Resize
    D. Crosshair

5. Which dialog box allows you to change the margins of a publication?
    A. Layout Guides
    B. Page Layout
    C. Print
    D. Save As

6. Which of the following file formats is NOT compatible with Microsoft Publisher?
    A. PDF
    B. TIF
    C. GIF
    D. BMP

PROJECTS

At the end of each lesson, you will be asked to complete one or more projects to reinforce what you learned in the lesson. Fewer explanations are given in the projects—you are, after all, applying skills you acquired in the lesson. As you go on to future lessons, the skills you gained in this lesson will be tested again and again. Try to remember as much as you can, but know that you can look back into the lessons for help when you need it.

SCANS **PROJECT 1-1**

As a volunteer for a local fishing club, you have agreed to design an advertisement for an annual event for children. Create a publication that measures 4.75 inches wide and 7.5 inches tall. Set 0.25-inch margins (layout guides) on all sides. You will create four different text box frames. Each one will be as wide as the left and right margins but of different height. Change the view, if necessary, so you can see what you will be keying.

Use a font that fits the occasion. The font used in Figure 1-24 is Comic Sans MS. The sizes may vary depending on the font chosen.

FIGURE 1-24
Completed Project 1-1

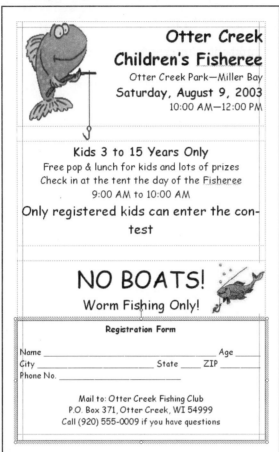

1. The first text box frame starts at the top margin guide. Make it 1.75 inches tall.

2. Right align the following paragraphs and format the text as shown in parentheses.
   Otter Creek (20 pt. bold)

   Children's Fisheree (20 pt. bold)

   Otter Creek Park—Miller Bay (12 pt.)

   Saturday, August 10, 2003 (14 pt. bold)

   10:00 AM-12:00 PM (12 pt.)

3. Create the second text box frame to start at 2.25 inches. Make it 1.75 inches tall.

4. Center align the following paragraphs and format them as shown in parentheses.
   Kids 3 to 15 Years Only (14 pt. bold)

   Free pop & lunch for kids & lots of prizes (12 pt.)

   Check in at the tent the day of the Fisheree (12 pt.)

   9:00 AM to 10:00 AM (12 pt.)

   Only registered kids can enter the contest (16 pt.)

5. Create the third text box frame to start at 4.250 inches. Make it 0.875 inch tall.

6. Center align the following paragraphs and format them as shown in parentheses.
   NO BOATS! (28 pt.)

   Worm Fishing Only! (16 pt.)

7. Create the last text box frame to begin at 5.25 inches. It should measure 2 inches tall and end at the bottom margin guide.

8. Key the paragraphs and format them as shown in parentheses. The lines are created using the Shift and Underline keys and they may vary in length from those showing in Figure 1-24.
   Registration Form (center align, 10 pt. bold)

   Name _____ **Age** _____ (left align, 10 pt.)

   City _____ **State** _____ **ZIP** _____ (left align, 10 pt.)

   Phone No. _____ (left align, 10 pt.)

   Mail to: Otter Creek Fishing Club (center align, 10 pt.)

   P. O. Box 371 Otter Creek, WI 54999 (center align, 10 pt.)

   Call (920) 555-0009 if you have questions (center align, 10 pt.)

9. Turn on a ¾ pt. border for the bottom text box frame.

10. Insert a 1.4 inches wide and 2 inches tall picture in the upper-left corner. Put it on top of the text frame. Insert the fish fishing.gif graphic from the data files.

11. Insert the **fish and worm.jpg** graphic from the data files in the right side of the third text box frame. *Challenge*: Change the text wrap for the graphic to None so that it does not push the text over.

12. When you finish, save the publication as **fisheree ad *xxx***, substituting your initials for *xxx*. Print it and close it.

SCANS PROJECT 1-2

Your mother is a member of the Otter Creek Garden Club and she has asked you to create an ad for their upcoming annual plant sale. Create a custom publication that measures 4.75 inches wide and 4 inches tall. Set 0.25 inch margins (layout guides) on all sides. Create a text box frame that snaps to the margin guides.

1. Change the view, if necessary, so you can see what you will be keying.

2. Key and format the text in Figure 1-25. You choose the fonts. The two fonts used in the figure are Script MT Bold and Arial. You must keep the finished ad the original size, so choose your font sizes carefully.

3. Go to the data files and insert the picture file POTDPLNT.WMF on top of the text box frame and size it to fit to the left of the text as shown in Figure 1-25. It should push the text to the right.

4. When you finish, save the publication as **plant sale ad *xxx*** substituting your initials for ***xxx***. Print it and close it.

FIGURE 1-25
Completed Project 1-2

SCANS PROJECT 1-3

Get together with two or three of your classmates. Choose a real or imagined upcoming event at your school that needs publicity. Create an advertisement for the school newspaper. Save it, print it, and close it.

CRITICAL *Thinking*

ACTIVITY 1-1

Desktop publishing documents are "nonlinear," which means that they are constructed using blocks (or frames) of text and graphics that are placed in any order the designer chooses. How is this different from word processing?

FLYERS

OBJECTIVES

Upon completion of this lesson, you should be able to:

- Search the Clip Organizer for desired clip art and add clip art to a publication.

- Search the Microsoft Design Gallery Live for desired clip art.

- Move, resize, rotate, and flip a clip art frame.

- Use the Character Spacing feature to format text.

- Use the ruler guides to position a frame.

- Add and format a WordArt frame.

- Change the bullet symbol.

- Layer and group objects.

- Wrap text around a clip art frame and WordArt frame.

Estimated Time: 4 hours

VOCABULARY

Flip

Flyer

Grouping

Kerning

Layering

Rotate

Ruler guides

Scaling

Text wrap

Tracking

WordArt

What Is a Flyer?

A *flyer* is a publication that announces an event or advertises a special limited-time promotion of a single product or service. It is printed on one side of a single sheet of paper and is usually hung on walls or bulletin boards, placed on counter tops, or inserted into newspapers or shopping bags. It is used to generate interest in an organization or event.

Design Considerations for a Flyer

To be effective, a flyer must include the following objects:

- A large headline that can be read at a distance

- Minimum body copy

- Some graphic objects or attention-getting visuals

- Description of the product or event

- Price information (if applicable)

- Company or organization name prominently placed

- Company address, phone and fax number positioned near the company logo or name

  Other suggestions for design include the following:

- Use font styles that represent the product advertised. Use enough contrast between the headline and text to make the headline stand out.

- Make the information brief and easy to read.

- Use a single, dominant color that is easy to read if it is used as text color or background fill for text box frames.

- Choose an appropriate paper color.

- Consider larger-sized paper such as 11 × 17.

- Make sure the page is not cluttered with excess text and graphic objects.

The Lesson Project

For this lesson, you will begin by creating a flyer for the City of Otter Creek that will promote the wearing of helmets when riding bikes (Figure 2-1).

FIGURE 2-1
Bike Helmet Flyer

Using the Clip Organizer

In the previous lesson you learned how to add a picture to a document using the Picture frame. In this lesson, you will learn how to use the Clip Organizer. The Microsoft Clip Organizer, included with Microsoft Office XP, is a stand-alone program that is used to organize media clips for Office documents. The Clip Organizer also comes with a variety of media clips for your use.

How clips are Organized

When Clip Organizer is first used after it has been installed, it scans your computer for media files and organizes media clip shortcuts into collections (folders). When you are in the Clip Organizer, you can preview, open, or insert a media file into your document without having to go to the actual storage location on your computer. The clips are organized into four types of collections:

- **My Collections**, which include clips you have stored on your hard disk.

- **Office Collections**, which are clips that come with Microsoft Office XP as well as clips on the Clip Organizer CD.

- **Web collections**, which is a link to an online source provided by Microsoft content partners.

- **Shared Collections**, which are clips that are found on a shared network drive within your organization. (Your network administrator has to have created such a collection.)

To insert a clip art object, click the Clip Organizer Frame on the Object toolbar and the Insert Clip Art task pane will appear at the left side of your screen. This task pane is illustrated in Figure 2-2.

FIGURE 2-2
Insert Clip Art Task Pane

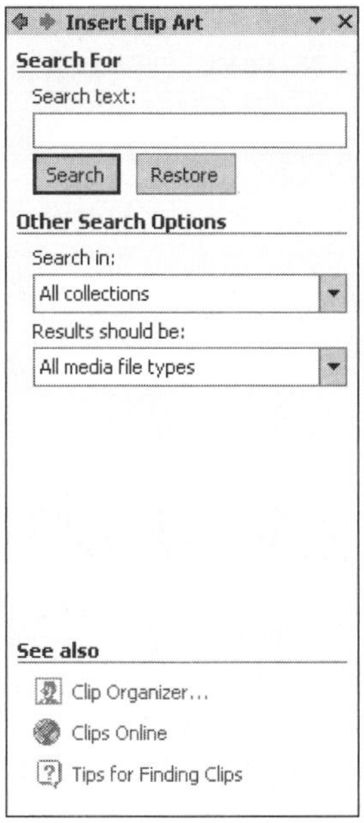

Search for a clip by keying in the Search text box a word or phrase that describes the clip you want. You can limit where you want the search carried out by specifying the collection to be searched in the *Search in* drop-down list. You can limit the type of media to be searched in the *Results should be* drop-down list. The choices for types of media include the following:

- All media file types
- Clip Art
- Photographs
- Movies
- Sounds

When the specifications have been entered or chosen, click Search to see the results. The results of the search will be shown in the same pane as thumbnail (very small) images. Figure 2-3 shows the possible results of a search for *helmets*. You can scroll down to see additional images.

FIGURE 2-3
Results of Search in Clip Organizer

Modifying Your Search

If you do not like the choices presented in the Insert Clip Art task pane, you can modify your search specifications by clicking the Modify button below the thumbnail images.

Adding a Clip to Your Document

Once you have found a clip you like, you may either click it to select it or drag it onto your open document. If you want to add several clips, hold the CTRL key down as you select additional clips and drag them all at once into your document. (If you do this, the clips end up stacked on top of each other, and you need to move them off the pile and into the document one by one.)

STEP-BY-STEP 2.1

1. Start Microsoft Publisher.

2. Click **Blank Publication** under the New section of the task pane.

3. Click the **Clip Organizer Frame** tool on the Object toolbar. If the Add Clips to Organizer dialog box appears, click **Later**.

4. Key **helmet** in the Search text box.

5. Click **Search**. Look at the results.

STEP-BY-STEP 2.1 Continued

6. Click **Modify**.

7. Key **bikes** in the Search text box and click **Search**.

8. Scroll, if necessary, to find an image that contains a bike rider who looks like a young person and is wearing a helmet. (You may not find the image shown in Figure 2-1.)

9. Drag the image onto your document and release the left mouse button anywhere in the document. Click anywhere in the scratch area to deselect the image.

10. Save the file as **bike helmets *xxx*** (where *xxx* are your initials). Keep the publication open and read on.

Additional Clip Options

A gray bar with an arrow appears beside the selected clip in the Clip Art task pane. When you click the arrow, Publisher displays a menu of choices that relate to what can be done with that clip (see Figure 2-4). These choices include:

FIGURE 2-4
Drop-Down List for a Clip

■ **Insert**—Insert the clip into the document.

■ **Copy**—Puts a copy of the selected clip into the Office Clipboard.

■ **Delete from Clip Organizer**—Deletes the shortcut to the clip that is showing in the Clip Organizer. It does not delete the actual stored file.

- **Open Clip In**—Opens the clip in an image-editing program such as Microsoft Photo Editor.

- **Tools on the Web**—If you are connected to the Internet, a window will open that will give you links to an online clip gallery, to articles relating to the Office programs, and to the Picture It program. (See Figure 2-5.)

- **Copy to Collection**—Copy the selected image to another collection or create a new collection to which the image can be copied.

- **Move to Collection**—Move a selected image to another collection or create a new collection to which the image can be moved.

- **Edit Keywords**—Keywords are stored with the image that describes the image. These help when searching for clips. This option lets you add, edit, or delete keywords. This can only be done on your personal collections. Keywords can also be changed in the Properties dialog box.

- **Find Similar Style**—This will bring up other images created in the same artistic style but not necessarily matching the keyword.

- **Preview/Properties**—This dialog box shows the properties of the image such as the type of file, size, and properties.

FIGURE 2-5
Tools on the Web Dialog Box

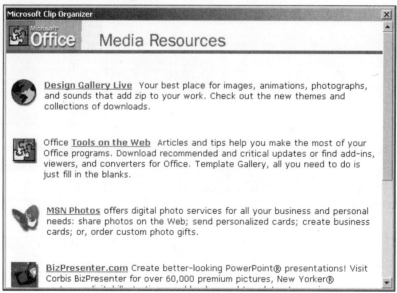

STEP-BY-STEP 2.2

1. Click on the down arrow next to any image in the Insert Clip Art task pane. Click the **Insert** command. Did the image appear in the document page?

2. Click again on the down arrow next to any image, then click **Tools on the Web**. It should take you to the window displayed in Figure 2-5.

STEP-BY-STEP 2.2 Continued

3. Close the Tools on the Web window by clicking the **X** in the upper-right corner of the window. (You will learn more about this later in the lesson.)

4. Save the publication and keep it open as you read on.

Viewing Clips by Collections

At the bottom of the Insert Clip Art task pane under See also is the Clip Organizer command. Clicking on this command will result in the opening of the Microsoft Clip Organizer as shown in Figure 2-6. Once you're in Clip Organizer, you can search for clips or browse the collections.

FIGURE 2-6
Clip Organizer Viewed by Search

There are two different views in the Clip Organizer. One is by Search, (shown in Figure 2-6). This is similar to the Insert Clip Art task pane. You can key keywords into the Search text box and click Search. You can also limit the search to certain collections and types of media files as you did in the Insert Clip Art task pane.

The other view is by Collection Lists. The collections have a plus or minus to the left of the collection name. A plus indicates subfolders. Clicking the plus will expand the main collection folder and list the subfolders. Some subfolders also contain folders. A minus indicates that the main folder (or collection) is expanded. You should see subfolders listed under the main folder name. In this view you can choose a collection as well as a folder in that collection and simply browse through the images until you see one you like. These would be very broad categories. In Figure 2-7 the Office Collection is selected and the Animal folder is selected.

FIGURE 2-7
Clip Organizer Viewed by Collections

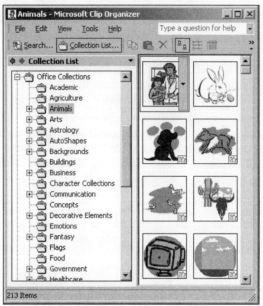

Notice that in the lower-right corner of some of the thumbnail images are little icons that tell you where the clip is located or if it is an animated *.gif*.

STEP-BY-STEP 2.3

1. If necessary, select **Task Pane** from the **View** menu.

2. Change the task to **Insert Clip Art** from the down-pointed triangle at the top of the Task Pane.

3. Click **Clip Organizer** at the bottom of the Insert Clip Art task pane. If you are prompted to add clips, click **Later**.

4. Click **Search** at the top of the Clip Organizer.

5. Key **bikes** in the Search text box, if necessary, and click **Search**.

6. Find another bike image in which the biker is wearing a helmet.

7. Drag the image, using your left mouse button, anywhere onto the document page.

8. Open the Clip Organizer window from the Task Bar. Then click **Collection List** at the top of the left pane of the Clip Organizer.

STEP-BY-STEP 2.3 Continued

9. Click the **Office Collections folder**. Click the **+** to expand the folder, if necessary.

10. Scroll down to the **Sports** subfolder. Click on the **+** to expand the Sports subfolder.

11. Click on the **Equipment** subfolder.

12. Scroll through the images until you find an image with a bike helmet or a biker wearing a helmet.

13. Drag the image anywhere onto the document page.

14. Reopen the Clip Organizer, if necessary.

Using the Help Feature in the Clip Organizer

Because Help may be a new feature for you, we'll learn to use the Help feature in the Clip Organizer dialog box. Help is a separate program within the Office Suite. You will see an Ask a Question text box in the upper-right corner. Key a question in that box and press Enter. You will get a bulleted list of possible answers. Clicking a bulleted item will open a help pane with instructions or information related to your bulleted choice (see Figure 2-8).

FIGURE 2-8
Help Pane

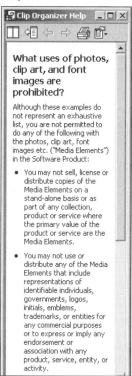

If keying in a question does not get you the answer, other sources of information are available. If your Clip Organizer Help looks like Figure 2-8, you can click the Show button at the top. This expands the Help window to show three other tabbed pages. (See Figure 2-9.)

- Contents is like a table of contents in a book. You can *browse* through different chapters and read the help information. Each chapter has a plus to the left. Clicking the plus expands the chapter into subchapters.

- Answer Wizard is similar to the Ask a Question text box. Key in a question and click Search. The results show in the Contents pane.

- Index allows you to key a word that describes the help you are seeking and click Search. You will see a list of terms related to the word you keyed. Click a word in the list of results that show in the Contents Pane.

FIGURE 2-9
Showing the Three Tabbed Pages in Help

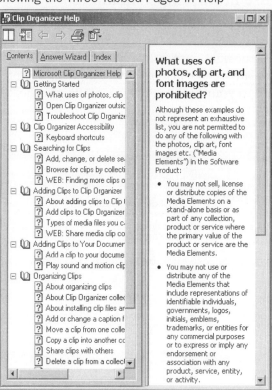

STEP-BY-STEP 2.4

1. With the Clip Organizer window open, key **how do I copy an image** in the Ask a Question box. Press **Enter**.

2. Click the bulleted item that reads **What uses of photos, clip art, . . .**

3. Read the results in the Contents pane.

4. If the Clip Organizer pane is a single pane, click the **Show** button at the top of the Contents pane.

STEP-BY-STEP 2.4 Continued

5. Click the **Contents** tab and expand the chapters.

6. Click one of the subchapters and read the information in the Contents pane.

7. Click the **Answer Wizard** tab and key the same text as in step #1 of this exercise. Click **Search**.

8. Click the **Index** tab. Key **image** and click **Search**.

9. Click any of the resulting topics showing in the bottom of the pane and read the information provided.

10. Close the Help window and the Clip Organizer window by clicking the **X** in the upper-right corner.

11. Make sure the Insert Clip Art task pane is still showing.

Using Clips Online

Below the Clip Organizer link at the bottom of the Insert Clip Art task pane is the Clips Online command. This link takes you to the Microsoft Design Gallery Live, which is an Internet site containing more clips. You have to be connected to the Internet for this feature to work.

When you click the Clips Online command, you will see the window that is showing in Figure 2-10. (NOTE: Before this window appears, you may see a window with terms for using the online clip art. If this window appears, click Accept.)

In the left side of the window are options for keying a keyword, where to search, what format the media should be in, and the chronological order of the stored images. The number of pages of images available will show in the upper-right corner. The example showing in Figure 2-10 is page 8 of 26. To move forward from page to page, click the >> symbol or select a page number from the drop-down list next to the current page number.

FIGURE 2-10
Microsoft Design Gallery Live

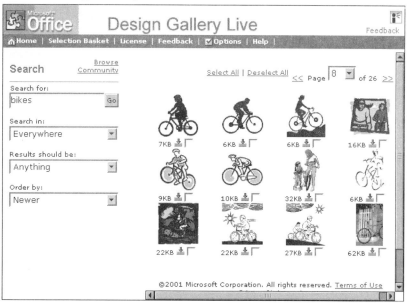

As you move from page to page, if you see any images you like you should click in the option box under the image to insert a check mark. The checked images are the ones that will be downloaded to a collection folder on your computer. You can deselect an unwanted image by clicking it again. The check mark will disappear.

When you are done making your selection(s), click the Download # clips which is at the top middle of the window. You will see the window in Figure 2-11. This window indicates how many clips are selected, their total size, and the approximate time it will take for them to download from the Internet to your computer.

FIGURE 2-11
Download Window

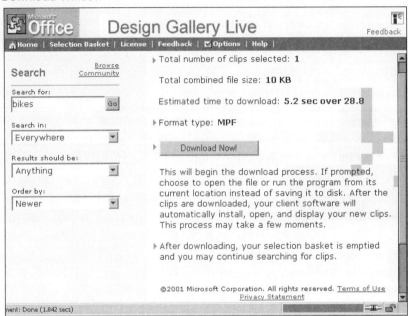

The images you selected in the Design Gallery Live will appear in a special Downloaded Clips collection in the Clip Organizer and will be placed in a folder that matches the keywords that are assigned to the image in the Design Gallery Live. In Figure 2-12, the bike clip was downloaded to the Transportation folder in the Downloaded Clips folder, which is a subfolder under My Collections.

FIGURE 2-12
Downloaded Clip Art

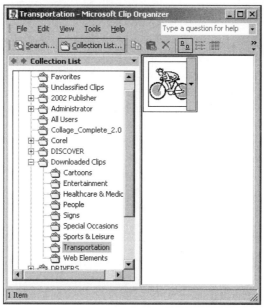

STEP-BY-STEP 2.5

1. Click **Clips Online** in the toolbar above the image pane in the Equipment window.

2. If a window appears asking if you agree to the use of the clip art you are about to see online, click **Accept**.

3. In the Design Gallery Live, key **bikes** in the Search for text box. (Do not change any other options.) Click **Go**.

4. Look through as many pages as you wish. Click on the **>>** to go forward and **<<** to move backward through the pages of images.

5. Click in the box below any desired images so a check mark appears. (The image in Figure 2-1 is on page 8. Choose it, if you wish.)

6. Click **Download # Clips**.

7. In the next window, click **Download Now!**

8. Notice the images that are now in one or more subfolders under the Downloaded Clips folder. Close the Design Gallery and drag one of the images anywhere onto the document page.

Modifying a Clip Art Frame

You can move, size, and delete clip art frames the same way you did text and picture frames. First you must select the frame. Then resize it by moving your mouse pointer over a handle until you see the word Resize. Hold down your left mouse button and drag out or in. You can move it by pointing to any border of the clip art frame until you see an icon labeled Move along with four arrows. Hold down the left mouse button and move the object around on the document page or onto the scratch area for use later. To delete a clip art object, select it and press the Delete key.

You are going to delete all but one clip art frame and use the remaining frame as part of your flyer. You will keep the one you think would be a good graphic for a flyer about bike helmets.

Flipping or Rotating the Graphic

When adding a graphic to a flyer, make sure that it is facing into the publication. This leads the reader's eye onto the information in the publication, not away from it. Depending on what graphic you select, you may need to *flip* it horizontally to face the other direction or you may need to *rotate* it so it is turned on its side or is upside down. Both of these changes to images are done using the Rotate or Flip feature in the Arrange menu. The choices you have from this menu are shown in Figure 2-13.

FIGURE 2-13
Rotate or Flip Menu

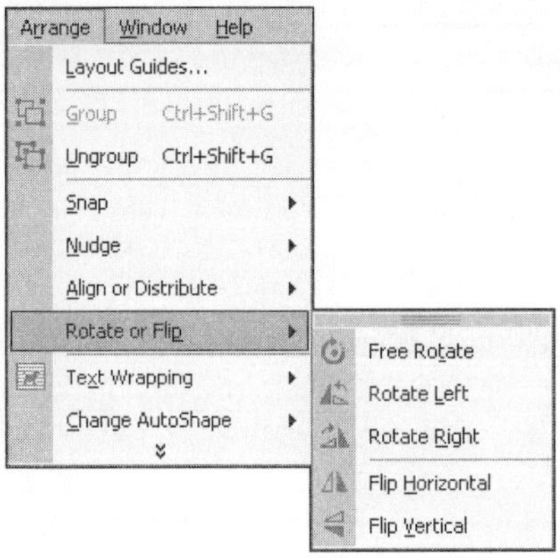

- **Free Rotate**—Use the Rotate tool to turn the object clockwise or counter clockwise by the desired amount.

- **Rotate Left**—Turn the object to the left 90 degrees per click.

- **Rotate Right**—Turn the object to the right 90 degrees per click.

- **Flip Horizontal**—Make a mirror image of the object on the horizontal axis.

- **Flip Vertical**—Make a mirror image of the object on the vertical axis.

STEP-BY-STEP 2.6

1. With **bike helmet** *xxx* open in the window, select and delete all but one clip art frame by clicking on a clip art frame and pressing **Delete**. (Your clip art does not have to be the same as the one in Figure 2-14.)

FIGURE 2-14
Publication with Clip Art

2. From the **Arrange** menu, choose **Layout Guides**.

3. Change all four margins to **0.5** inch.

4. If necessary, flip the graphic so that it is facing in toward the publication by selecting the object and choosing **Flip Horizontal** from the **Rotate or Flip** feature in the **Arrange** menu.

5. Move the graphic so that it snaps to the left margin guide and bottom margin guide in the lower-left corner of the document page.

6. Resize the graphic so that it measures approximately **4.5** inches wide and **3.25** inches tall. (Use the Measurements toolbar to help you or watch the Object Size Box in the lower-right status bar.)

7. Your publication should look something like Figure 2-14 except that you may have a different graphic. If, after resizing, your graphic is in a different position than the graphic in the figure, position the graphic again.

Adding Text to the Flyer

Now you will add the text to the flyer that explains the free offer of bike helmets. You will create a text frame using the Text Box tool and key and format the text. The frame will cover part of the graphic, but you will learn how to wrap the text around the graphic.

Changing Character Spacing

Up to now you have changed the size of text to make it stand out. Another feature in Publisher that provides formatting of characters is the Character Spacing feature. It is located in the Character Spacing dialog box, which is opened from the Format menu. You want to use this feature for only a very small amount of text, such as a headline. Changes in character spacing to large amounts of text make the text very hard to read.

The choices in the Character Spacing dialog box shown in Figure 2-15 include the following:

FIGURE 2-15
Character Spacing

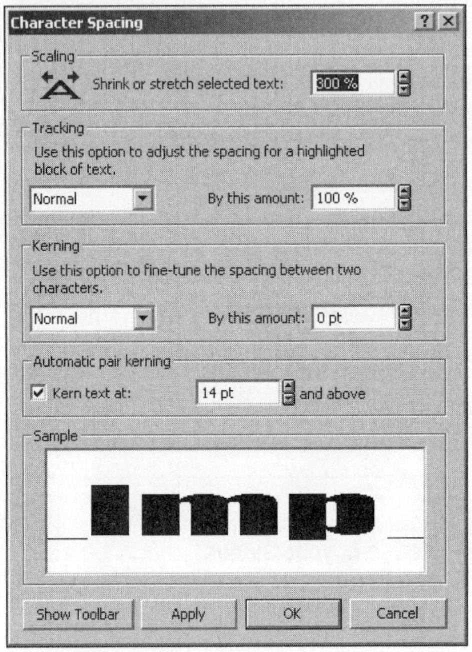

- *Scaling*—Changes the size of the letters by shrinking and stretching the letters from 0.1% to 600% in width without making the letters taller.

- *Tracking*—Affects the space between two or more adjoining letters in a block of text. There are five tracking options: Normal, Tight, Very Tight, Loose, and Very Loose. You can also choose *Custom* to set your own spacing.

- *Kerning*—Affects the space between letter pairs when the type size is 14 pt. or greater. You can add space between pairs of letters or you can decrease space resulting in letters overlapping.

The same feature found in the Character Spacing dialog box are available on the bottom half of the Measurements toolbar.

STEP-BY-STEP 2.7

1. Select the Text Box tool from the Object bar. Create a text that measures **7.5** inches by **7.5** inches and starts at the upper-left corner where the left margin guide and top margin guide meet.

STEP-BY-STEP 2.7 Continued

2. Choose Center Alignment. Key and format the text as shown in Figure 2-16.

FIGURE 2-16
Keyed and Formatted Text

FREE (Impact, 72 pt., scaling set to 300%)
Bike Helmets . . . (Impact, 60 pt. bold)
Bring your child . . . (Arial, 26 pt. bold)
Protect your . . . (Arial, 36 pt. italics)

3. Save the file again.

Adding Another Text Frame

You do not have to put all of your text in one text frame. You can have several text frames on one page. Draw and position each frame and add the text.

S TEP-BY-STEP 2.8

1. With **bike helmets** *xxx* open in the window, click the **Text Box** tool from the **Object** toolbar.

2. Click in the lower-right corner of the document page and draw a frame that measures **2.25** inches wide and **0.75** inches tall. Use the Measurement toolbar to help you. Choose Character Spacing from the Format menu for scaling.

3. Key the following text and format it with Arial, 12 pt. bold, and right alignment:
For more information,
Contact Debbie or Lily at:
Phone: (920) 555-5080

STEP-BY-STEP 2.8 Continued

4. If your frame is too small, a box with an "A" will appear at the bottom of the frame as shown in Figure 2-17. Resize the text frame so that all the text shows. (Sometimes even blank lines created by pressing Enter will cause this to happen.)

FIGURE 2-17
Text Frame Adjustment

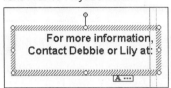

5. Move the text box so that the lower-right corner of the frame snaps to the lower-right corner on the document page at the intersection of the right margin guide and bottom margin guide.

6. Save the file and keep it open.

Using Ruler Guides

In the next exercise, you are going to add another picture frame to the document page. In order to position it in the exact location, you'll use a very useful feature called *ruler guides*. These guides look like green dotted lines and are used to help position objects on the page. To use a ruler guide, hold the Shift key and point at the horizontal or vertical ruler so that you see an adjust icon. Drag the guide to the desired position. When a ruler guide is placed on the document page and the Snap to feature is turned on, the ruler guides become "sticky" and objects snap to the guides.

The last step for the flyer is to add the city's logo. You'll drag horizontal and vertical ruler guides into your document. Then you will line up the new picture along the ruler guides.

STEP-BY-STEP 2.9

1. With **bike helmets** *xxx* still open in the window, hold the **Shift** key and point to the horizontal ruler guide with the mouse pointer until you see the adjust icon and a tool tip labeled *Create Horizontal Guide*.

2. Drag the guide down to **8.5** inches on the vertical ruler. Release the mouse.

3. Holding down the Shift key, drag a guide from the vertical ruler over to **6.25** inches on the horizontal ruler.

4. Click the Picture Frame tool.

5. Draw the frame beginning where the two ruler guides intersect and continue extending down and to the right until the frame is approximately 1 inch square.

STEP-BY-STEP 2.9 Continued

6. Insert **Otter Creek Logo.jpg** from your prerecorded data files, as shown in Figure 2-18.

FIGURE 2-18
Object Sticking to Ruler Guides

7. Using the Measurement toolbar, resize the frame to be **1.5** inches wide and **1** inch tall, if necessary.

8. Your publication should now resemble Figure 2-19. Save the publication again as **bike helmets** *xxx* and print it. Close the file.

FIGURE 2-19
Completed Bike Helmet Flyer

Adding WordArt to a Publication

Up to this point, you have been using the text box frame to create text for headlines and titles. While you can vary the font design and size, you are somewhat limited in the formatting of the text. *WordArt* is a utility that makes text look like a graphic. It is used primarily for headlines, banners, and titles. WordArt uses the same fonts as those used in a text box frame but contains special effects that make the fonts appear different and graphic-like. *Halloween Extravaganza* in Figure 2-20 is an example of WordArt.

FIGURE 2-20
Completed Halloween Project

Creating WordArt Frames

To create a WordArt frame, select the Insert WordArt button on the Object toolbar. When you release the mouse button, a grid of style choices appears in a window titled *WordArt Gallery*. From this gallery you may choose the orientation (vertical or horizontal), shape, color, and style of the WordArt object (see Figure 2-21). Your design choices can be altered later using the WordArt toolbar.

FIGURE 2-21
WordArt Gallery

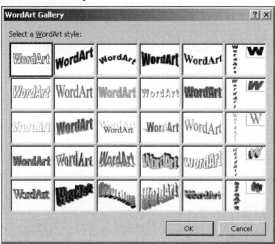

After making a choice from the WordArt Gallery, a small dialog box appears instructing you to enter *Your Text Here*. In addition to keying text in the Your Text Here dialog box, you can select the font design and size. You can also insert special characters in the text, such as a trademark or copyright symbol. Publisher will autofit the text into the frame.

Once the text has been entered and the font design and size have been chosen, click OK or click the X in the dialog box to close it. At that point, the WordArt frame will appear in the document page and a new WordArt toolbar will appear (see Figure 2-22). You can change the shape, the direction of the text, the *text wrapping* (how the text frames form their shape around the WordArt frame), the alignment and character spacing, the line thickness of the text and its color, or turn on shading or a shadow. All of these special effects are easy to use.

FIGURE 2-22
WordArt Toolbar

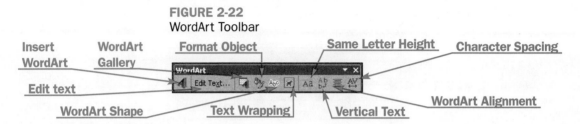

STEP-BY-STEP 2.10

1. Create a new document and choose Blank Publication. Change all four margins to **0.3** inch in the Layout Guides dialog box.

2. Choose the Insert WordArt tool and choose the third shape in the first row. Click **OK**.

3. Key the text: **Halloween Extravaganza**

4. Choose the font **Chiller**, size **36**. Click **OK**.

5. With the WordArt chosen, choose **WordArt Shape** from the WordArt toolbar. Choose the fourth shape in the fourth row. It is labeled **Deflate Bottom**.

6. Resize the object by dragging the bottom-left handle down and to the left until the object measures approximately **5.325** inches wide and **3.65** inches tall.

7. Move the WordArt object to the upper-left corner so that the frame is at the top of the paper and snaps to the left margin guides. (It is ok that the frame is outside the margin guide as long as none of the contents extend beyond the no-print zone of your printer. Most laser printers have a no-print zone of 0.25 inch. Check with your instructor to find out what the no-print zone is on the printer you are using.)

8. With the WordArt object still selected, click the WordArt shape button and choose **Cascade Up**.

9. From the WordArt toolbar, click **Format WordArt**. Choose the **Colors and Lines** tab, and change the Fill color to gray or silver. Click **OK** and close the WordArt toolbar.

> **Computer Concepts**
>
> Use the Measurement tool bar to achieve a specific size or location for an object.

10. Save your publication as **Halloween *xxx*** (where *xxx* are your initials). Save often! Keep it open for the next exercise.

Layering and Grouping Objects

A common design technique is *layering* objects. This means one object is on top of one or more objects. This is typically done with graphics and WordArt. When two or more objects are layered, a decision has to be made as to which object is on top. You may have numerous layers, one for each object, and you get to control the order of the layers.

To send an object to the front or back, select the object to be layered and choose Order from the Arrange menu or click the down arrow next to the Bring to Front button on the Standard toolbar. The choices are illustrated in Figure 2-23. The first two choices will bring an object to the front of all the layers or send an object to the back of all the objects. The Bring Forward and Send Backward options will move the object forward and backward only one layer at a time.

> **Computer Concepts**
>
> If you need to edit an object that is layered at the bottom, send the objects on top to the bottom until the desired object is on top.

FIGURE 2-23
Bring to Front Button

Once the objects are layered as desired, they can be *grouped* using the Group feature. Grouping locks objects together to ensure that they can be moved and sized together. All the objects that are to be grouped need to be selected first. Do this by selecting one object and holding the Shift key as you select the other objects.

FIGURE 2-24
Group Objects Icon

When more than one object is selected, a Group Object button automatically appears in the lower-left corner of the selected objects as shown in Figure 2-24. Clicking on this button will group the objects. When objects are grouped there will only be one set of handles surrounding the grouped objects, and an ungroup icon will appear at the bottom-right corner of the grouped object (see Figure 2-25). Clicking this icon will ungroup the objects. If one of the grouped objects needs to be edited, the group needs to be ungrouped first so the individual object can be selected and edited.

FIGURE 2-25
Ungroup Objects Icon

You are going to add a graphic to the publication and group it with the WordArt object.

STEP-BY-STEP 2.11

1. With **Halloween *xxx*** open in the window, use the Clip Organizer Frame tool to open the Insert Clip Art task pane. Key **Halloween** in the Search text box and click **Search**.

2. Locate a picture with a black cat and drag it onto the document page. If necessary, flip it horizontally so that the cat is looking into the page.

3. Use the Measurement tool bar to resize the clip art to approximately **3.725** inches wide and **5** inches tall.

4. Move it to **0.725** inches on the vertical ruler and snap it to the left margin guide.

5. With the clip-art frame still selected, open the **Arrange** menu and choose **Order**. Choose **Send to Back** so that it goes behind the WordArt object.

6. With the clip-art frame still selected, hold the **Shift** key and click the WordArt frame. A Group Objects button will appear as shown in Figure 2-26.

FIGURE 2-26
Two Objects Selected

7. Click the **Group Object** icon. The two objects are now grouped and an Ungroup Object button appears.

8. Save the file again with the same name.

Changing a Bullet Symbol

You are going to add two text box frames. One will contain a bullet list. In Lesson 1, you added bullets to two lines in the Bus Ad exercise by clicking the Bullet button on the Formatting toolbar. In the next Step-by-Step, you will add bullets, but will also change the bullet symbol to more appropriately fit the theme.

Changing the bullet format is done in the Indents and Lists dialog box (Figure 2-27) chosen from the Format menu. You have a choice of formatting normal (no bullets), Bulleted list, and Numbered list. When the Bulleted list is selected, the New Bullet button appears. This opens a grid of symbols that are available in different font sets.

FIGURE 2-27
Indents and Lists Dialog Box

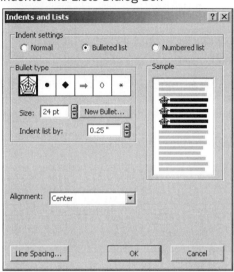

STEP-BY-STEP 2.12

1. Create a text box frame that measures **4.85** inches wide and **2.875** inches tall. Add the following text and format as shown in parentheses. All the lines are center aligned.
   Otter Creek Zoo (Berlin Sans FB Demi, 48 pt., orange font color)
   Children's Halloween Party (Berlin Sans FB Demi, 28 pt., orange font color)
   Saturday, October 25, 2003 (Berlin Sans FB Demi, 24 pt., black font color)
   6 to 10 pm (Berlin Sans FB Demi, 24 pt., black font color)
   Sunday, October 26, 2003 (Berlin Sans FB Demi, 24 pt., black font color)
   1 to 5 pm (Berlin Sans FB Demi, 24 pt., black font color)

2. Move the text box to align at the right margin guide and **3** inches on the vertical ruler.

3. If the grouped object is covering up the text box frame, bring the text box frame to the front.

4. Create another text box frame that measures **5.6** inches wide and **4.575** inches tall. Add the following text and format as shown in parentheses. Align the frame at **1.5** inches on the horizontal ruler and **6** inches on the vertical ruler. Choose center alignment and format all lines with Berlin Sans FB Demi.
   Pumpkin Carving (26 pt., orange font color)
   Halloween Costume Contest (26 pt., orange font color)
   Graveyard Scavenger Hunt (26 pt., orange font color)
   Bob for Eyeballs (26 pt., orange font color)
   Scary Face Painting (26 pt., orange font color)
   Much More... (26 pt., orange font color)

STEP-BY-STEP 2.12 Continued

5. Leave a blank line and change to right alignment. Key and format the following text:
   Admission Cost per Day: (18 pt., black font color)
   50¢ for children under 12 (18 pt., black font color) (For the ¢ sign, open the Insert menu and choose Symbol. Scroll to below the lowercase letters and click the ¢ symbol. Click Insert and then Close.)
   $1.00 for adults (18 pt., black font color)

6. Leave a blank line and add the final two lines.
   Sponsored by Otter Creek Department of Parks (Berlin Sans FB Demi, 14 pt., orange font color)
   And local civic groups (Berlin Sans FB Demi, 14 pt., orange font color)

7. Select the six lines at the top of the text box frame. Click the **Bullet** button.

8. From the **Format** menu, choose **Indents and Lists**.

9. Click **New Bullet**.

10. From the Font drop-down list, choose **Webdings** and choose a symbol that represents Halloween. Click **OK** twice.

11. Save the file.

Changing the Text Wrap for Picture and Clip Art Frames

When picture and/or clip art frames are added to a publication that contains text frames, the design may need the text to wrap around the picture or through the picture or stop above the picture and continue below the picture. This is called *text wrap*. These wrap choices are available in the Text Wrap feature chosen from the Picture toolbar (see Figure 2-28).

FIGURE 2-28
Text Wrap Options

Computer Concepts

When text wrap is set to None, you can move an object very close to a text box frame. One way to do this is to use the arrow keys on your keyboard to "nudge" an object one pixel at a time.

STEP-BY-STEP 2.13

1. Insert three more clip-art objects that go well with the design. Look at Figure 2-20 for ideas.

2. The clip-art frame in the upper-right corner should measure approximately **2.5** inches square and it should have a square text wrap.

3. The clip-art frame in the lower-right corner should measure approximately **2.5** inches wide and **2** inches tall. It should have square text wrap. This will push the right-aligned text in toward the center of the text box frame. This is intentional.

4. The little graphic to the left of the bulleted items should measure approximately **2** inches wide and **1.1** inches tall. The text wrap for this text box frame is set at none so that it can be placed very close to the text without rearranging the text lines. You may need to send this new clip-art frame to the back.

5. Save your publication again as **Halloween *xxx*.** Print it and close it. Your completed flyer should look similar to Figure 2-20 when you are finished.

SUMMARY

In this lesson, you learned:

- You can search for clip art using the Clip Organizer.
- You can search for clip art using the Microsoft Design Gallery Live.
- Flipping clip art reverses the direction the picture is facing.
- Moving and resizing a clip art frame uses the same procedure as doing so for a text frame.
- You can make text look larger and change the space between characters using Character Spacing.
- Ruler guides help you position a frame in an exact location.
- WordArt makes text stand out and is good for headlines and titles.
- Bullet symbols can be changed from the default setting and can add greatly to the design of a flyer.
- Objects can be layered and grouped to create a graphic object that can be moved and sized as one object.
- The text wrap feature determines how close text in a text box frame can be to a Picture, clip art, and WordArt frames.

VOCABULARY *Review*

Define the following terms:		
Flip	Layering	Text wrap
Flyer	Rotate	Tracking
Grouping	Ruler guides	WordArt
Kerning	Scaling	

REVIEW *Questions*

TRUE / FALSE

Circle T if the statement is true or F if the statement is false.

T F 1. When you draw a picture frame, Publisher takes you directly to the Clip Organizer.

T F 2. The Flip Horizontal command turns a Clip Organizer frame 90 degrees.

T F 3. Deleting a picture from the Clip Organizer does not delete it from your computer system.

T F 4. Clips downloaded from the Design Gallery Live are stored in the Downloaded Clips folder in My Collections.

T F 5. To use a ruler guide, you must hold down the Ctrl key and point at the horizontal ruler or vertical ruler so that you see an adjust icon.

T F 6. The WordArt feature can make text look like a graphic.

T F 7. Individual objects can be edited in a grouped object.

T F 8. The only two options for moving an object in front of or behind another object are Bring to Front and Send to Back.

T F 9. Find Similar Style options for clip art brings up images created in the same style that match the keywords.

T F 10. Kerning changes the size of the letters by shrinking or stretching the letters.

FILL IN THE BLANK

Complete the following sentences by writing the correct word or words in the blanks provided.

1. The two views of the Clip Organizer are _____ and _____.

2. The star icon in the lower-right corner of a clip in the Clip Organizer indicates that the clip is a(n) _____.

3. The feature in the Character Spacing dialog box that adjusts the spacing between a pair of letters is _____.

4. You must be connected to the _____ to use the Microsoft Design Gallery Live.

5. The Flip feature makes a _____ image of the object when it is flipped.

6. The various designs from which to choose for WordArt can be selected from the _____.

7. The feature that determines how close a picture, clip art, or WordArt object can be positioned near a text box frame is called _____.

8. _____ words that describe the content of a graphic are stored with each picture in the clip Organizer.

9. The _____ tabbed page in the Help dialog box allows you to key a word that describes the help you need.

10. Clips selected in the Microsoft Design Gallery Live are placed in a special _____ collection.

PROJECTS

SCANS PROJECT 2-1

You have been asked to create a flyer for the Senior Prom, a special night the Otter Creek High School Honor Society is going to conduct for senior citizens at the Otter Creek Seniors Center. This flyer will be posted at the Seniors Center.

1. Create a blank document measuring 8½ by 11 inches.

2. Set the margins at 0.5 inch each in the Layout Guides dialog box.

3. Search for a clip art using **dancers** as your keyword. Choose an appropriate clip art for the occasion.

4. Size the clip to approximately 2.5 inches by 2.5 inches. Snap it to the left and top margin guides in the upper-left corner.

5. Create a text box frame to the right of the clip art that extends to the right margin guide and is 2.5 inches tall.

6. Key the words **Senior Prom** and format the text as follows: Broadway, 72 pt., bold, center alignment, scaling at 130%. If you don't have Broadway, choose another decorative font that will fit the occasion.

7. Bring down a ruler guide from the horizontal ruler to 3.5 inches on the vertical ruler.

8. Create another text box frame starting at the ruler guide that measures 7.5 inches wide and approximately 4.75 inches tall. Set center alignment.

9. Key the date and time on two separate lines and format with Arial, 48 pt. bold.
   Otter Creek Seniors Center (Arial 36 pt. bold)
   Dance to the music of the (Arial, 32 pt.)
   Melo Tones (Arial, 32 pt. bold, italic, and 150% scaling)
   Refreshments
   Cost $1 at the door (Arial, 32 pt.)

10. Create another text box frame that measures 5.0 inches wide and 1.5 inches tall and position it at the lower-left corner where the left margin guide and bottom margin guide intersect.

11. Key the following lines and format with Arial, 18 pt. bold, and left alignment:
    Sponsored by:
    Otter Creek High School Honor Society
    And
    The Otter Creek Seniors Center

12. Create a clip organizer frame in the lower-right corner that measures approximately 2.0 inches wide and 2.0 inches tall.

13. Search for a clip art using **music** as your keyword. Choose an appropriate clip art for the occasion.

14. Save your publication as **Senior Prom** *xxx* (where *xxx* are your initials). Print it and close it. Your finished project should look something like Figure 2-29.

FIGURE 2-29
Completed Project 2-1

PROJECT 2-2

The Otter Creek High School senior class has been asked to help with a yearly popular family activity in Otter Creek called the Quarry Quest, where families can visit the local quarry to learn about quarry activities and look at the equipment. You have been asked to create the flyer that will be posted at the various public places, including the schools.

You need to include certain text, but how you design it is up to you! The flyer in Figure 2-30 is just an example of what you can do.

HINT: To get a clip art frame close to the WordArt and text box frames, turn the text wrap to None. Also, the large capital letter in the paragraph containing the description is a separate rotated WordArt frame with the text wrap also turned to None. One last hint—the top two lines are separate WordArt frames, and the Quarry Quest WordArt frame is filled with a texture called Granite, which is found in Fill Effects under the Color drop-down list in the Fill dialog box.

Save the file as **Quarry Quest xxx** (where *xxx* are your initials).

FIGURE 2-30
Completed Project 2-2

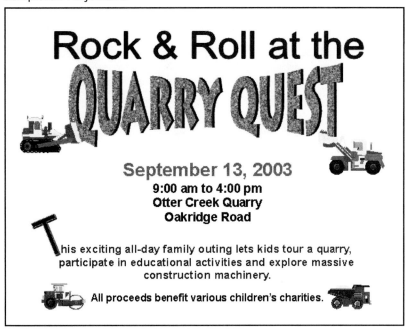

CRITICAL*Thinking*

ACTIVITY 2-1

A very important element of design is asking yourself the following question: Who is the intended audience? What special design considerations do you need to keep in mind when creating a publication for the audiences listed below?

- Children under 13
- Teenagers
- Young adults
- Baby Boomers (up to age 60)
- Senior Citizens (over age 60)

MENUS AND TABLES

OBJECTIVES

Upon completion of this lesson, you should be able to:

- Use a wizard to create a publication.

- Use wizard options to format a publication created with a wizard.

- Use the Picture toolbar to format a picture.

- Set up and format columns.

- Create a menu using the table object.

- Format a text box frame with reverse text.

- Align objects.

Estimated Time: 3 hours

VOCABULARY

Align

AutoFit Text

Cell

Distribute

Master page

Merge cells

Reverse text

Table

Watermark

Wizard

Using a Wizard

Up to this point you have been creating publications from scratch. You have been adding the frames and positioning and sizing them as directed. The *Wizard* feature in Microsoft Publisher will automatically design a publication containing preformatted objects for you. All you have to do is edit the objects to contain your information.

The big advantage to using a wizard, besides saving you time, is that the designs are created by graphic artists who know all about layout and design. Your publication will look like you spent hours creating it when it only took minutes!

In the following exercises, you will create a menu for a special event at the Otter Creek Seniors Center. Study the parts of Figure 3-1. As you can see, it will contain objects you have already worked with in previous lessons. In addition, you will work with a new object called a *table*, which is a format for organizing text in rows and columns.

FIGURE 3-1
Completed Menu

Starting the Wizard

When you start Publisher, you will see a screen similar to the one shown in Figure 3-2. You choose the type of publication and the style within the publication type. This is an example of a wizard. When using a wizard, you may be asked for some Personal Information. If you fill it in with information such as name, address, phone number, etc., that is always the same, Publisher will use this information in frames that require such data, thus saving you from having to enter it each time. You will not use the Personal Information feature until later in the book.

FIGURE 3-2
New Publication Window

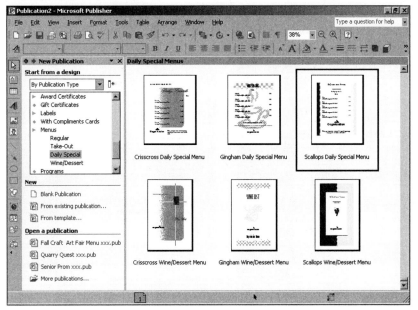

STEP-BY-STEP 3.1

1. Start Publisher. If Publisher is already running, open the **View** menu and choose **Task Pane**, if it is not already open.

2. Select **Menus** in the New Publication type list in the left pane. (Menu in this case refers to a bill of fare at a restaurant, and not a menu you might find in a software program.) Notice that Menus expands to show a submenu. (A triangle to the left of Menu is an indication that there is a submenu.)

3. Select **Daily Special**.

4. Click **Scallops Daily Special Menu**.

5. The publication builds and a prompt asks you if the wizard may fill in your name, address, and other information, click **OK**.

6. When the Personal Information dialog box opens, click **Cancel**. You will see a menu similar to the one in Figure 3-3. Keep the publication open.

Making Changes in the Wizard

Once the Publisher Wizard has created your publication, it will look much like Figure 3-3. The wizard offers you four ways to change the publication. These options are listed in the left pane. Design changes can be made before you edit the frames or after. If you change the design after you have edited all the frames, the new design may delete or move some of the edited frames, thus undoing changes you made. The changes you can make to the publication created by a wizard are listed in Table 3-1:

FIGURE 3-3
Publication from Wizard

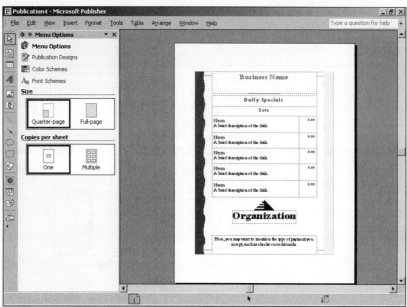

TABLE 3-1
Publication Choices After the Wizard is Created

PUBLICATIONS PANE OPTIONS	DESCRIPTION
Menu options	These options will vary depending on the design chosen. They may include size of the publication, adding or deleting components, and number of copies per page.
Publication Designs	These are the designs available in the New Publications window.
Color Schemes	This is a defined set of colors that is available for every publication. Certain colors are used for different text objects, WordArt objects, and graphic objects. If you don't like the choices in the list, you can create a custom color scheme.
Font Schemes	This is a defined set of fonts associated with a publication. Within each font scheme, a major font is used for titles and headings, and a minor font is used for body text or captions.

To change the publication design, simply click Publications Design and choose the desired new design. The contents in the right pane reflect the change. In addition to changing the Publication Design, the color scheme, and the font scheme, you can change other flyer options including adding graphic objects, a customer address, or a tear off (such as a coupon or telephone number for future reference).

S TEP-BY-STEP 3.2

1. With the Scallops menu showing in the document page, click **Publication Designs** near the top of the left pane to display the options shown in Figure 3-4.

FIGURE 3-4
Publication Designs Pane

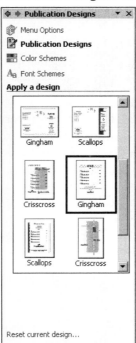

2. Scroll through the list and find **Gingham** in the fourth row of choices**.**

3. Click the **Gingham** menu and the right pane will display the new design.

4. From the **Menu Options**, choose **Full Page** in the **Size** category.

5. From the **Color Schemes**, try out different color schemes. Then choose **Trout**.

6. From the **Font Schemes** option, try out different font schemes and then choose the **Punch** set of fonts.

STEP-BY-STEP 3.2 Continued

7. Close the task pane by clicking the **X** in the upper-right corner of the pane.

8. Keep the publication open and read on.

Editing the Frames in a Publication Created by a Wizard

With your publication showing, you can edit it much like you edited your earlier publications:

- Frames can be moved using drag and drop.

- Frames can be deleted by right-clicking the frame and choosing Delete Object.

- New frames can be added by selecting the object tool and drawing the frame in the publication.

- Text can be edited in a text box by selecting the text inside a text box frame and keying your own text. As you select frames and add your own text, you will see that some frames will automatically resize the font to fit to the frame. This is called *AutoFit Text*. Text may automatically shrink because the Shrink Text On Overflow or Best Fit option is selected for that frame. The Shrink Text on Overflow option will reduce the font size until there is no text in the overflow area. The Best Fit option shrinks or expands the text to fit in the text box frame as you resize the frame. AutoFit Text options can be changed in the Format menu as illustrated in Figure 3-5.

FIGURE 3-5
AutoFit Text

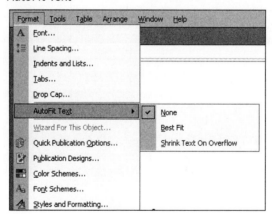

- The format of text can be copied to other selections of text. To do this, select the formatted text and choose the Format Painter option from the Standard Toolbar. Drag the mouse pointer across the text you want to format. To copy formatting to several occurrences of text, double-click the Format Painter to keep it on as you use it. Then click the button again to deselect the option when you are finished.

- Graphics can be replaced by selecting the graphic frame and adding your own picture or clip.

In the next Step-by-Step, you will edit a wizard-prepared publication.

S TEP-BY-STEP 3.3

1. Right-click the *organization* logo frame near the bottom of the menu and choose **Delete Object** to remove it. Do the same with the *business address* frame, *business phone numbers* frame, and the *payment* frame. (Remember to press F9 to zoom closer so you can see the contents of the frames.)

2. Move the *business name* frame to the bottom center of the checkered design graphic object.

3. Save the publication as **Fall Art & Craft Fair Menu** *xxx* (where *xxx* are your initials). If you are prompted to save the logo to the personal information set, click **No**.

4. Select the **Daily Specials** text in the top text frame, and key **Luncheon Menu**.

5. Select the new text and change the size of the font to 28 pt.

6. Resize the frame to be **0.5** inch tall. (HINT: View the Measurements toolbar to help you.)

7. Select the **Date** in the second text frame, and key the following two lines. The text will become very small to fit the two lines into the frame.
October 11, 2003
Lunch served 11:00 am to 12:30 pm

8. With the frame selected, click the **Format** menu and choose **AutoFit Text** and choose **Best Fit**. (At this point the font will not change.)

STEP-BY-STEP 3.3 Continued

9. Resize the frame to be **6** inches wide and **0.75** inch tall. (If at this point the font does not get larger, resize the frame to be smaller at about **0.68** inch. The font should change to a larger size. Then resize the frame to **0.75** inch again and center it.) Your publication should look much like Figure 3-6.

FIGURE 3-6
Edited Text Frames

10. Select **Business Name** in the bottom text frame. Resize the frame to **6** inches wide and key the following text in place of the existing text: ***Coffee available from 9 a.m. to 2 p.m.** Center the frame.

11. Save **Fall Art & Craft Fair Menu *xxx*** and keep it open as you read on.

Edit the Graphic

The next steps involve changing the graphic. The graphic is layered behind the table and it is very lightly colored. It almost looks like a *watermark*, which is a semi-transparent image used for stationery and as a special effect for publications. You are going to search for a fall image to replace the coffee cup and make the image a little darker using the Picture toolbar shown in Figure 3-7.

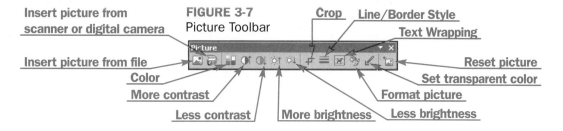

FIGURE 3-7
Picture Toolbar

Study Table 3-2 to learn the functions of the buttons on the Picture toolbar.

TABLE 3-2
Picture Toolbar Tools

BUTTON	DESCRIPTION
Insert Picture From File	Opens the Insert Picture dialog box
Insert Picture From Scanner	Activates scanner or digital camera connection for capturing a picture
Color	Lets you choose from Automatic (default color assigned to picture when it was saved), Grayscale, Black & White, Washout (like a watermark)
More Contrast	Increases the contrast between the light and dark colors
Less Contrast	Decreases the contrast between light and dark colors
More Brightness	Increases the intensity of the color of the picture
Less Brightness	Decreases the intensity of the color of the picture
Crop	Lets you "hide" part of the picture
Line/Border Style	Applies a border around the picture frame at various thicknesses
Text Wrapping	Sets a wrap around a picture frame when it is next to another frame
Format Picture	Opens the Format Picture dialog box
Set Transparent Color	Lets you choose one color in a picture to be turned off so the background color shows through
Reset Picture	Sets formatting back to the original settings

STEP-BY-STEP 3.4

1. With **Fall Art & Craft Fair Menu *xxx*** open in the window, point below the table in the publication and double-click the picture.

2. In the Insert Clip Art task pane, key **fall** in the **Search for** text box and click **Search**.

3. Choose a picture that is a simple design. Try several until you find one that doesn't take away from the text but adds interest.

4. With the picture showing in the middle of the publication, look at the Picture toolbar. (If the Picture toolbar is not showing, open the View menu, choose **Toolbars**, and choose **Picture**.)

5. Click the **Less brightness** button a few times to make the picture a little darker. (You may need to change this later.)

6. Resize the picture to measure approximately **6** inches wide and **5.6** inches tall. If necessary, move it so it is centered on the page. Save the publication and keep it open as you read on.

Editing a Table

A *table* is an object that contains rows and columns. Where the row and column meet is referred to as a *cell*. Text is usually keyed in the cell, but pictures could be added as well. The advantage of using tables is that text is lined up in the rows and columns and is easy to read.

When you are done keying text in one cell, press Tab to move the cursor to the next cell to the right. The arrow keys can also be used to move from cell to cell. After text is keyed, the cells can be selected individually, or whole rows and columns can be selected so text can be formatted. To select a row or column, point to the left of the row or just above the column until a thick black arrow shows. When you click, the row or column is selected. You can also use the Select feature in the Table menu.

Computer Concepts

If you hold down the Shift key as you drag, you will not resize the entire table—only the row or column.

The height of the rows and width of the columns can be adjusted to accommodate more text or to make them smaller. This is done by pointing to the row or column border you want to resize and dragging the resize icon. Because the table is a frame, it can be resized like any other frame. Additional rows and columns can be added to the table using the Insert Column or Insert Row buttons. A new row can be added to the end of the table by simply pressing Tab from the lower-right cell in the table. To add a row in the middle of the table, select a row near where the new row is to be inserted and choose Rows Above or Rows Below from the Insert feature in the Table menu. To add new columns, select a column next to where the new column will be inserted and choose Columns Left or Columns Right from the same menu.

You will add text to the existing table created by the wizard, add additional rows, and format text in the next Step-by-Step.

STEP-BY-STEP 3.5

1. With **Fall Art & Craft Fair Menu xxx** open in the window, select the text in the first cell and key **BBQ SANDWICH**.

2. Press **Tab** and key **$3.00**. (The font will be much smaller. You will fix this later.)

3. Press **Tab**. Continue keying the text as shown in Table 3-3. (For the cent sign, open the **Insert** menu and choose **Symbol**. Locate the cent sign, click **Insert**, and then click **Close**.) When you finish the (SODA) row, press **Tab** to start a new row. (The text you key will be formatted differently from the other text. You will format the new rows shortly.)

TABLE 3-3
Table Containing Text

ITEM	PRICE
BBQ SANDWICH	$3.00
HOT DOG	$2.00
STRAWBERRIES & ICE CREAM	$2.50
COOKIE	50¢
SODA	50¢
COFFEE*	50¢

4. To insert a row above the COOKIE row, click in the COOKIE row, open the **Table** menu, choose **Insert**, and choose **Rows Above**.

5. Key **CHIPS**. Press Tab and key **$1.00**.

6. To format the cells, click in a formatted word, such as *Sandwich*. Double-click the **Format Painter** (it's the paintbrush) on the Standard toolbar. The button should remain depressed and the mouse pointer should look like a paintbrush.

7. Drag across the words **CHIPS** and **COFFEE*** and all the money amounts. They should all be Gill Sans Ultra Bold, 12 pt.

8. Click the **Format Painter** button to turn the painter off.

STEP-BY-STEP 3.5 Continued

9. Select the column with the dollar amounts by pointing above the column until you get a thick black arrow pointing down. Click to select the column. Click the **Right Alignment** button on the Formatting toolbar. The table should now resemble Figure 3-8.

10. With the table frame selected, open the **Table** menu, choose **Select**, and choose **Table**. Change the font size to 14 pt.

11. Save the file with the same name. Keep the publication open and read on.

FIGURE 3-8
Completed Table

BBQ SANDWICH	$3.00
HOT DOG	$2.00
STRAWBERRIES & ICE CREAM	$2.50
CHIPS	$1.00
COOKIE	50¢
SODA	50¢
COFFEE*	50¢

Adding WordArt Objects

You can make titles and important headings stand out by using WordArt, as discussed in Lesson 2. In the next Step-by-Step, you will adjust the position of objects in a publication and add two WordArt frames. Remember that when you aren't told exactly what button to choose, you can point to the buttons and read the description of each one.

STEP-BY-STEP 3.6

1. Drag the table frame down on the page so that it begins at **3.625** inches on the vertical ruler.

2. Drag the frame containing the date and time down to **2.750** inches.

3. Drag the frame containing Luncheon Menu to **2.000** inches. Deselect the frame.

STEP-BY-STEP 3.6 Continued

4. Create a WordArt frame and choose the fifth style in the second row. Key the text: **Fall Art & Craft Fair** and choose Gill Sans Ultra Bold.

5. Size the frame so that it starts in the upper-left corner where the left- and top-margin guides meet, extend it to the upper-right margin and make it as tall as the checkered graphic in the background.

6. Select the WordArt frame, if necessary. Click the **Format WordArt** button on the WordArt toolbar. Change the Fill Color to **Accent 1** and the Line Color to **No Line**. Click **OK**.

7. Click the **WordArt Shape** button and choose **Deflate Top**.

8. Create and format another WordArt frame at the bottom of the page just as you did the one at the top. Key the following text: **Otter Creek Seniors Center**. Select **Deflate Bottom** for the shape.

9. Arrange the objects at the bottom so your completed publication resembles Figure 3-9. Save the publication again as **Fall Art & Craft Fair Menu *xxx***, print it, and close it.

FIGURE 3-9
Completed Menu Project

Working With Columns

Up to this point, your publications have had only one column. Many of your objects are as wide as the area between the right and left margins. Another option is to use columns, which are often used in newsletters and brochures. Columns provide shorter line lengths, making the text easier to read. In the next exercise you will create a one-page publication that is set up in two columns. The default width setting for columns is equal width but some publications warrant uneven columns to add a little more interest. The publication in Figure 3-10 has uneven column widths.

FIGURE 3-10
Completed Immunization Schedule

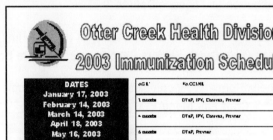

Columns are set in the Layout Guides dialog box chosen in the Arrange menu. You cannot change the widths of the columns, however, in the Layout Guides dialog box. This must be done in the Master Page of a publication.

The *master page* is the layer beneath the foreground page. When you want certain elements—layout guides, text, pictures, or graphic objects—to appear in the same place on every page, you position them on the master page. To show the master page, you select it from the View menu. You can tell you are in the master page view because you will see the letter *R* on the page navigation button rather than a page number. In this lesson, you will only use the master page to adjust the width of the columns. You will learn how to add objects to the master page in Lesson 6.

STEP-BY-STEP 3.7

1. Create a new blank publication.

2. In the Layout Guides dialog box, set the left, right, top, and bottom margins to **0.5** inch each.

3. Set the number of columns to **2**. Click **OK**.

4. From the **View** menu, choose **Master Page**. Notice the **R** in the page navigation button.

5. Hold down the **Shift** key and point to the column guide in the middle of the page until you see an **ADJUST** icon. (This is the same icon you see when you drag down a ruler guide.)

6. Hold down the mouse button and drag to the left until the column guide lines up at approximately **3.625** inches on the horizontal ruler. Watch the object position box in the lower-right corner of the screen.

7. Go to the **View** menu and return to the foreground page by deselecting **Master Page**. You should now see a **1** in the page navigation button.

8. Create a WordArt object and choose the first choice in the WordArt gallery. Key the following text in two lines in the same frame, and then click **OK**.
   Otter Creek Health Division
   2003 Immunization Schedule

9. Move the WordArt frame to the top margin and resize it so that it starts at **2** inches on the horizontal ruler at the top margin guide and extends to the right margin guides and measures approximately **1.25** inches tall.

10. To the left of the WordArt frame starting at the upper-left corner where the left- and top-margin guides meet, add an appropriate clip-art object using the search term **immunization**. Resize the clip-art object to measure approximately **1.3** inches wide and **1.3** inches tall. (HINT: Use the Measurement toolbar.)

11. Compare your publication with the one showing in Figure 3-11.

12. Save your publication as **Immunization Schedule xxx**.

FIGURE 3-11
Publication Showing Columns

Creating and Formatting Tables

Your first table was created for you automatically when you created the menu using a wizard. In the next publication, you will create tables from scratch. The publication in Figure 3-10 contains two tables. Each table has two columns and 9 or 10 rows. Tables can be created using the Insert Table button on the Objects toolbar or by using the Insert command on the Table menu. Either method will display the Create Table dialog box (see Figure 3-12). If you know the exact number of rows and columns you want in your table, you can use the spin buttons to increase or decrease the numbers showing in the dialog box.

FIGURE 3-12
Create Table Dialog Box

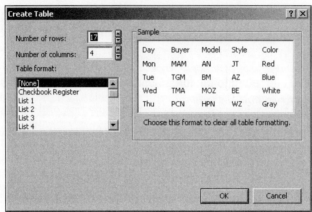

You can also choose a table format in the left pane of the dialog box. The format chosen will show in the preview window. Using a pre-designed format speeds up the formatting process.

Once the table is created, you can resize the columns and rows. You can also *merge cells*, which means joining two or more adjacent cells to form one cell. Lastly, you can format the borders of the cells. This requires selecting rows and/or columns. Do this by pointing outside the row or column until you see a heavy black arrow. Drag the arrow down the rows or across the columns to select them. Then open the Format menu and choose Table. In the Colors and Lines tabbed page, either choose from the preset options or choose individual borders. Then choose a color and weight. Let's learn as we work on the publication in the next Step-by-Step.

S TEP-BY-STEP 3.8

1. With **Immunization Schedule *xxx*** showing in the window, drag down horizontal ruler guides to help you with positioning your table frame. Position them at **2.125** inches, **6.5** inches, **7.25** inches, and **9.5** inches.

2. Click the **Insert Table** button on the Objects toolbar. Start drawing a table at the left side of the right column at the **2.125**-inch ruler guide. Size the table to stretch to the right pink margin guide and down to **6.125** inches or **4** inches tall.

3. When the Create Table dialog box shows, click **9** rows and **2** columns. Select the **List 1** table format. Click **OK**.

STEP-BY-STEP 3.8 Continued

4. Point to the column guide separating the first and second columns. When you see a double headed arrow, hold the **Shift** key and drag left until the column guide lines up with **5** inches on the horizontal ruler guide as shown in Figure 3-13.

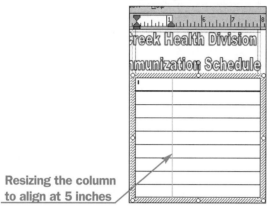

FIGURE 3-13
Adjusting the Column Width

Resizing the column
to align at 5 inches

5. Key the data in Table 3-4 into the first eight rows:

TABLE 3-4
Text for Step 5

AGE	VACCINE
2 months	DTaP, IPV, Comvax, Prevnar
4 months	DTaP, IPV, Comvax, Prevnar
6 months	DTaP, Prevnar
12 months	MMR, Varicella, IPV
15 months	DTaP, Comvax, Prevnar
4-6 years	DTaP, IPV, MMR
11+ years	Td Booster, Hep B (if hasn't had series)

6. Select both cells in the last row and click **Merge Cells** from the **Table** menu.

7. Key the following text:
   *U.S. Public Health Service and the American Academy of Pediatrics recommend the above schedule.

8. Create another table the width of the left column starting at the **7.25**-inch ruler guide. Extend it to the bottom margin guide.

9. In the Create Table dialog box, key in **10** rows and **2** columns and choose **List with Title 1** in the Table format pane. Notice that the two cells in Row 1 were merged to form one cell.

STEP-BY-STEP 3.8 Continued

10. Key the data in Table 3-5.

TABLE 3-5
Text for Step 10

DEFINITIONS	
DTaP	Diptheria/Tetanus/Acellular Pertussis
Td	Tetanus/Diptheria
IPV	Inactivated Polio Vaccine
Hib	Haemophilus Influenza b
MMR	Measles/Mumps/Rubella
Hep B	Hepatitis B
Varicella	Chicken Pox Vaccine
Comvax	Hepatitis B and Hib
Prevnar	Pneumococcal Conjugate

11. Select Rows 2-10. From the **Format** menu, choose **Table.**

12. Choose the **Colors and Lines** tab and click the Grid preset button (the third button in the lower-right corner).

13. In the Line section, choose the color **black** and a weight of **1 pt**. Click **OK**.

14. Hold the **Shift** key while you use the mouse to grab the line between columns. Move it to the left so none of the cells except the first one at the right wrap to a second line. Save the file.

Formatting a Text Box with Reverse Text

It is a common formatting design to fill a text box with black fill color and change the text font to white. This is called *reverse text*. When formatting a light-colored text to appear in a dark-colored background, it is a good idea to bold the text as well.

STEP-BY-STEP 3.9

1. With **Immunization Schedule *xxx*** open in the window, create a text frame that extends across the first column beginning at the **2.125**-inch horizontal ruler guide. Make it **5** inches tall.

STEP-BY-STEP 3.9 Continued

2. Turn on center alignment and key the following text:
DATES
January 17, 2003
February 14, 2003
March 14, 2003
April 18, 2003
May 16, 2003
June 20, 2003
July 18, 2003
August 15, 2003
September 19, 2003
October 17, 2003
November 21, 2003
December 19, 2003
TIMES
9:30 to 10:30 AM and
3:30 to 5:30 PM

3. Select and format the text as follows: Arial Black, 14 pt., white font color.

4. Select the text frame containing the text and choose **Black** from the Fill Color dialog box.

5. Create another text frame in the right column that starts at the **6.5**-inch horizontal ruler guide and extends to the right margin guide. Make the frame **2.25** inches tall.

6. Key the text shown below. Format the first line in bold and the next three statements as a bulleted list, using a bullet of your choice.
Parents, please note the following:
It is necessary to bring your child's immunization record to the clinic for each visit. We shall update your records.
Hepatitis B vaccine is required for kindergarten, 1st, 2nd, 3rd, 7th, 8th, 9th, and 10th grades starting the 2003-2004 school year.
Vericella (chicken pox vaccine) is recommended for children who have no reliable history of chicken pox.

7. Insert a clip-art frame in the upper-left corner of the text box you just added. Use **shot** as your search text.

8. Resize it to approximately **0.9** inch square. Move the clip up so that about a third of the image is above the top of the text box.

9. Create a small text frame in the right column at **8.5** inches on the vertical ruler. Extend it across the column, and make it approximately **0.4** inch tall. Center the following text:
Call (920) 555-5080 for more information

10. Format the text as follows: Arial Black, 12 pt.

11. Select the text frame. Click the **Line/Border Style** button, and select **¾ pt**.

12. Save the file.

Aligning Objects

The last objects to be added are the address of the Otter Creek Health Division and the Otter Creek logo. Since these two objects will be close together, they would look better if they were aligned at the tops of each of the frames. This can be done manually by using the mouse to line them up or by using the Align or Distribute feature. (*Align* means the top, bottom, left, or right borders of two or more objects are even. *Distribute* means that two or more objects are equally spaced apart vertically or horizontally.) Multiple objects can be selected and aligned at various different positions. The choices are found in the Align or Distribute submenu of the Arrange menu (see Figure 3-14).

FIGURE 3-14
Align or Distribute Submenu

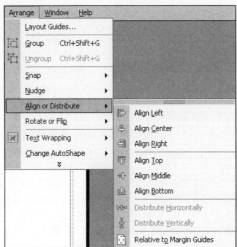

As shown in Figure 3-14, objects can be aligned horizontally (three choices) or vertically (three choices). The Center commands, for example, are ideal for centering objects on top of each other.

The distribute choices arrange objects an equal distance from one another. To use the distribute choices, Relative to Margin Guides must be selected. (The Relative to Margin Guides option should be used with care, because it affects all alignment and distribution choices.)

STEP-BY-STEP 3.10

1. Create a picture frame in the lower-right corner of the publication that measures approximately **1.05** inches square.

2. Insert the **Otter Creek Logo.jpg** graphic file from your prerecorded data files.

3. Create a text box frame to the left of the picture frame that measures **2.5** inches wide and **1** inch tall.

4. Key the following text:
Otter Creek City Hall
215 Washington Avenue
Fourth Floor

STEP-BY-STEP 3.10 Continued

5. Format the text as follows: Arial Black, 12 pt., and right align.

6. Move the text frame as close as possible to the picture frame.

7. Hold the **Shift** key while you click to select the text frame and the picture frame. Both should be selected.

8. From the **Arrange** menu, choose **Align or Distribute** and **Align Top**.

9. Look back at Figure 3-10 and compare your completed publication with the figure. Is it similar? Do you wish to make some adjustments?

10. Save, print, and close the file.

SUMMARY

In this lesson, you learned:

■ You can use a Wizard to create a publication.

■ You can edit a publication that was created using a Wizard.

■ The appearance of a picture can be altered using the Picture toolbar.

■ A document can be formatted into columns.

■ Columns can be resized.

■ It is easy to create and format tables.

■ You can create a text box with reverse text (white on black).

■ Objects in a publication can be aligned in a number of ways.

VOCABULARY *Review*

Define the following terms:

Align	Master page	Table
AutoFit Text	Merge cells	Watermark
Cell	Reverse text	Wizard
Distribute		

REVIEW *Questions*

WRITTEN QUESTIONS

Write a brief answer to the following questions.

1. What are some of the advantages of using a Wizard to create a publication?

2. What is a watermark?

3. What is a table?

4. In what two ways can a table be created?

5. What is the purpose of the Table AutoFormat command?

6. What are the two directions objects can be aligned?

7. How do you format reverse text?

8. How can you resize columns in a document that are set up using the Layout Guides dialog box?

9. How can you resize columns in a table without changing the size of the entire table?

10. How do you merge cells in a table?

11. What are five formatting commands found on the Picture toolbar?

12. What is the box called where a column and row meet in a table?

MATCHING

Match the correct term in Column 2 to its description in Column 1.

Column 1	Column 2

_____ 1. Frames that automatically resize the font to fit the frame

_____ 2. The menu where you choose the desired new design after a wizard is complete

_____ 3. A tool used to copy text and paragraph formatting

_____ 4. The dialog box used to set the number of columns in a publication

_____ 5. Where you place objects you want to appear on every page, such as a page number or graphic

_____ 6. The button you press when you want multiple cells in a column to be one cell

_____ 7. A text box that is filled with black color and contains text that is white in color

_____ 8. Arranging objects to be an equal distance from one another either horizontally or vertically

A. Reverse text

B. AutoFit Text

C. Distribute

D. Merge cells

E. Format painter

F. Publication designs

G. Master page

H. Layout Guides

PROJECTS

PROJECT 3-1

The annual Otter Creek Senior Summer Olympics is going to be held in July. You have been asked to create a schedule that can be posted at the Otter Creek Seniors Center. Many activities are scheduled, so the listing needs to be easy to read and understand. You will create a table to contain the information that will include the date, time of the event, name of the event, and the location in the city where it will be held. The table will take up most of the one-page publication. It will look much like Figure 3-15.

FIGURE 3-15
Completed Senior Olympic Schedule

1. Create a blank publication.

2. Set the margins to 0.3 inch for all four sides.

3. Bring down a ruler guide from the horizontal margin to 2.25 inches on the vertical ruler.

4. Create a table that starts at the 2.25 inches ruler guide and size it to fit from the left margin to the right margin and down to the bottom margin.

5. When the Create Table dialog box appears, key 34 rows and 4 columns and choose None for the Table Format. (If you see a prompt about increasing the size of the table, click Yes.)

6. Hold the Shift key as you resize the columns so the entire table does not "shift." Move the column guides to the following points on the horizontal scale: 1.5 inches, 2.5 inches, and 4.75 inches

7. Key the text in Table 3-6, leaving a blank row between the days as shown in Figure 3-15.

TABLE 3-6
Schedule data

DAY	TIME	EVENT	LOCATION
Friday, July 11	10:00 AM	Water games & relays	YMCA (324 Lincoln Avenue)
	10:45 AM	Water exercise	YMCA
	1:00 PM	Contract bridge	Otter Creek Seniors Center (220 N. Campbell Road)
	1:00 PM	Table tennis	Otter Creek Seniors Center
Monday, July 14	8:00 AM	Walk for fun	South Park (625 Willow Boulevard)
	9:30 AM	Opening ceremony	South Park
	10:00 AM	Softball throw	South Park
	10:30 AM	Frisbee throw	South Park
	11:30 AM	Noon picnic lunch	South Park
	12:30 PM	Brown bag bingo	South Park
	1:30 PM	Toss 'em (similar to Jarts)	South Park
Tuesday, July 15	8:00 AM	Miniature golf	Creek View Par 3 (345 Hickory Heights)
	10:30 AM	Free throw	Recreation Gym (425 Archery Lane)
	10:30 AM	Bottle Bowling	Recreation Gym
	1:30 PM	Dartball	Recreation Gym
Wednesday, July 16	8:30 AM	Bean bag toss	South Park
	10:00 AM	Horseshoes	South Park
	10:00 AM	Lawn dice	South Park
	1:30 PM	Sheepshead	Otter Creek Seniors Center
	1:30 PM	Kings in the corner	Otter Creek Seniors Center
	1:30 PM`	Euchre	Otter Creek Seniors Center
Thursday, July 17	8:00 AM	Shuffleboard	Recreation Gym
	1:30 PM	Cribbage	Otter Creek Seniors Center
	1:30 PM	Canasta	Otter Creek Seniors Center
	1:30 PM	Pinochle	Otter Creek Seniors Center
Friday, July 18	7:00 AM	Golf	Otter Creek Municipal Golf Course (233 Ash Street)
	8:30 AM	Putting	Otter Creek Municipal Golf Course

8. Now that you have the text in the table, format it using shading, font changes, and reverse text. Select the first row and the blank rows between the days and fill them with a medium shade of gray.

9. Select the first row and format the text to be center-aligned, Arial, 14 pt., white, and bold.

10. Select the times data and format the text using Arial, 10 pt., and right align.

11. Select the event and location text and format the text using Arial, 10 pt., and left align.

12. Select the cell that contains **Friday, July 11** and the three blank cells below and merge the four cells. Format the text using Arial, 16 pt., and center align. Repeat this formatting for the remaining dates.

13. Press Ctrl+A twice to select all the cells in the table. Turn on the grid border by choosing Format, Table, Colors and Lines. Click the grid button that is in the lower-right corner of the dialog box and choose a weight of 0.25.

14. At the top of the publication, add a WordArt frame that measures approximately 6 inches wide and 1 inch tall. Snap it into the top- and right-margin guides. Key the text: **2003 Otter Creek Senior Summer Olympics**. You choose the color.

15. Create a text box frame under the WordArt frame that contains the following three lines of centered text:
**Register by Monday, June 30, 4:30 PM at the Otter Creek Seniors Center,
220 N. Campbell Road, Otter Creek
$2.00 Entry Fee**

16. Format the first two lines of text using Arial, 12 pt. bold.

17. Format the third line of text using Arial, 14 pt. bold.

18. Add a clip art of your choice using the search text of **torch**. Align it to the left of the WordArt frame and text box frame as shown in Figure 3-15. Resize the clip art if necessary.

19. Save the publication as **Senior Olympic Schedule xxx**. Print the file and close it.

SCANS PROJECT 3-2

Create a table that will be used in a newsletter for the Otter Creek Police Department. It will include statistics on the bike patrol activities along with a graphic. It should look similar to Figure 3-16, but feel free to be creative!

FIGURE 3-16
Possible Completed Project

Bike Patrol Activity Highlights (May—September)	
Complaints investigated	86
Citations issued	38
In-jail arrests	6
Traffic stops	55
Assisted other units	41

1. Create a blank publication that is 8½ x 11 inches.

2. Set layout guides at 0.5 inch on all sides.

3. Bring down a ruler guide to 7.5 inches on the vertical ruler.

4. At 2 inches on the horizontal ruler and at the 7.5 inches ruler guide, create a table that extends to the right margin and down to the bottom margin.

5. In the Create Table dialog box, enter 6 rows and 2 columns. Choose None for table format.

6. Merge the cells in the first row.

7. Center the following two lines of text in the first row:
    Bike Patrol Activity Highlights
    (May – September)

8. In the remaining five rows, key the text in Table 3-7.

TABLE 3-7
Text for Project 3-2

Complaints investigated	86
Citations issued	38
In-jail arrests	6
Traffic stops	55
Assisted other units	41

9. Change the font for the entire table to a sans serif font.

10. Change the size of both lines of the title to 18 pt., medium blue color.

11. Change the remaining cells to 16 pt.

12. Select the entire table and turn on the grid border. Set the color to a medium blue.

13. Center align the numbers in the second column.

14. Insert an appropriate graphic to the left of the table. The sample shown includes a graphic that was sent to the back and made lighter using the More Brightness button on the Picture toolbar.

15. Save the file as Bicycle Patrol *xxx*.

16. Print the file and close it.

CANS PROJECT 3-3

One of the Wizards available in Microsoft Publisher is the Calendar Wizard. A calendar basically is a big table. Create a calendar as follows:

1. Use the Start a publication from design option and choose Full Page from the Calendar type.

2. Create a one-month calendar for the month of your next birthday. You choose the design.

3. Mark the day of your birthday by keying the text, **My Birthday**, in the appropriate cell.

4. Save the file as **My Calendar**. Print the file and close it.

CRITICAL *Thinking*

CANS ACTIVITY 3-1

You have probably created tables in other software programs, such as Microsoft Word or Corel WordPerfect, or you have worked with rows and columns in a spreadsheet program such as Microsoft Excel. List what you see as the similarities in creating tables in Publisher and these other programs. List what you see as the differences.

INVITATIONS AND POSTCARDS

OBJECTIVES

Upon completion of this lesson, you should be able to:

- Use a wizard to create a publication.
- Use wizard options to format a publication created with a wizard.
- Turn off hyphenation.
- Create and format autoshapes.
- Fill WordArt with Gradient.
- Save an object as a picture file.

Estimated Time: 3 hours

VOCABULARY

AutoShapes

Gradient

Invitation

Opaque

Postcard

Save As Picture

Transparent

Invitations

I*nvitations* are used to invite people to special occasions. Your company may have a special sale, special promotion, open house, special event, or any number of occasions that require an invitation. Microsoft Publisher provides a wizard to create various styles of invitations in a card format as well as the folded card layout using the blank publication option. You could also use the postcard publication as an invitation. In addition, it is not uncommon today (although it is a little tacky) to receive a fax as an invitation to a workshop or special promotion. In this lesson, you will use a wizard and a folded card blank publication for invitations.

Invitations can be formal or informal, depending on the occasion and the invitees. The paper on which invitations are printed also makes a big difference in the type of impression they send. Using thicker paper, such as medium stock or cover stock, will give the invitation a more formal look. The finish of the stock will also make a difference—an uncoated finish may be smooth or textured; whereas, coated finishes will be glossy. Having the invitation machine-folded is important for a more professional look.

Create an Invitation Using a Wizard

Your first invitation will be to members of the Otter Creek Seniors Center to announce a birthday party celebration. Pages 2 and 3 of this invitation are shown in Figure 4-1. Publisher provides personal as well as business-type invitations. You are going to choose a birthday invitation and modify it for the special birthday party.

FIGURE 4-1
Finished Pages 2 and 3 of Invitation

FIGURE 4-1
Finished Pages 2 and 3 of Invitation

STEP-BY-STEP 4.1

1. Create a new publication using the **Invitation Cards** publication from the Publication Type list in the New Publication pane.

2. From the **Birthday Party** category, choose **Slice of Cake Birthday Party Invitation**.

3. If the message appears telling you that the Wizard will fill in your name, etc., click **OK**. When the Personal Information dialog box appears, click **Cancel**.

4. In the Task Pane, choose **Quarter-page top fold** from the Size and fold section.

5. On page 1, select the text **You're invited...** and change the font to Broadway.

STEP-BY-STEP 4.1 Continued

6. Look at the page numbered navigation buttons at the bottom left of the window. Click 2 to turn to page 2 and replace the placeholder text in each box with the following text:

Invitation Title: **25 years old!**

Describe the event: **The Otter Creek Seniors Center is celebrating its 25th birthday and would like you to attend!**

Contact Person: Delete this box by right-clicking and choosing Delete Object.

Date: **January 25, 2003**

Time: **1 PM—3 PM**

Describe the location:

Otter Creek Seniors Center

220 N. Campbell Road

7. Format the text in all the text frame boxes using the Broadway font. Change the size of the text to the following point sizes starting at the top text box: 28, 12, 20, 20, 12.

8. You may have to resize the boxes and move them up and/or down to display all of the text.

9. Turn to page 3 and select the words **"To a birthday bash!"** and change the font to Broadway.

10. Press **Enter** at the end of the line you just formatted, and key the text:
Cake and ice cream for everyone! It will break into two lines. Check your pages 2 and 3 with Figure 4-1 to see if you are on the right track.

11. Turn to page 4 and create a small text box centered above the graphic. Key the text:
Designed by (your name).

12. Select the text and format the font as Broadway, size 10 point.

13. Save the publication as **Seniors Center Birthday Invitation** *xxx*, where *xxx* are your initials. Keep it open for the next Step-by-Step.

> **Note** ☑
>
> By default, automatic hyphenation is turned on for text box frames. This means that hyphens will be placed in words based on spelling rules. If you want to control what words are hyphenated, click Manual.

To Hyphenate or Not to Hyphenate

When a text box frame contains a lot of text such as you would see in a newsletter, hyphenation is generally turned on so that the right margin is less jagged.

When a text box frame is smaller, such as a pull quote or the description found in the invitation you just created, a hyphen is more noticeable. Since the text is generally centered in these smaller text box frames, automatic hyphenation should be turned off. This is done in the Hyphenation dialog box (Figure 4-2), which is opened from the Language submenu found in the Tools menu. To turn off the automatic hyphenation for a particular text box frame, deselect the Automatically hyphenate this story option. This has to be done for each individual frame that is affected; it is not a *global* function that affects all text box frames. You will experiment with this feature in the next Step-by-Step.

FIGURE 4-2
Hyphenation Dialog Box

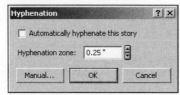

S TEP-BY-STEP 4.2

1. Select the text box frame describing the event on page 2.

2. From the **Tools** menu, choose **Language**.

3. From the submenu, choose **Hyphenation**.

4. Deselect the **Automatically hyphenate this story** option and click **OK**.

5. There should be no hyphenated words now in this text box frame.

6. Save the file again with the same name. Close the file for now. You will make one more change later, and then you will print it.

Creating AutoShapes

*A*utoShapes is a utility used to create various geometric shapes. These shapes can be used to enhance the design of a publication or to create your own graphics. The shapes are organized in categories that include lines, connectors, basic geometric shapes, block arrows, flowchart elements, stars and banners, and callouts. There is also a link to AutoShapes contained in the Clip Art Organizer.

Adding AutoShapes to Your Document

To add an AutoShape, click AutoShapes on the Objects toolbar (see Figure 4-3), select a category, point to a shape and see a tool tip describe the shape. When you find the shape you want, click to select it. Then, using your mouse pointer on the document page, hold the left mouse button and drag the mouse diagonally until you have the object size you want.

FIGURE 4-3
AutoShapes Submenu

Reshaping AutoShapes within Your Document

Once certain AutoShapes are drawn, they can be reshaped using the yellow adjustment handle. Position the mouse pointer over the adjustment handle until the mouse pointer turns into the adjust pointer. Then click on the handle and drag the mouse to change the shape. (See the sample in Figure 4-4.) Some shapes do not have adjustment handles, while others have more than one adjustment handle.

FIGURE 4-4
Sun Shape Before and After Adjustment

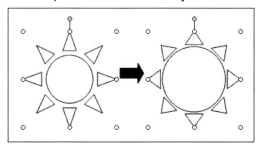

Changing an AutoShape

You can change an AutoShape to another shape entirely. Select the shape and open the Arrange menu. Choose Change AutoShape. You will see a submenu that contains the various categories from which to pick a different shape.

Adding Text to an AutoShape

Text can be added to the shape by selecting the shape and keying the desired text. The advantage of adding it to the shape instead of adding a text box as a layer on top of the shape is that if you rotate or flip the shape, the text will also rotate or flip. Let's try out some of these features.

STEP-BY-STEP 4.3

1. Create a blank publication.

2. From the AutoShapes button on the Objects toolbar, choose **Stars and Banners**.

3. Look for and click **Explosion 1**.

4. Anywhere on the document page, drag the mouse pointer diagonally until the object measures approximately **1.5** inches wide and **1.5** inches tall.

5. Zoom in to see it better by pressing **F9**.

6. With it still selected, key **25**. Select the text you just keyed, change to center alignment, and change the font to Lithograph or Wide Latin.

7. Keep clicking the **Increase Font Size** button (a big **A** with an arrow on the Formatting toolbar) until the text doesn't all fit in the shape. Once it is too large, click **Decrease Font Size** to make it fit. It should be approximately size 28 pt.

8. Change the font color to **white**.

9. Change the AutoShape fill color to **black**.

10. With the AutoShape selected, point to the rotate button (the green button at the top of the frame) and drag it slightly to the left. It should resemble Figure 4-5.

FIGURE 4-5
Rotated Explosion AutoShape

11. Save your work as **AutoShape Practice xxx** and keep it open for the next Step-by-Step.

Adding Shadows to AutoShapes

You can give AutoShapes a 3-D effect by adding shadows to them. Select the shape and choose a shadow from the Shadow button on the Formatting toolbar. You may choose the side on which the shadow will appear as well as the depth of the shadow from the submenu. You can also turn on the Shadow Settings toolbar from the submenu, which allows you to adjust the shadow even more as well as choose a different shadow color.

S TEP-BY-STEP 4.4

1. Create another AutoShape anywhere on the document page choosing the **Up Ribbon** from the **Stars and Banners** category.

2. Make it approximately **3.5** inches wide and **1.0** inches tall.

3. Notice this shape has two yellow diamonds. Try them out and see what they do. Click the **Undo** arrow on the Standard toolbar to cancel the adjust changes. (HINT: You can click on the down arrow next to the Undo button and select Adjust Objects. When you release the mouse button, all changes will be undone.)

4. Resize the entire object to be **4.5** inches wide.

5. Create a WordArt object choosing the fourth shape in the top row.

6. Key the text **25 Years** and click **OK**.

7. Drag the WordArt object to the top of the ribbon. Center it. Adjust the size and placement.

8. Select the AutoShape and fill it with a gray color.

9. Click the **Shadow Style** button. It is near the right on the Formatting toolbar (Figure 4-6). Choose the second shadow in the second row.

FIGURE 4-6
Shadow Submenu

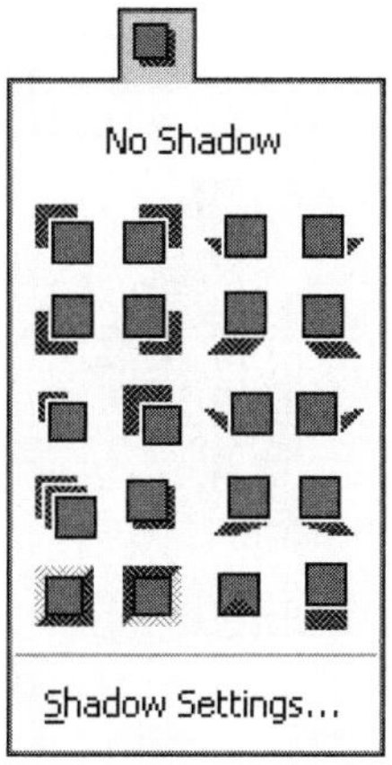

10. Select both shapes and click the **Group** button.

STEP-BY-STEP 4.4 Continued

11. Your shape should resemble Figure 4-7. Keep your **AutoShape Practice *xxx*** publication open for more AutoShape exercises.

FIGURE 4-7
Up Ribbon AutoShape

Applying Fill Colors and Fill Effects

Up to now if you have changed the color of an object, you have chosen a color from the Fill Color tool on the Formatting toolbar. There are two other choices on that palette—More Fill Colors and Fill Effects. Figure 4-8 shows the dialog box that appears when you choose More Fill Colors. It contains additional colors available in the standard color choices. Custom choices provide you with the opportunity to make your own color.

At the bottom of the dialog box is the option to increase the transparency percentage of the chosen color. This basically makes the color lighter so that if the filled object is layered on top of another object and/or text, the bottom layer will be more visible.

FIGURE 4-8
More Fill Colors Dialog Box

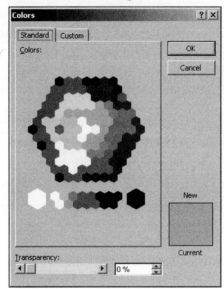

Fill Effects brings up the dialog box in Figure 4-9. This dialog box offers many different types of gradients, textures, patterns, pictures, and tints/shades. One of the interesting designs is the gradient. *Gradient* is a fill effect that uses tints or shades of one or more colors to create special patterns within an object. One or two colors can be chosen along with many different shading styles. The easiest way to choose gradient colors, however, is to use the Preset colors. These come in an array of combinations of colors bearing such names as Rainbow, Brass, Chrome, Gold, Daybreak, Horizon, and more. These combinations are great!

Let's try some of these options in the next Step-by-Step.

FIGURE 4-9
Fill Effects Dialog Box

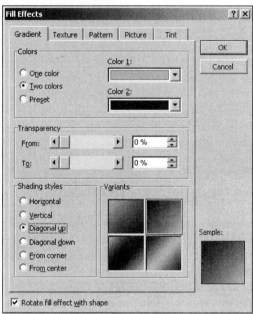

STEP-BY-STEP 4.5

1. With **AutoShape Practice *xxx*** open in the window, click the AutoShapes tool, and choose **Block Arrows**.

2. Choose the **Striped Right Arrow** shape and draw an arrow that is approximately **2.5** inches wide by **1.5** inches tall.

3. From the down arrow beside **Fill Color**, choose **Fill Effects**.

4. On the **Gradient** page, choose **Two colors**.

5. Choose **Accent 4** for Color 1; choose **Main** for Color 2.

6. Choose **Vertical** for shading styles.

7. Look at the square samples at the right. Choose the second option on the top row. Click **OK**.

STEP-BY-STEP 4.5 Continued

8. Your shape should resemble Figure 4-10. Click the **Save** button on the Toolbar, but keep your publication open.

FIGURE 4-10
Gradient Fill in AutoShapes

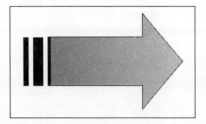

Fill Effects can also be applied to WordArt objects. This can be very effective for titles created with WordArt. We'll try this in the next Step-by-Step.

STEP-BY-STEP 4.6

1. Create a WordArt object choosing the second style in the top row.

2. Key your name and click **OK**.

3. Move the WordArt toolbar out of the way.

4. From the **Fill Color** down arrow, choose **Fill Effects**.

5. On the **Gradient** page, choose **Two Colors**.

6. Choose **Main** as Color 1; choose **Accent 5** as Color 2.

7. Choose **From center** as the shading style.

8. Choose the second illustration on the right. Click **OK**. Look at the results of your formatting.

9. To explore this feature further, click to select your WordArt object. Then click the down arrow again for **Fill Color**.

10. Choose **Fill Effects** and then **Preset**.

STEP-BY-STEP 4.6 Continued

11. Experiment with different designs and settle with the one you like best. Your WordArt may resemble the object in Figure 4-11.

12. Save the publication again as **AutoShapes Practice *xxx*** and print it. Close the file.

FIGURE 4-11
WordArt with Fill Effects

Modify an Invitation

Now that you have experience with AutoShapes, you will make one change to the invitation you created earlier in this lesson.

S TEP-BY-STEP 4.7

1. Open the **Seniors Center Birthday Invitation**. Click to select the grouped objects on Page 1 surrounding the birthday cake.

2. Ungroup the object by clicking the **Ungroup Objects** button.

3. Click away from the selected objects and select the AutoShape to the right of the birthday cake object.

4. Click the **Fill Color** down arrow and select **Fill Effects**.

5. Choose **Gradient** and then **One color**.

6. Choose **Accent 4**.

7. Choose **From center**; click the option on the right with the darker color in the center. Click **OK**.

8. Save the file again, print it and fold it. How does it look? Close the file.

Use the Side-Fold Card for an Invitation

You used the Wizard to create an invitation. Now it's time for you to venture out on your own and create an invitation using the side-fold card page setup. This special page setup will generate four pages, just like the one you created using the Wizard. It will still print on one 8½ × 11 sheet of paper, but it will fold on the side instead of the top. Figure 4-12 illustrates what the front of the invitation may look like when you finish.

FIGURE 4-12
Page 1 of Side-Folded Invitation

S TEP-BY-STEP 4.8

1. Create a new blank publication using the default 8½ × 11 page.

2. From the **File** menu, choose **Page Setup**.

3. From the **Publication type**, choose **Folded card**.

4. From the **Page size**, choose **Side-fold card**. Click **OK** and click **Yes** to the message asking to automatically insert pages. (Look at the rulers. Your "page" is now 4.25 inches wide and 5.5 inches tall.)

5. On page one, insert a clip-art object that contains a picture you select after searching for **orchestra** in the Clip Organizer. (If the Add Clips to Organization dialog box appears, click **Later**.)

6. Display the Picture toolbar, and change the color of the picture to **Grayscale**. Size and position the object attractively.

STEP-BY-STEP 4.8 Continued

7. Create a text box frame centered below the picture containing the following text:
Let our music put you in the mood!

8. Choose an appropriate font and format the text box frame using reverse text (white text on a black background).

9. Save your publication as **fund raiser invitation xxx**. Keep it open to prepare other pages.

STEP-BY-STEP 4.9

1. With the fundraiser invitation open in the window, turn to page 3. Create a text box frame in the middle of the page and key the following text:
Followed by great food!

2. Format the font design and font size the same as you did on Page 1, but do not format it using reverse text.

3. Add a divider above and below the text. (HINT: Go to the Clip Organizer and search for **divider**. Insert and size the divider. Copy the divider to the clipboard, and then paste another copy into the publication. Move the copy to the desired location.)

4. On Page 2, create three text box frames. Format the text using Arial and choose an appropriate size.

5. In the top frame, key the following text:
Victims of Violence
Fund Raiser

6. In the middle frame, key the following text:
The Otter Creek Symphony Orchestra
And
Local Area Restaurants
Are privileged to present a concert and desserts
For your pleasure
All proceeds go to the Victims of Violence Fund

7. In the third frame, key the following text and bold the text to the left of the colon.
Chairperson: Heather Mannerly
Contact: 920-555-4001
Date: March 22, 2003
Time: 7 PM
Location: Otter Creek Performing Arts Center
Tickets: $25/person

STEP-BY-STEP 4.9 Continued

8. Copy one of the dividers you added on Page 3, and paste it at the top, middle, and bottom of Page 2. (See Figure 4-13 for an example.)

FIGURE 4-13
Pages 2 and 3 of Side-Folded Invitation

9. On Page 4, paste a divider at the bottom margin and center a small text box frame above it to contain the following text:
Created by
(your name)

10. Save the file again as **fund raiser invitation *xxx*** and print the file. Fold it and check the formatting. How does it look? Close the file.

Create a Postcard

*P*ostcards are used to send greetings, to announce activities and events, and to send brief messages. While they can be the plain "vanilla" type that may be used to announce a meeting, they can also be very artistic! Postcards are always printed on heavier stock paper to withstand the automated mail handling system. Generally, one-half of one side needs to be left blank for the mailing address, postage, and postmark.

Postcards can be created using a wizard or you can begin with a blank publication. If you start with a blank publication, the postcard size must be chosen from the Page Setup dialog box. Two pages are needed for a postcard. One page is for the front of the card and the other page is for the back, half of which will be empty.

In the next Step-by-Step, you will create a postcard from a blank publication, and you will use the tricks you learned in previous exercises when working with WordArt and AutoShapes. Before beginning, study Figure 4-14. Note how attractive it is. How much of that do you think you could do without help?

STEP-BY-STEP 4.10

1. From the **File** menu, choose **New**. Click **Blank Publication**.

2. Open the **File** menu, choose **Page Setup** and then **Postcard**.

3. Choose **1/4 page Letter** in the **Page size** list. Make sure **Landscape** is chosen and click **OK**.

4. Using the Clip Organizer, search for **balloons**.

5. Choose a single- or two-balloon clip art and drag it into the upper-left corner of the document. Resize it to be about **1.5** inches tall and proportionately wide.

6. With the clip-art object selected, click **Copy**.

7. Click **Paste** and move the second copy to the right of the first copy.

8. Make enough copies to fit across to the right margin.

9. Make the center clip-art objects just a little less tall by dragging up from the bottom-middle handle. This will give the balloons in the middle the illusion of flying higher than the ones on the side.

10. Save your postcard as **Humane Society Postcard *xxx***. Keep it open in the window so you can add some text to the card.

STEP-BY-STEP 4.11

1. Create a WordArt frame, choosing the third box in the second row.

2. Key **Grand Opening** and choose Kabel Ult BT as the font (or something similar that you will use throughout the publication).

3. Resize the object to be the same width as the balloon objects and move it up over the top of the balloons.

4. Change the WordArt shape to the **Inflate Top** shape.

5. Choose the **preset** gradient color **Early Sunset**. Set both of the transparencies in the gradient dialog box to **0%** so the vividness of the colors will show.

6. Create another WordArt shape choosing the third box in the first row.

7. Key **Saturday November 8, 1 PM – 4 PM** and choose Kabel Ult BT as the font.

STEP-BY-STEP 4.11 Continued

8. Resize the object to be the same width as the top WordArt shape, choose the **Deflate Bottom** shape, and move it below the first WordArt shape (see Figure 4-14).

FIGURE 4-14
Front of Finished Postcard (Page 1)

9. Create a text box frame to fill the remaining space in the postcard to the bottom margin.

10. Center the following text:
    Otter Creek Humane Society
    2345 Alpine Road
    Public is Invited

11. Format all three lines using the Kabel Ult BT font and choose center alignment.

12. Select the first line and increase the size to fit the width of the text box frame.

13. From the **Format** menu, choose **Font**.

14. Turn on **Outline** and **Shadow**.

15. Format the second and third lines to be a larger font as well, but not larger than the first line.

16. Create a rectangle (from the objects toolbar) that covers the entire postcard, out to the edges of all four sides.

17. With the rectangle selected, click the arrow beside the **Fill Color** button and choose **Fill Effects**. From the Texture page, choose **Newsprint**. Click **OK**.

STEP-BY-STEP 4.11 Continued

18. Send the rectangle to the back. Your first page should resemble Figure 4-14.

19. Save the publication again as **Humane Society Postcard xxx**. Keep it open.

STEP-BY-STEP 4.12

1. Study Figure 4-15—the back of the card. From the **Insert** menu, choose **Page**.

2. Choose **After current page** and **Insert blank pages**. Click **OK**.

3. Create a rectangle over the left half of the page all the way to the top and bottom edges of the page. Fill it with **Newsprint** texture.

4. Search for one or two clip art objects (**dogs**, or **cats**, or **animal shelters**) to place in the shaded area. Resize the clip art, if necessary.

5. Create AutoShapes of your choice to put behind the clip art that helps the clips stand out. Fill the AutoShapes with colors of your choice.

6. Create a text box frame in the center and key the following text. Format the text with Kabel Ult BT to match the font on the first page.
Please come and see our new facilities!

7. Fill that text box frame with a color of your choice.

8. Center a text box at the bottom of the shaded half and add the following text. Format the box using reverse text (white text on a black background).
Sponsored by Friends of Otter Creek Humane Society

STEP-BY-STEP 4.12 Continued

9. Your second page should resemble Figure 4-15. Save the file.

FIGURE 4-15
Back of Finished Postcard (Page 2)

10. From the File menu, choose **Print**. Click **Change Copies Per Sheet**.

11. Choose **Print one copy per sheet**. (NOTE: Normally you would print multiple copies per sheet to keep the printing costs down. For this exercise, you are selecting only one to speed up the printing in your classroom.) Click **OK**.

12. Click **OK**, and then save and close the file.

Creating Logos

Y ou have learned how to format WordArt in two lessons, and you have learned how to use the AutoShapes. Now you are going to combine the two to create a logo for the Otter Creek Bicycle Patrol.

After you create the logo and group the objects, right-click to display a shortcut menu offering the *Save as Picture* command (Figure 4-16). This command allows you to save your picture as a separate graphic file. (If you do not group the objects, only one object will be saved as a picture.) You must choose a picture file format from the Save As dialog. The most common formats that are compatible for documents as well as Web pages are *.gif, .jpg*, and *.png*. Formats vary in resolution as well as file size. A comparison of the sizes of a graphic saved in different formats is shown in Table 4.1.

> **Hot Tip**
>
> When you create a logo, you can save the image as a graphic file. The image can then be used in Publisher as well as other software programs if they are compatible with the graphic format you use. This is a new feature in Publisher, and you will find it VERY useful!

FIGURE 4-16
Save As Picture Command

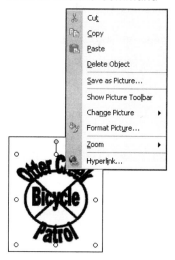

TABLE 4.1
Graphic File Comparisons

FILE FORMAT	FILE SIZE
.GIF	9KB
.JPEG	9KB
.PNG	30KB
.TIF	16KB
.BMP	50KB
.WMF	42KB

In addition to considering a file, note that when you create a picture and save it using a *.jpg* format, it will have an *opaque* background. This means you will not be able to see a layer behind it through the picture you created because it has a solid background. The *.gif* format, however, has a *transparent* background with no background color, so you can see the layer behind it. This may be important in your design planning.

STEP-BY-STEP 4.13

1. To create the Bicycle Patrol logo, create a blank publication using the default letter size.

2. From the **Flowchart** category in the AutoShapes tool, choose the **Summing Junction** shape.

3. Resize the shape to be **0.75** inch for both the width and the height. (HINT: Hold the **Shift** key as you resize so the shape will be a perfect circle.)

4. With the AutoShape object selected, change the line thickness to **2¼ pt** using the **Line/Border Style** button.

5. Create a WordArt shape and choose the third shape in the top row.

6. Key the following text on three separate lines as shown:
   Otter Creek
   Bicycle
   Patrol

7. Click **OK**.

8. From the WordArt toolbar, choose the **WordArt Shape** button. Choose the **Button (Pour)** shape.

9. Resize the WordArt object working with the height and width so that it is slightly larger than the AutoShape object.

10. Move the WordArt object on top of the AutoShape object. The center of the WordArt object should be about the same width as the center of the AutoShape object, and the centers should layer right on top of each other.

11. Select both objects. (NOTE: You may have to use your mouse pointer to draw a marquee around the two objects so that when you release your mouse button, both objects are selected.)

12. Make sure the centers of both objects are aligned exactly using the **Arrange** menu and choosing **Align or Distribute**. Then choose **Align Center**.

STEP-BY-STEP 4.13 Continued

13. Click the **Group Objects** button that appears in the lower-right corner of the two selected objects. Your logo should resemble the center part of Figure 4-17. Complete the next Step-by-Step to save the object as a picture.

FIGURE 4-17
Logo on AutoShape

STEP-BY-STEP 4.14

1. Right-click the grouped object and choose **Save as Picture**.

2. Save the object with your other publications. Name the file **bicycle patrol logo**. Before clicking Save, click the **Save as type** arrow at the bottom (see Figure 4-18) and choose **JPEG File Interchange Format** to save it as a *.jpg* file.

FIGURE 4-18
File Formats

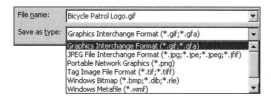

3. Close the publication and don't save the changes.

4. Create a blank publication using the default letter size.

5. Create an AutoShape of your choice that measures approximately **2.5** inches wide by **2.5** inches tall. Fill it with a color of your choice.

6. From the **Insert** menu, choose **Picture** and **From File**.

7. Locate your newly created logo. Click **Insert**.

8. Move the logo on top of the AutoShape. Notice that it is opaque.

9. Select both objects. Use the **Arrange** menu to align the objects vertically (middle) and horizontally (center).

10. Print the file. Close the publication, but don't save the changes.

SUMMARY

In this lesson, you learned:

- To use a wizard to create an invitation.
- The format of the publication created by a Wizard can be changed using the Wizard options.
- Why you should turn off hyphenation for text box frames that contain a small amount of text.
- To create and format AutoShapes.
- The color scheme that is being used in a WordArt object can be filled with the Gradient tool found in the Fill Effects dialog box.
- A graphic object created in Publisher can be saved as a picture file for use in other publications.

VOCABULARY *Review*

Define the following terms:

AutoShapes	Opaque	Save As Picture
Gradient	Postcard	Transparent
Invitation		

REVIEW *Questions*

TRUE/FALSE

Circle T if the statement is true or F if the statement is false.

T F   1. Postcards should be printed on heavy stock paper.

T F   2. A graphic object created in a Publisher document can be saved as a separate file.

T F   3. Gradient fill can only be applied to AutoShapes.

T F   4. Every AutoShape object has an adjustment handle.

T F   5. Hyphenation formatting applies to an entire text frame box.

T F   6. A picture saved with a *.jpg* format will have a transparent background.

T F   7. The color of a shadow applied to an object can be changed.

MULTIPLE CHOICE

Select the best response for the following statements.

1. Hyphenation is chosen from the Language portion of the _____ menu.
   A. Tools
   B. View
   C. Edit
   D. Table

2. AutoShapes is chosen from which of the following toolbars?
   A. Standard
   B. Formatting
   C. Objects
   D. Graphics

3. You can add a shadow to an AutoShape. You must choose the feature from which toolbar?
   A. Standard
   B. Formatting
   C. Objects
   D. Graphics

4. Fill color is chosen from which of the following toolbars?
   A. Standard
   B. Formatting
   C. Objects
   D. Graphics

5. When working with gradients, you may chose from all of the following EXCEPT
   A. Preset
   B. One color
   C. Two colors
   D. Three colors

WRITTEN QUESTIONS

Write a brief answer to the following questions.

1. Why is it a good idea to turn off automatic hyphenation on a smaller text box frame?

2. Is it better to key text into an AutoShape or to create a separate text box frame or WordArt frame and layer it on top of the AutoShape?

3. What are the choices for color when using Gradient fill?

4. Why would you want to save a graphic object created in Publisher as a separate graphic file?

5. Why is it necessary to group the objects before saving them as a picture?

6. What are the three common graphic formats that are compatible for documents as well as Web pages?

7. What adjustments can you make to shadow settings?

8. After you have chosen the AutoShape you'd like in your document, how do you tell Publisher what size you'd like the shape to be?

PROJECTS

PROJECT 4-1

SCANS

In this project, you will create a postcard for an annual bike auction. You will have a chance to apply many of the skills you learned in this lesson. Figures 4-19 and 4-20 illustrate a possible design.

FIGURE 4-19
Possible Design for Page 1 of Postcard

1. Create a blank publication. Choose postcard as the publication type.

2. Create a WordArt shape of your choice. Key the following text: Annual Bike Auction

3. Make it as wide as the margins and a proportionate height.

4. Format it as you desire.

5. Add a text box frame below the WordArt frame that contains the following text, centered:
Saturday, October 25, 2003
10–11 AM

6. Make the text a sans serif font (such as Arial) and large enough to be read easily.

7. Add a clip-art object that contains a bike. Move the bike below the text box frame.

8. Add an AutoShape of your choice behind the bike and as much of the other objects as you like. Format the AutoShape to enhance the design.

9. Save the file as **bike auction postcard** *xxx*.

10. Insert another page. On the second page, create a text frame in the left half of the page.

11. Key the text as shown in Figure 4-20; format the first four lines in bold and choose center alignment.

FIGURE 4-20
Page 2 of Postcard

**The Otter Creek Bicycle Patrol
Annual Bike Auction
Saturday, October 25, 2003
10—11 AM**

Rain or shine, dozens of bikes will be auctioned and can be inspected starting at 9:00 AM.

Terms: Cash or check and all purchases must be removed at the time of the auction.

The Victim Support Services will have bike locks for sale for $30.

A catering truck will be available with food and refreshments.

For more information, call 920-555-5080.

12. Insert the logo you created earlier in the lesson (bicycle patrol logo.jpg) in the lower-left corner of Page 2. You may need to resize it so all the text fits as well as the logo.

13. Save the file again as **bike auction postcard xxx.**

14. Print the file and close it.

 PROJECT 4-2

On your own you will create an invitation. The only requirements are as follows:

1. It must be from a blank publication.

2. You can choose the top-fold card size or the side-fold card size.

3. It should be an invitation to an event that is taking place in your school or community.

4. Save the file with file name Project 4-2 xxx and print it.

CRITICAL *Thinking*

 ACTIVITY 4-1

Search for job postings for Desktop Publishers. What are the requirements needed for these positions?

BROCHURES

LESSON 5

OBJECTIVES

Upon completion of this lesson, you should be able to:

- Set up a custom layout.
- Insert a text file.
- Copy and modify WordArt objects for consistency.
- Add a drop cap to a publication.
- Group and move a panel of objects.
- Create and edit a brochure from a Wizard.
- Insert a Design Gallery Object.
- Change line and paragraph spacing.

Estimated Time: 3 hours

VOCABULARY

Brochure

Design Gallery Object

Drop cap

Gutter

Panel

What Is a Brochure?

A *brochure* is a publication that is used to convince readers that you have something that they need. That something could be useful information, opportunities for enhancement, entertainment, a product, or some service.

The readers have to see right away what they will get from reading the brochure, as well as what it will cost them. This can be a real challenge because when people look at a brochure cover they don't read it, they glance at it. So it has to catch their attention, first of all, and then motivate them to pick it up.

Generally a brochure presents only one idea to one audience. It can vary in size from an 8½ × 11-inch paper with a trifold to several pages. The more benefits you want to convey, the longer the brochure.

The cover generally includes a title, headline, and an appropriate graphic. The inside lists the benefits and features starting with the strongest benefit first. The number of benefits will be a determining factor as to the length of the brochure. It shouldn't be too long, however. It should be just long enough to get them to decide if they want more information or want to take action on the information presented. The benefits may need to be categorized in subtopics or bulleted items if you have a lot of them.

Try to make the style of writing somewhat casual, like a conversation. Use *you* to make it more personal.

In this lesson, you will first create a two-page brochure that can be printed back-to-back. The purpose of the brochure is to convince people to donate money to the Otter Creek Zoo by buying bricks on which their names or names of loved ones will appear. These bricks will be laid out at the zoo for others to see. One page will include the cover panel, mailing panel, and back panel. The second page will include the inside panels. A panel is just another word for column. Each page will be set up with three columns.

Because brochures are often kept for a longer period of time—for future reference or until a decision is made concerning the information presented—they should be printed on paper heavier than bond paper.

Setting Up the Layout

You have learned to set up columns using the Arrange menu and Layout Guides dialog box. In this lesson, you will set up one page with columns as well as column guides to indicate the white space between the columns, known as the *gutter*. The gutter is especially important in a brochure design because that is where the page is folded. Usually you want to avoid folding text in the gutter because the fold makes the text difficult to read. After you have set up one page, you will insert the second page and copy the objects, which will save you the time of having to set up the second page.

The rule of thumb for figuring the width of the gutters is to double the left (or right) margin. So if you have a left margin of 0.25 inch, the gutter between columns should be 0.5 inch. The gutter will be indicated with the use of the ruler guides. Figure 5-1 shows the layout for the first page, including the columns, margins, and gutters.

FIGURE 5-1
Page 1 Layout

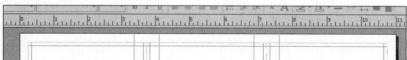

S TEP-BY-STEP 5.1

1. Create a new blank publication using the default 8½ x 11-inch size.

2. From the **File** menu, choose **Page Setup**. On the Layout page, click **Landscape**. Click **OK**.

3. From the **Arrange** menu, choose **Layout Guides**. Change the four margins to **0.25** inch each.

4. Change the number of columns to **3**. Click **OK**.

5. Increase the zoom so you can see 16 increments between inches on the horizontal ruler. This makes it easier to move the ruler guides by incremental amounts.

6. Drag a vertical ruler guide to approximately **7.625** inches on the horizontal ruler.

STEP-BY-STEP 5.1 Continued

7. Drag three more vertical guides to the following locations **6.875** inches, **4.125** inches, and **3.375** inches.

8. From the **Insert** menu, choose **Page**.

9. Choose **1** page after the current page and **Duplicate all objects on page**. Click **OK**. Now you have two pages in your publication.

10. Save the file as **Zoo Brochure xxx**, where *xxx* are your initials. Keep it open for the next Step-by-Step.

Add Objects to Page 1

Let's add objects to the publication, beginning with the first page. The left *panel* (or first column at the left) is the part of the brochure that folds into the center. The middle panel (or second column) will be left blank for the mailing information. The right panel (or third column) is the cover of the brochure. The ruler guides will serve as margins for the columns in which they are placed. For the outside edges, you will use the blue or pink guides as the guides to which the objects will be snapped. How close you can go to the edges of the paper will depend on your printer, so you may have to make adjustments after sending your first draft to the printer.

In past exercises, you keyed your text. In this lesson, you will insert some text files from the prerecorded data files that accompany this textbook. Microsoft Publisher is compatible with the following file formats and will, in most cases, keep the character and paragraph formatting applied to the original text. This list can vary depending on what programs you have installed on your computer.

■ Publisher files (files with a *.pub* extension)

■ Plain Text (files with a *.txt* extension)

■ Rich Text Format (files with an *.rtf* extension)

■ Hypertext Markup Language files (files with an *.html* or *.htm* extension)

■ Microsoft Word for Windows versions 2.0, 6.0, Word 95, Word 97, and Word 2000 (files with a *.doc* or *.dot* extension)

■ Microsoft Word for Macintosh versions 4.0, 5.0, 5.1, 6.0, and Word 98

■ Microsoft Works for Windows versions 3.0 and 4.0 word-processing files (files with a *.wps* extension)

■ WordPerfect for MS-DOS version 5.1

■ WordPerfect for Windows versions 5.0, 5.1, 6.0, 7.0, and 8.0

■ Microsoft Excel for Windows versions 2.0, 2.1, 3.0, 4.0, 5.0, Excel 95, and Excel 97

For this brochure, you will insert Word (.doc) files. The advantage of using a program such as Word or WordPerfect is that you can do all the formatting in the word processing program. The text will already be formatted when the file is inserted into Publisher. When you finish the left panel, it will look much like Figure 5-2.

FIGURE 5-2
Left Panel of Page 1

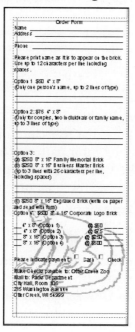

STEP-BY-STEP 5.2

1. Create a text box frame in the left panel on page one that fits from the left, top, and bottom pink guides and the green ruler guide at the right side of the left panel.

2. With the text box frame selected, open the **Insert** menu, choose **Text File**, go to the prerecorded data files, and insert **Order Form.doc**.

3. If you get a message about a text file converter that needs to be installed, choose to install it now.

4. If you get a message **The inserted text doesn't fit in this box. Do you want to use autoflow?**, click **No**. You may have to make your frame just slightly larger to fit in all the text.

5. With the frame still selected, choose ½ **pt** from the **Line/Border Style** button on the Formatting toolbar. This border will help set off the information in the order form.

6. Choose a clip-art object to insert in the bottom of the left panel using the Clip Organizer Frame. Key the word **animal** in the **Search For** text box. Size it to be as wide as the column and about **2.5** inches tall.

7. Change the text wrap to **None** using the Text Wrap button on the Picture toolbar.

8. Change the color of the animal to **Grayscale**.

STEP-BY-STEP 5.2 Continued

9. Use the **Send to Back** button to send the picture behind the text. You should be able to make out the shape of the animal, but it should not prevent you from being able to read the text. You can use the **Brightness** buttons or **Contrast** buttons on the Picture toolbar to make the clip art more or less noticeable.

10. Save the file again as **Zoo Brochure xxx**. Keep the publication open for the next exercise.

On the right panel (or third column) we'll add five WordArt objects. Since they are all going to be the same style, font design, and font color, we'll just create one and make four copies. Then we'll edit the text in each of the other four. Follow the steps in Step-by-Step 5.3 to create a panel that looks like Figure 5-3.

FIGURE 5-3
Right Panel of Page 1

STEP-BY-STEP 5.3

1. With **Zoo Brochure xxx** open to the third panel, create a WordArt object using the first style in the fourth row.

2. Key the text **Leave** and choose the font named Dauphin. (If you don't have that font design, choose another appropriate display font.) Click **OK**.

3. Make the object approximately **2** inches wide and **0.75** inches tall and move the object to the right pink guide at **0.625** inch on the vertical ruler.

4. Using the WordArt toolbar, click the **Format WordArt** button. Choose the Colors and Lines page. In the Fill section, click the arrow for the drop-down list and choose **Fill Effects**. In the texture choices, choose **Granite**. Click **OK** twice.

STEP-BY-STEP 5.3 Continued

5. With the WordArt object selected, click **Copy** on the Standard toolbar.

6. Click **Paste**. Move the copied WordArt object about a quarter inch away from the left green guide at approximately **2.25** inches on the vertical ruler.

7. Click **Paste** again. Move the second copied WordArt object to approximately **3.875** inches on the vertical ruler and snap it to the blue guide at the right of the panel.

8. Click **Paste** again. Move the third copied WordArt object to approximately **5.625** inches on the vertical ruler and snap it to the blue guide at the right of the panel. Click **Paste** one more time. Move the fourth copied WordArt frame to the bottom pink guide and stretch it from the green guide at the left to the blue guide at the right.

9. Change the text in each of the pasted WordArt frames using the **Edit Text** button on the WordArt toolbar each time.
   WordArt frame 2:   A
   WordArt frame 3:   Lasting
   WordArt frame 4:   Impression
   WordArt Frame 5:   Otter Creek Zoo

10. Resize the frame so that all the first letters are approximately the same height *except* the bottom frame. Leave the bottom frame at approximately **0.75** inch tall. (You will have to make the frame with the *A* less wide so it is not so stretched. Look at Figure 5-3 for guidance.)

11. Now you will insert a graphic file from your data files named **Paws**. Using the **Insert** menu, choose **Picture** and then choose **From File**. This file should be in the same location as your other data files.

12. Using the **Set Transparent Color** button on the Picture toolbar, click in the white background of the graphic to hide the background. Click the third button on the Picture toolbar and change the color of the clip art to **Grayscale**.

13. Resize the picture to be **1.5** inches wide and **1.5** inches tall and move the picture behind the first WordArt object so that it snaps to the right margin and top margin guides.

14. Send it behind the WordArt frame. If the picture is too dark, lighten it up.

15. Make three copies of the graphic and move them behind the next three WordArt frames. Lighten or darken them as you feel is necessary. They don't all have to be the same shade of gray.

STEP-BY-STEP 5.3 Continued

16. Your finished first page should resemble Figure 5-4. Save the file again as **Zoo Brochure *xxx*** and keep it open to format page 2.

FIGURE 5-4
Completed Page 1

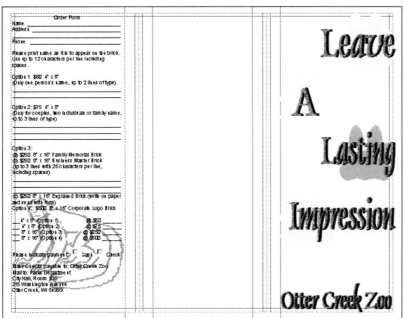

Add Objects to Page 2

The second page will contain the information about the types and costs of the bricks that can be purchased. Instead of creating separate text box frames for the left and center panel, you are going to combine them with one big text box frame. This is a common design if you don't have extensive text that is hard to read through the gutter.

You will copy a WordArt object from Page 1 and paste it twice on Page 2 to provide consistency in design. You will also copy the Paw graphic object.

STEP-BY-STEP 5.4

1. With **Zoo Brochure *xxx*** showing in the window, click the Page 2 indicator.

2. Create a text box frame that starts at **1.5** inches on the vertical ruler and extends from the blue guide at the left margin to the green guide at the right side of the middle panel and down to the bottom pink guide.

3. Insert the text file from your data files named **Types and Costs of Bricks.doc**. If you get a message **The inserted text doesn't fit in this box. Do you want to use autoflow?**, click **No**.

4. If you do not see the last paragraph in the text box frame that reads ***The only exception to the 12 characters rule is if your last name is longer**, make the frame longer. It is ok if the frame extends out of the page as long as the text doesn't.

STEP-BY-STEP 5.4 Continued

5. Copy one of the WordArt objects on Page 1 and paste it on Page 2.

6. Move it to the upper-left corner of Page 2 and resize it so that it extends to the same green guide that marks the right margin of the middle panel.

7. Click the **Edit Text** button on the WordArt toolbar and key **Help pave the way...**

8. Resize the frame to be approximately **1** inch tall.

9. Create a line under the title of the story (*Types and Costs of Bricks*) using the **Line** tool. Begin at the left pink guide. Hold the shift key while you extend the line to the right of the middle panel. Choose **2¼ pt.** from the **Line/Border Style** button.

10. Leave the publication open.

Using Drop Caps

A new feature you will use is a *drop cap*, which is a large letter at the start of a paragraph. This, too, is a common design. You do have to be careful not to overuse it. Use only one drop cap per story. If a page contains multiple new story frames, only include one drop cap per column.

When you create a drop cap, click in the paragraph where you want to add the drop cap and select Drop Cap from the Format menu. You will see the dialog box showing in Figure 5-5 that lets you choose the design. You can further customize it by clicking on the Custom Drop Cap tab. If you want to remove the drop cap, you must click in the paragraph containing the drop cap, open the Drop Cap dialog box, and click Remove. (See Figure 5-6 to preview the second page of the brochure.)

FIGURE 5-5
Drop Cap Dialog Box

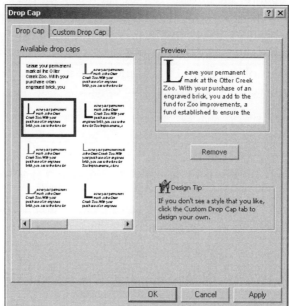

STEP-BY-STEP 5.5

1. Create a text box frame in the right panel that begins at the 7.625-inch ruler guide and extends from the top margin to approximately **6 inches** on the vertical ruler.

2. Insert the text file named **Leave your mark.doc** from the prerecorded data files.

3. Click in the first paragraph. Open the **Format** menu and choose **Drop Cap**. Click the **Custom Drop Cap** tab.

4. Click the third *W* box and change the setting below it to **1** line. Be sure the font is **Times New Roman** and the color is **black**.

5. Click **OK** to return to your document. Does the Drop Cap look like the one in Figure 5-6?

6. Copy two WordArt frames from page one and paste them at the bottom of the right panel. Make the top WordArt frame **1.5** inches wide and **0.65** inches tall. Edit the text to read **At the**.

7. Make the bottom WordArt frame **3.0** inches wide and **0.65** inches tall. Edit the text to read **Otter Creek Zoo**.

8. Copy a **Paw** graphic from the first page and paste it on Page 2. Move it to the upper-left corner and send it behind the other objects.

9. Paste the **Paw** graphic again and place it in the upper-right corner of the right panel. Send the **Paw** graphic behind the other objects.

10. Insert another animal graphic that you change to **Grayscale** or **Washout** and send it to the back of the right panel. Resize the graphic, if necessary.

STEP-BY-STEP 5.5 Continued

11. Check your Page 2 against Figure 5-6. Save the file and print it.

12. Check to see that everything fits on the page and that you can read the text with graphics behind it. Make any necessary adjustments and save the publication again.

13. Print your final copy either printing back-to-back or on two separate pages, depending on your printer's capabilities. Fold the brochure as a trifold. Close the file.

FIGURE 5-6
Completed Page 2

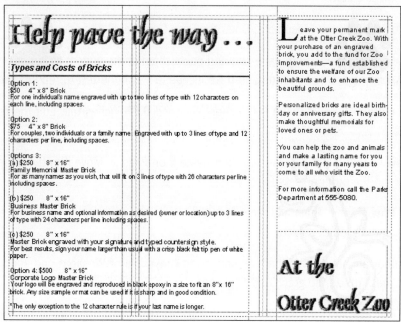

Rearranging Panels

You are no doubt very proud of your completed brochure. Your boss tells you, however, that she would prefer to have the order form on Page 2 in the right panel so that it is across from the prices. Also, perhaps the text on the right panel of Page 2 would make more of an appeal if it were the first panel readers see when they open the brochure. Fortunately, you know how to group objects so this will be an easy task!

To make this even easier, you will want to change your view to a small enough magnification that you can see the entire brochure and have enough Scratch Area (the gray background behind the document page) to move the grouped objects. From there they can be moved back onto the desired panels.

The following Step-by-Step will guide you in laying out your screen and objects as shown in Figure 5-7.

FIGURE 5-7
Desktop Layout with Grouped objects

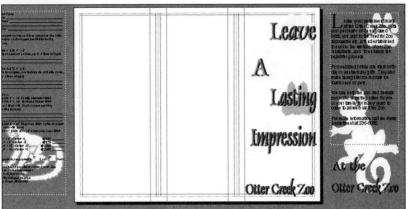

STEP-BY-STEP 5.6

1. Open the publication **Zoo Brochure xxx**.

2. Change the Zoom to **33%**.

3. Switch to Page 2, if necessary.

4. With your mouse pointer, drag an elastic box around all the objects in the right panel (the text frame with the drop cap, the two graphics, and the two WordArt objects).

5. Click the **Group** button and move the grouped objects out to the right of the document page onto the Scratch Area.

6. Switch to Page 1.

7. With your mouse pointer, drag an elastic box around all the objects in the left panel (the form and the animal graphic).

8. Click the **Group** button and move the grouped objects out to the left of the document page onto the Scratch Area.

9. Still on Page 1, move the grouped object at the right side of the Scratch Area containing the text frame with the drop cap, the two graphics, and the two WordArt frames onto the left panel on Page 1, taking care to lay it out within the appropriate ruler and margin guides.

STEP-BY-STEP 5.6 Continued

10. Your edited Page 1 should now look like Figure 5-8. Save the file as **Revised Zoo Brochure xxx**.

FIGURE 5-8
Revised Page 1

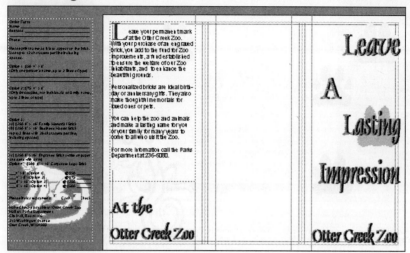

11. Switch to Page 2 and move the grouped object containing the form and animal graphic to the right panel of the form, taking care to lay it out within the appropriate ruler and margin guides.

12. Save the file again.

STEP-BY-STEP 5.6 Continued

13. The revised Page 2 should resemble Figure 5-9. (It is not necessary to ungroup the objects you have moved.)

14. Print the file and fold it. Close the file.

FIGURE 5-9
Revised Page 2

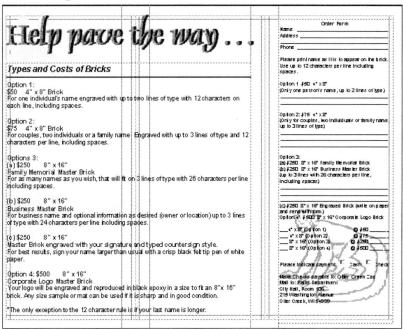

A Brochure from a Wizard

You have had practice using the Wizard tool before, so you should be good at it now! Sometimes the graphic design used in a Wizard is just so good it really is to your advantage to use it. On the other hand, you may end up making so many changes you may wonder why you used a Wizard to begin with. The Otter Creek Arbor Club has decided to help improve on the beauty of Otter Creek by promoting the planting of trees. These trees can be purchased and planted in memory of a loved one. A small plaque is put on the tree with the name of the person who is being commemorated. The purpose of the brochure is to tell people about the program and try to convince them to buy a tree to be planted.

Run the Brochure Wizard

Publisher makes several different types of brochures available. These are informational, price list, event, fund-raiser, special paper informational, and special paper price list. Each subcategory includes special panels. If you use the latter two categories with the special paper, Publisher can display some of the patterns available from PaperDirect and Avery, so you can see how your document will look with that special paper in the background. Then you have to load that special paper in your printer before you print. Just because you are creating a fund-raising brochure, though, does not mean you have to choose that subcategory. You may choose any design you like and do your editing.

As with previous Wizards, you click the design you want, and Publisher builds your publication. When you get the prompt from Publisher telling you that it can fill in the personal information, you have no choice but to click OK. We have not covered personal information yet, but we will in a later lesson. Click Cancel to bypass the Personal Information dialog box. The two-page brochure will be displayed with brochure options in the task pane at the left side of the screen. From that point, you edit the objects to customize the brochure to your preferred design. Hopefully, that doesn't involve too many changes! Figure 5-10 shows you the first page of the brochure you will create using the Wizard.

FIGURE 5-10
Completed Page 1 of Wizard Brochure

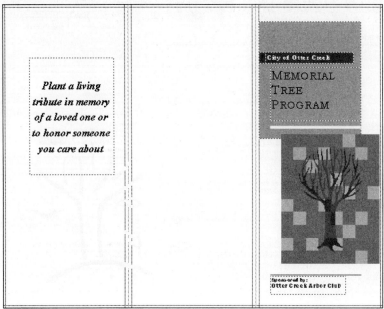

Insert a Design Gallery Object

Before you start the publication, you need to learn about a very unique feature of Publisher called the *Design Gallery Object*. These objects are mini-Wizards used to create design objects within a publication. Once the object is created, you can edit it just like you can edit the publication

Wizard. The Design Gallery Object tool is located on the Objects toolbar. When you choose it, the Microsoft Publisher Design Gallery dialog box opens as shown in Figure 5-11. You can choose from the Objects by Category page, Objects by Design page, or from objects you have created yourself.

After you choose the object, click Insert Object and the object is created. A Wizard button appears below the object. You may click that button to edit the Wizard options related to the specific object you created. You can edit any object within the created Design Gallery Object as well.

FIGURE 5-11
Microsoft Design Gallery Dialog Box

STEP-BY-STEP 5.7

1. Beginning in a new Publisher window, open the **File** menu and choose **New**.

2. Choose **Brochures** and then **Informational**. Click the **Bars Informational Brochure**.

3. Click **OK** when you see the message telling you that Publisher can fill in the name, etc.

4. Click **Cancel** when the Personal Information dialog box appears.

5. You are not going to change any of the options in the Task pane, so you can close that by clicking the **X** in the upper-right corner of the Task pane.

6. It doesn't matter where you start, so we'll begin in the right panel. Select the text in the text box frame containing the business name and key **City of Otter Creek**.

7. Select the **Product/Service Information** text and key the following text in three separate lines:
Memorial
Tree
Program

STEP-BY-STEP 5.7 Continued

8. Right-click on the text box frame containing the business tag line and choose **Delete Object**.

9. Select the text box frame containing the telephone number at the bottom of the panel and resize it to be **0.5 inches** tall.

10. Delete the phone number and key the following text in two lines:
    Sponsored by:
    Otter Creek Arbor Club

11. Change the bottom line of text to 12 pt. Select both lines and change the font design to Franklin Gothic Heavy.

12. Select the clip-art frame, click the **Clip Organizer Frame** tool, and search for **tree**.

13. Choose the clip art you like. Resize the picture to be approximately **2.8 inches** wide and **3.6 inches** tall. Move it toward the right margin, as shown in Figure 5-10.

14. Save your publication as **Memorial Tree Brochure xxx**.

STEP-BY-STEP 5.8

1. In the middle panel, delete the four text box frames, taking care **NOT** to delete the picture that is showing in the left and middle panels.

2. Select the clip-art frame in the left and middle panels and search for a **tree** from the Clip Organizer that is very simple in design. It will keep the same color as the original clip art being replaced. If not, you will have to experiment with the Washout or Grayscale options in the Color button on the Picture toolbar.

3. In the left panel, delete both text box frames.

4. Click the **Design Gallery Object** button near the bottom of the Object toolbar and select the **Pull Quotes** category.

5. Select the **Bars Pull Quote** object and click **Insert Object**.

6. Move the frame to the center of the left panel at approximately **1.5 inches** on the vertical ruler.

7. Select the text in the object and key the following text:

   Plant a living tribute in memory of a loved one or to honor someone you care about

8. Select the text and resize it to 22 pt. Center and resize the object frame to show all the text.

9. Change the **Fill Color** to **No Fill**.

10. Save your publication using the same name. Your Page 1 should resemble Figure 5-10 with the exception of the clip art. Do not save the publication to the Personal Information set, if prompted.

Change Line and Paragraph Spacing

You can see how easy it is to edit the objects created by the Wizard. Let's proceed to the second page. You'll use the ruler guides to help line up text box frames vertically, and you'll delete some existing frames and add new ones. First, however, you need to learn about the line and spacing feature.

You will find that on Page 2, when you create a new text box frame, the spacing will be too wide between lines and paragraphs, and the text won't fit in the text frame. To change the spacing between lines within paragraphs and to change the space above and below paragraphs, use the Line Spacing feature found in the Format menu. You may change the spacing either before or after inserting the new text.

STEP-BY-STEP 5.9

1. Turn to Page 2. Bring down a ruler guide from the horizontal ruler to **1.625** inches on the vertical ruler and another one at **2.5** inches.

2. Starting with the left column, delete the top text box frame containing the Main Inside Heading and delete the clip-art object.

3. Move the text box frame so the top is at the **2.5-inch** ruler guide.

4. Select and delete the text in the frame.

5. Insert the text file from your data files named **Tree Introduction.rtf**. Resize the text box frame from the bottom so it's only tall enough to fit the text.

6. Create a text box frame below the edited frame in the left panel that measures approximately **2.625** inches wide and **1.375** inches tall. You may have to adjust the size after you have keyed the text.

7. To change the line and paragraph spacing, open the **Format** menu and choose **Line Spacing**. Change the Between lines to **1 sp** and the After paragraphs to **0 pt**. Click **OK**.

8. Center the text shown below and format it using Franklin Gothic Heavy, 18 pt.
   Bur Oak
   In Memory of
   Joseph John
   2003

9. With the frame selected, choose **Line/Border Style** on the Formatting toolbar and choose the second **4½ pt. double border**.

10. Insert a clip-art object above the larger text box frame and search for a **tree** clip art of your choice.

STEP-BY-STEP 5.9 Continued

11. Resize the clip-art object to be approximately **2.2** inches wide and **1.65** inches tall. Using the Picture toolbar, change the color to **Grayscale**.

12. Save your publication again as **Memorial Tree Brochure *xxx***.

STEP-BY-STEP 5.10

1. With **Memorial Tree Brochure *xxx*** open in the window, delete all text box frames and clip-art frames in the middle and right panels.

2. Create a text frame in the middle panel that extends from the **2.5-inch** vertical ruler guide to the bottom of the column. Resize the width of the frame to be **2.625** inches wide to match the text box frame in the left panel and center it.

3. Insert the text file named **Tree Choices.rtf** from the data files. Adjust the size of the frame, if necessary, to fit in the panel.

4. Add a text box frame in the middle panel that starts at the **1.625-inch** vertical ruler guide that measures approximately **2.5** inches wide and **0.5** inches tall.

5. Key the text **Tree Choices** and change the font to Garamond, size 20 pt. font, and italics.

6. Align the new text box frame at the same position on the left as the bottom frame.

7. Create a text box frame in the right panel that starts at the **2.5-inch** vertical ruler guide and extends to the bottom of the panel. This frames needs to be a little wider than the other two, so make it approximately **3** inches wide and center it.

8. Go to your data files and insert the text file named **Tree Form.rtf**. Repair the telephone number—**5081**.

9. Work with the line and paragraph spacing until all the text shows in the frame. It is ok that the frame extends outside of the panel as long as all the text shows.

10. Create a text box frame starting at **1.625** inches that measures approximately **2.75** inches wide and **0.75** inch tall.

11. Change the line spacing to **1 sp**. and the After paragraph spacing to **0 pt**.

12. Key the text on two lines as shown below and change the font to Garamond, size 20 pt. and italics.
Please Forward the
Completed Application to:

13. Align the new text box frame at the same position on the left as the bottom frame.

14. Insert a clip art using **tree** in the Search For text box in the right panel. Find one that is a simple design. Change the color to **Washout** or **Grayscale**. Resize the clip art to fill the frame as much as possible without distorting it. Send the picture to the back.

STEP-BY-STEP 5.10 Continued

15. Draw a horizontal line above the top two text box frames that extends from the left of the text box frame in the middle panel, to the right edge of the top text box frame in the right panel.

16. Change the **Line/Border Style** of the new line to ¼ **pt**. size, if necessary, and change the color to **Accent 1** color using the **Line Color** button on the Formatting toolbar.

17. Check your Page 2 with Figure 5-12. If you like it, save the file again as **Memorial Tree Brochure** *xxx* and print the two pages. Fold the brochure and close the file.

FIGURE 5-12
Completed Page 2 of Wizard Brochure

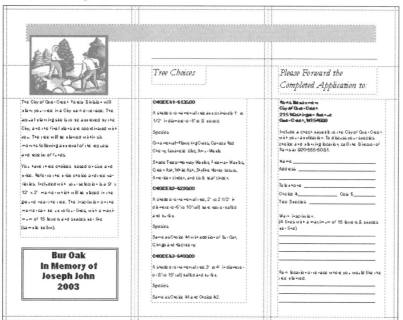

SUMMARY

In this lesson, you learned:

- You can create a brochure based on a custom layout of three columns and use ruler guides to act as margins.

- Text files created in various other software programs can be inserted into a text box frame.

- Copying a WordArt object that is formatted the way you want it and modifying the text in the copied objects can provide consistency in design and save time.

- A drop cap can enhance the design of a text box frame if used sparingly.

- If you have to rearrange a panel of objects, group them first and move them to the Scratch Area until you are ready to move them to a different panel.

- You can create a brochure using the Wizard and then modify the objects, which saves time setting up the layout and overall design.

- A Design Gallery Object can be inserted into a publication to bring attention to important information.

- If a text box frame contains extra line or paragraph spacing, you can use the Line Spacing dialog box to change the spacing.

VOCABULARY *Review*

Define the following terms:

Brochure	Drop cap	Panel
Design Gallery Object	Gutter	

REVIEW *Questions*

FILL IN THE BLANK

Complete the following sentences by writing the correct word or words in the blanks provided.

1. The white space between the columns is called the _____.

2. Use the _____ to create design objects within a publication.

3. You must have a _____ created in your publication before you can insert text.

4. A _____ is a large letter at the beginning of a paragraph.

5. The _____ button is used to send a picture behind another object.

6. When moving objects around on different pages, the _____ is where you can place them as you make your final design decisions.

7. The _____ button is used to hide or turn off one color in a clip-art object.

8. Use _____ to indicate where the gutter is in a brochure.

9. The part of the Publisher window where objects can be temporarily placed until they are put in the publication is the _____.

10. The Line Spacing dialog box may be chosen from the _____ menu.

11. Choosing to add spacing between paragraphs from the line spacing dialog box is similar to pressing the _____ key.

12. When preparing a trifold brochure like the ones in this lesson, you would normally use _____ page orientation.

13. In order to move several objects at one time, you must select and then _____ the objects.

MULTIPLE CHOICE

Select the best response for the following statements.

1. Which of the following file formats is NOT compatible for text box frames with Microsoft Publisher?
   A. Plain (ASCII) text
   B. Microsoft PowerPoint (.PPT)
   C. Rich Text Format (.rtf)
   D. Microsoft Word 2.0 and later

2. The Design Gallery Object button is located where?
   A. Insert menu
   B. Objects toolbar
   C. Standard toolbar
   D. Picture toolbar

3. What is the name of the guides that are used to line up objects and act as temporary margins within a column?
   A. Ruler
   B. Column
   C. Margin
   D. Page

4. If you have a left margin of 0.3 inch in a brochure, the gutter between each column should be what according to the rule of thumb of design?
   A. 0.5 inch
   B. 0.6 inch
   C. 0.75 inch
   D. 1.0 inch

5. If you decide you don't want a drop cap, how do you get rid of it?
   A. Delete it
   B. Choose Remove from the Drop Cap dialog box
   C. Cover it up with a text box frame
   D. Change the text font

6. In what menu will you find the Layout Guides dialog box?
   A. Format
   B. Insert
   C. Arrange
   D. Tools

7. What appears at the bottom of a Design Gallery Object for the purpose of editing the object?
    A. Text box frame
    B. Wizard button
    C. Handle
    D. Close button

PROJECTS

SCANS PROJECT 5-1

In this exercise, you will review and practice creating a brochure from scratch. It is for the Health Service Division of the City of Otter Creek. Due to budget restrictions, it will be printed on color bond paper and only black and shades of gray will be used. We will begin by setting up the layout for the brochure.

Setting up the Layout

1. Create a new publication based on the 8½ × 11- inch document size.

2. Change the orientation to landscape.

3. Change the margins to 0.3 inch and the number of columns to 3.

4. Drag the ruler guides to allow for the necessary amount of gutter space as you did in the first brochure in this lesson.

5. Using the Line tool, draw a line at 1.5 inches on the vertical ruler across the top of the page from the far left margin to the far right margin.

6. Change the line style to a double line.

7. Bring down a ruler guide from the horizontal ruler to 1.375 inches on the vertical ruler.

8. Bring down another ruler guide from the horizontal ruler to 1.75 inches on the vertical ruler.

9. Insert a new page and copy all the objects.

10. Turn off the automatic hyphenation for the entire publication by going to the **Tools** menu and choosing **Options**. In the Edit page, turn off the option to automatically hyphenate in new text boxes. This will save a lot of hassle later!

11. Save the file as **Health Services Brochure xxx**. Leave it open to continue with adding objects to Page 1.

Page 1 of the Brochure

Left Panel

1. Study Figure 5-13. Then turn to page 1 of **Health Services Brochure *xxx***. At the top of the left panel, create a text box frame that measures 2.875 inches wide and 0.5 inches tall. Line it up on top of the ruler guide at 1.375 inches and at the left column guide (blue).

FIGURE 5-13
Page 1 of the Health Services Brochure

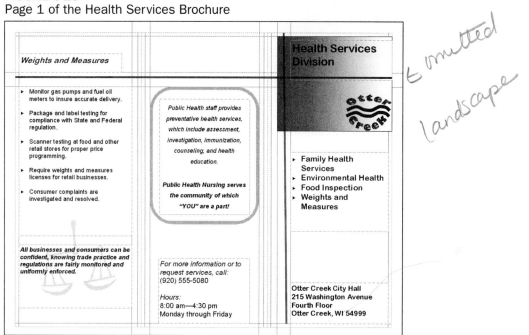

2. Key the text **Weights and Measures**. Change the font design to Arial Rounded MT Bold and the font size to 16 pt. Turn on italics. (This will be the "master" text box frame you will copy for the other titles on Page 2.)

3. Create a text box frame in the left panel starting at the 1.75-inch ruler guide and at the left column guide and extending to the ruler guide that marks the right margin of the left panel. Size it to be approximately 4 inches tall.

4. Insert the text file named **Weights and Measures.rtf** from the data files.

5. Select the paragraphs and turn on the bullet button. Choose a bullet that you like. (You will use the same bullet through the brochure for consistency.)

6. Create another text box in the left panel that starts at approximately 6.0 inches on the vertical ruler and extends between the column guide and ruler guide and is approximately 1.685 inches tall.

7. Key the following text and format the text using Arial, size 12 pt., bold, and italic:
All businesses and consumers can be confident, knowing trade practice and regulations are fairly monitored and uniformly enforced.

8. Insert a clip art that you searched for using the word balance on top of the text box frame you just created. Change the color, if necessary, to either Washout or Grayscale. Send the picture to the back.

9. Save the file again as **Health Services Brochure *xxx*.**

Middle Panel

1. Create a text box frame in the bottom of the middle panel that measures approximately 2.5 inches wide and 1.725 inches tall. Snap it to the bottom column guide and center it within the panel.

2. Left align the following text and format it using Arial, 14 pt.
   For more information or to request services, call:
   (920) 555-5080
   Hours:
   8:00 am–4:30 pm
   Monday through Friday

3. Format the lines ending with a colon using italics.

4. Using the Design Gallery, choose the Capsules Pull Quote and insert it in the center of the middle panel.

5. Size it to be approximately 3.275 inches tall and the width of the middle column.

6. Center the following text and format it as Arial, 12 pt.
   Public Health staff provides preventative health services, which include assessment, investigation, immunization, counseling, and health education.

   Public Health Nursing serves the community of which "YOU" are a part!

7. Format the first paragraph using italics and the second paragraph using italics and bold.

8. Save the file.

Right Panel

1. On the right panel, create a vertical line using the Line tool. Extend the line from the top column guide to the bottom column guide at approximately 7.75 inches on the horizontal ruler. Change it to a double line style, if necessary.

2. Drag a ruler guide from the vertical ruler to 7.875 inches on the horizontal ruler.

3. Create a text box frame that measures approximately 1.15 inches tall and extends from the ruler guide at 7.875 inches and the top column guide to the right column guide.

4. Key the following text and format it using Arial Rounded MT Bold, 22 pt.
   Health Services
   Division

5. Create a rectangle starting at the top column guide at 7.5 inches. Extend it to the right column guide and make it 2.5 inches tall.

6. Fill the rectangle with a gradient fill that puts the darker gray at the left side of the box. Send the rectangle to the back.

7. Insert the Otter Creek logo in the lower-right corner of the filled rectangle. You may need to use the Set Transparent Color tool on the Picture toolbar to turn off the background of the logo.

8. Create a text frame starting at 3.5 inches on the vertical ruler in the middle of the right panel that starts at the 7.875-inch ruler guide and extends to the right column guide and measures 2.125 inches tall.

9. Key the following text and format the font using Arial Rounded MT Bold, 16 pt.
   Family Health Services
   Environmental Health
   Food Inspection
   Weights and Measures

10. Select the paragraphs and turn on the bullets using the same bullet you used in the left panel.

11. There is one more text box in the right panel. Begin at 7.0 inches on the vertical ruler and at the ruler guide set at 7.875 inches and extend it to the right column guide and down to the bottom column guide.

12. Key the following text and format the font using Arial Rounded MT Bold, 14 pt.
    Otter Creek City Hall
    215 Washington Avenue
    Fourth Floor
    Otter Creek, WI 54999

13. Compare your Page 1 with Figure 5-13 and make any necessary changes. Save the file and take a break! You will continue with the second page in the next part of this exercise.

Page 2 of the Brochure

This page will be a little easier as there are fewer text frames that require keying text. Study the layout of Figure 5-14.

FIGURE 5-14
Page 2 of the Health Services Brochure

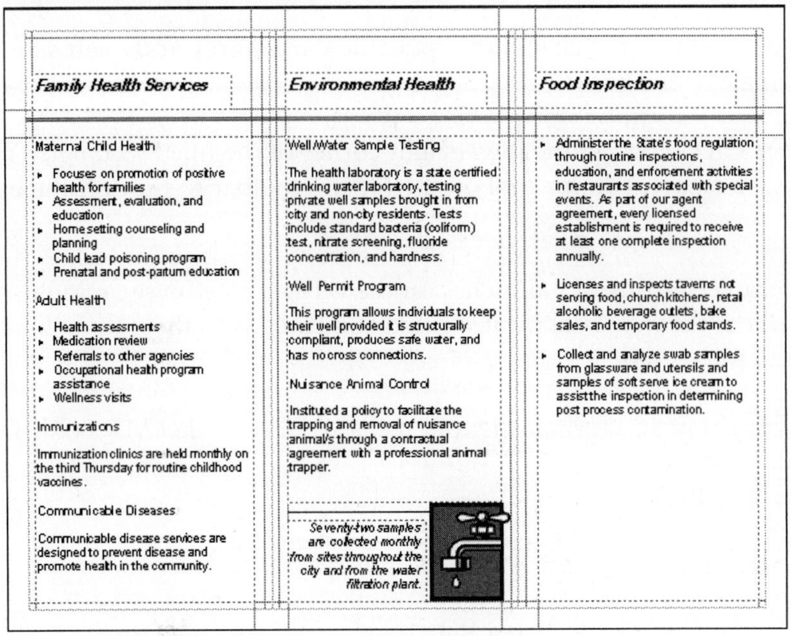

1. Copy the text box frame at the top of the left panel on Page 1.

2. Switch to Page 2 and paste the frame at the left column guide in the left panel so that the bottom of the frame snaps to the ruler guide at 1.375 inches.

3. Change the text to read: **Family Health Services**

4. Repeat the pasting at the top of the middle panel and the right panel. Change the text in the middle panel to read: **Environmental Health**. Change the text in the right panel to read: **Food Inspection.**

5. Create a text box frame in the left panel that starts at the 1.75-inch ruler guide and extends from the left column guide to the right ruler guide and down to the bottom column guide.

6. Insert the text file named: **Family Health Services.rtf** from the data files.

7. Select the paragraphs under the subtitle Maternal Child Care and turn on the same bullet you used earlier in the publication.

8. Select the paragraphs under the subtitle Adult Health and turn on the same bullet again.

9. Create a text box frame in the middle panel that starts at the 1.75-inch ruler guide and extends from the left column guide to the right column guide. Size it to be approximately 5 inches tall.

10. Insert the text file named **Environmental Health Services.rtf** from the data files.

11. Insert a small clip art using the word **water** in the **Search For** text box.

12. Position it in the lower-right corner of the middle panel as shown in Figure 5-14. Change the color to Grayscale.

13. Insert a small text box frame to the left of the clip art and right align the following text changing the font to Arial, 12 pt, italics.
Seventy-two samples are collected monthly from sites throughout the city and from the water filtration plant.

14. Draw a horizontal line above the small text box frame making it the width of the frame. Change it to ¾ pt. in the Line/Border Style drop-down list.

15. Insert a text box frame in the right panel starting at the 1.75-inch ruler guide and at the left ruler guide and extend it to the right column guide and down to the bottom column guide.

16. Insert the text file named **Food Inspection.rtf** from the data files.

17. Select all the paragraphs and turn on the same bullet you have used before on this page.

18. Check your finished Page 2 with Figure 5-14 and make any necessary changes.

19. Save your file and print and fold the two pages. Close the file. Congratulations on a job well done!

 PROJECT 5-2

Now it is time for you to do some creating on your own. Using a Brochure Wizard, create a brochure for an organization in your school or community. Get your instructor's permission before you begin. Use the Wizard to lay out the design, and edit the objects as necessary. Save the brochure as **Project 5-2 xxx**. Print it and fold it.

CRITICAL *Thinking*

 ACTIVITY 5-1

Now that you have used both the Wizard method and the from scratch method to create a publication, list and describe the advantages AND disadvantages of both methods.

NEWSLETTERS

OBJECTIVES

Upon completion of this lesson, you should be able to:

- Identify the parts of a newsletter.
- Describe the formatting considerations for a newsletter.
- Set up the master pages.
- Insert page number codes.
- Create, apply, and modify styles.
- Connect a file from one text box frame to another.
- Add continuation statements to text box frames.
- Add a caption to a picture.
- Set up and use tabs in a text box frame.
- Create a table of contents.
- Use the Design Checker to check for formatting problems.

Estimated Time: 5 hours

VOCABULARY

Continuation statements

Footer

Gray

Header

Master page

Mirrored guides

Newsletter

Overflow memory

Style

Tabs

Threaded

What Is a Newsletter?

A *newsletter* is a collection of stories, announcements, and explanations that is sent on a regular basis to a number of people. It is a communication tool that can help you build a profitable business, enable clients to know you better, update readers with new information about your organization, announce new products or services, and establish yourself as an expert in a particular field.

The audience can be employees of a company, members of an organization who receive the newsletter as part of their membership, subscribers who pay for the information, or potential customers.

Parts of a Newsletter

Newsletters are consistent in their elements. Readers expect to see certain elements in each issue and they expect to see them consistently in the same place. The typical elements that are included in most newsletters are described in Table 6-1.

TABLE 6-1
Parts of a Newsletter

PART	DESCRIPTION	DESIGN CONSIDERATIONS
Nameplate or banner	Newsletter's name found on the front cover.	It should grab the reader's attention and identify the purpose of the newsletter. It is usually placed at the top of the first page and may extend across the width of the page or at least be a very large-size font that is prominent.
Dateline or tagline	Short phrase that describes the purpose and audience and lists date of the issue.	These elements are placed next to the nameplate.
Headline	The title of the story.	Leads off a story in a text box frame and is a larger size font than the story text. It can be a different font design than the body text. All headlines are the same size and style of font for consistency.
Subheads	Label for part of a story when a story is very long.	Stands out from the body text by the being bold, italicized, or larger in size. It can be a different font design than the body text. All subheads are the same size and style of font for consistency.
Story	The text in the text box frame(s) that contains the story.	Use a size 10- or 12-point serif font, such as Times New Roman, for easy reading. Use the same size font for all of the stories for consistency.
Jump Line (called continuation statements in Publisher)	Statement that tells the reader where to turn for the rest of the story.	Use italics or parenthesis to set the jump line apart from the story. Appears at the end of a text box frame on one page and at the top of a text box frame on a continuing page.
Table of Contents	Lists the articles and features and their page numbers.	Placed on the front page in a small text box frame or table.
Pull Quote	Text pulled out from a story to catch the reader's attention.	Larger size font than the story and often outlined with a border or some graphic treatment so it stands out.
Caption	Explains a picture in a short sentence or paragraph.	Smaller size font directly under the picture.

TABLE 6-1 (Continued)
Parts of a Newsletter

PART	DESCRIPTION	DESIGN CONSIDERATIONS
Public Information	Identifies contact information for the newsletters and organization.	Placed on any page. Make the text box frame stand out with a border or shading.
Mailing Elements	Return address and space for a mailing label.	Usually half of the last page or the back cover is reserved for mailing information and postage.

Figure 6-1 shows you a partial page of a newsletter containing some of the possible newsletter elements.

FIGURE 6-1
Elements of a Newsletter

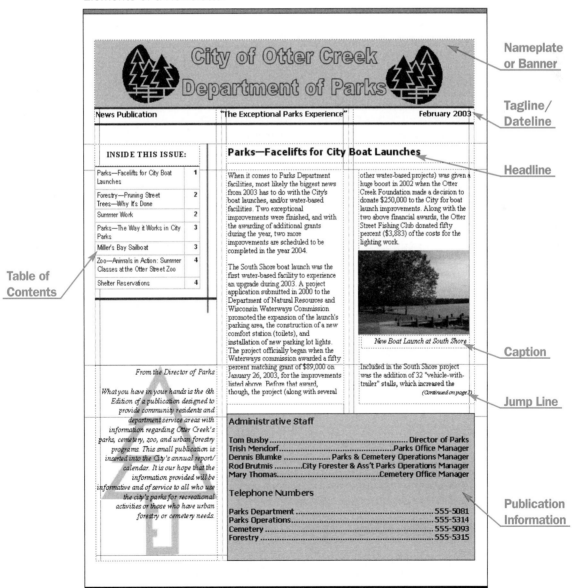

Layout Considerations

- **Columns**—One of the most important decisions regarding the design of a newsletter is the number of columns. Because newsletters are usually printed on 8½ × 11 paper, one column would be too wide. Even two columns can tend to be boring unless the two columns are offset by one narrow column at the left or right that is basically empty except for a few graphics, a pull quote, a very small story, or a table of contents. Using three or four columns is fairly common.

- **Background**—Elements that need to appear on every page, such as the newsletter title and a page number, are placed in the header or footer or on the background page of the publication.

- **White Space**—Try to avoid pages that look *gray*. Gray pages result from using all text and nothing else. Break up the pages with pictures, vertical lines between columns, or horizontal lines between stories. One of the most important design elements you can use in a newsletter is white space. You do not need to fill up every square inch of a page.

Setting Up a Newsletter

Now that you see what you need to include in a newsletter and have an idea of the formatting, let's begin creating one. Setting up a newsletter is very time consuming. Once you set up a newsletter page, you can base other newsletters on the first one. In other words, the first page can become a template. You start with page layout, which consists of the margins and the columns. Then you use the Master Page to set up the header and footer that will contain the name of the newsletter and the page numbers. (A *header* is information that appears at the top of every page; a *footer* is information that appears at the bottom of every page.)

The *Master Page* feature of Microsoft Publisher is a layer that contains only those items that you want to appear on every page. These items can be page numbers, logos, watermarks, or text. You can only add these objects or edit them when you are in the Master Page view.

To get to the Master Page of a publication, choose Master Page from the View menu. You may have a Right Master Page or both a Right and Left Master Page. This choice is made in the Layout Guides dialog box. If you want Right and Left Master Pages, you must choose Create Two Master Pages with Mirrored Guides. The *mirrored guides* indicate *opposite* margins guides, labeled Inside and Outside margins. This format is very noticeable in a textbook or magazine, for example, where the outside margins are on opposite sides of facing pages and inside margins are touching at the binding—thus mirrored. The outside margins could be wider than the inside margins or just the opposite. However, this is just one type of page layout. In our Step-by-Step, margins will be even all around because it is NOT a book.

STEP-BY-STEP 6.1

1. Start a new publication using the 8½ × 11 blank publication.

2. From the **Arrange** menu, choose **Layout Guides**. Change all the margins to **0.5** inch and key **3** in the Columns box.

3. At the right, choose the **Create Two Master Pages With Mirrored Guides** option and click **OK**.

4. From the **Insert** menu, choose **Page**. Key **3** in the Number of new pages box. Click **OK**. Keep the publication open.

The next step is to set up the Master Pages. When you choose Master Pages from the View menu, you will see two blank pages with R and L page navigator buttons in the lower-left corner of the screen. You'll add a page number at the bottom of each page and a newsletter title at the top of each page. To save time, you will create a text box frame for the left page, key any text needed, and copy it to the Clipboard. Then you'll paste the objects and drag them into place on the right page. You will do all necessary formatting in these text box frames. Rather than key an actual number when inserting page numbers, you'll insert a code that tells Publisher to put a real page number on the individual pages. The Page Number dialog box (Figure 6-2) is chosen from the Insert menu.

FIGURE 6-2
Page Number Dialog Box

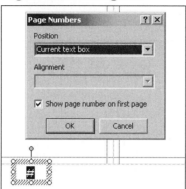

You also have the option in Publisher to turn off Master Page objects on the first page. Usually the banner takes the place of the title on the first page.

STEP-BY-STEP 6.2

1. From the **View** menu, choose **Master Page**. Look at the L and R navigation buttons in the lower-left corner of the window.

2. On the Left Master Page, center a text box frame just below the bottom margin guide of the middle column. Make the frame approximately **0.50** inch wide and **0.25** inch tall. (See Figure 6-2.)

3. Click the center alignment button and change the font to Tahoma, 12 pt. bold. Keep your insertion point in this text box frame.

4. From the **Insert** menu, choose **Page Numbers**. Make sure **Current text box** appears in the **Position** box. For now leave the option **Show page number on the first page** selected. Click **OK**.

STEP-BY-STEP 6.2 Continued

5. At the top margin of the middle column on the left page, create another text box frame that sits on the top margin guide (see Figure 6-3).

FIGURE 6-3
Newsletter Title on Master Pages

6. Make the text box frame approximately **3.0** inches wide and **0.25** inch tall.

7. Click the center alignment button and change the font to Tahoma, 10 pt. bold. Key the following text: **Otter Creek Parks News Publication**

8. Create a horizontal line that extends from the left margin guide to the right margin guide of the left page and sits on the top margin guide.

9. Select the text box frame you created, and use the arrow keys on your keyboard to nudge it up or down so that the words are just above the horizontal line you created.

10. Open the **View** menu and choose **Two-Page Spread** so you can see both Master Pages.

11. Select and copy the text box frame containing the page number code in the left page and paste it in the right master page at the bottom of the middle column. Make sure it is below the margin guide.

12. Select and copy the text box frame and horizontal line at the top of the left master page and paste them at the top of the right master page.

13. Exit the Master Page view by clicking **Master Page** from the **View** menu to turn it off.

14. Using the page navigators, turn from page 1 to the other three pages and look at the page numbers and newsletter titles.

15. Return to page 1. Open the **View** menu and choose **Ignore Master Page**. Do you still see the title and page number?

16. Save the file as **Parks Newsletter *xxx***, where *xxx* are your initials, and keep your emerging newsletter open.

Create the Banner and Tagline/Dateline

Adding or inserting objects to a document page is nothing new for you. Study Figure 6-4. You'll start off creating the banner and tagline/dateline. Then you will learn some new features for inserting text files that you have not used before.

FIGURE 6-4
Finished Banner and Tagline/Dateline

STEP-BY-STEP 6.3

1. With **Parks Newsletter xxx** open in the window, turn to page 1.

2. Create a rectangle at the top of the page starting at the left- and top-margin guides and extend the rectangle to the right margin and make it approximately **1.375** inches tall.

3. Fill the rectangle with a shade of gray. Change the border of the rectangle to **None**.

4. Create a WordArt object choosing the first style in the first row. Key on two lines, the following text:
   City of Otter Creek
   Department of Parks

5. Size the WordArt object to be approximately **4** inches wide and **1** inch tall.

6. Using the **Format WordArt** button on the WordArt toolbar, change the Fill Color to **No Fill**. Click **OK**.

7. Select the rectangle and the WordArt frame and align them (Arrange menu)—both vertically and horizontally—using **Align Center** and **Align Middle** from the Align or Distribute submenu. This is a two-step process.

8. Save the file again as **Parks Newsletter xxx**.

Now let's add some clip art to the banner.

STEP-BY-STEP 6.4

1. Open the Clip Organizer and key **tree** in the Search text box. Find a simple tree clip-art picture.

2. Drag the object to the right of the WordArt object you just created.

3. Resize the clip-art object to **1.125** inches wide and **1.125** inches tall.

4. Copy and paste the clip-art object. Drag it to the left of the WordArt object. Depending on the symmetry of the clip art you chose, you may have to flip it horizontally to make it mirror the one on the right side of the WordArt object.

STEP-BY-STEP 6.4 Continued

5. Line up the two clip-art objects with the WordArt object so that they are centered vertically and horizontally within the rectangle object.

6. Below the banner, create three text box frames placing one in each column. Key and format the text in Table 6-2.

TABLE 6-2
Text for the Banner

POSITION OF FRAME	TEXT TO KEY IN EACH FRAME	FORMAT
Left column	News Publication	Tahoma, 10 point, bold, left alignment
Middle column	"The Exceptional Parks Experience"	Tahoma, 10 point, bold, center alignment
Right column	February 2003	Tahoma, 10 point, bold, right alignment

7. Using the Line tool, draw a horizontal line above the width of the three text box frames. Change the line size to 2¼ pt.

8. Make a copy of the line you just created in the step above and paste it below the three text box frames.

9. Compare your banner and tagline/dateline to Figure 6-4. Save your newsletter using the same file name.

Create Styles

You have been doing a great job formatting text in these first six lessons. Since one of the design tips for newsletters is to be consistent in your treatment of various elements, a feature that helps ensure consistency is a style. A *style* is stored formatting characteristics that you can apply to text on a paragraph-by-paragraph basis. It can contain such formatting information as font design, font size, font color, indents, character and line spacing, tabs, and special formatting. Once you create and save a text style, you can apply it to any paragraph or table text within a publication. When creating style names, use words that best describe the part of the document you are formatting.

A big advantage to using styles is that if you decide you don't like the look of a style after you have applied it, you can edit the style. When you change the style, all the text in your document to which the style was applied is changed immediately. You don't have to manually change each occurrence of the formatted text.

The style can be created and applied using the Style box on the Formatting toolbar. If no style is applied, the word Normal will appear in the Style box. Once a style is created and applied, the name of the style will appear in the Style box when the text to which it is applied is selected. In Figure 6-5, the applied style is *Headline*.

FIGURE 6-5
Style Box

The easiest way to create a style is to use the Create Style By Example method. This involves formatting the designated text as you desire, selecting the formatted text, clicking in the Style box, keying the new style name, and pressing Enter. The Create Style By Example dialog box (Figure 6-6) will appear and that style name will be added to the list of styles in your document.

FIGURE 6-6
Create Style By Example Dialog Box

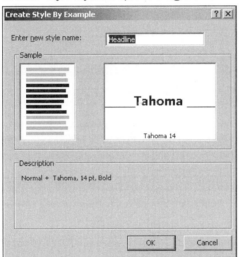

S TEP-BY-STEP 6.5

1. With **Parks Newsletter *xxx*** showing in the window, drag down a ruler guide from the horizontal ruler to **2.5** inches on the vertical ruler.

2. Create a text box frame beginning at the ruler guide you created and at the left margin of the middle column and extending to the right margin of the right column and measuring **0.375** inch tall.

3. Left align the following text in the text box frame:
Parks—Facelifts for City Boat Launches

4. Select the text and format it using Tahoma, 14 pt. bold.

5. Select the text you just formatted and click in the **Style** box. The word **Normal** should be selected.

6. Key the style name **Headline** and press **Enter**.

7. In the Create Style By Example dialog box, check the name of the style and the formatting showing in the Description part of the dialog box. If it matches Figure 6-6, click **OK**. If it doesn't, click **Cancel** and reformat the text again to match the step in this exercise.

8. Save the file and keep it open.

Create a New Style Using the Create a New Style Dialog Box

You can also create a style from scratch using the Create a New Style dialog box. To get to this dialog box, you have to choose Styles and Formatting from the Format menu. This feature opens up the task pane illustrated in Figure 6-7.

FIGURE 6-7
Styles and Formatting Task Pane

In this pane, you see a list of the tasks that are already part of a blank publication along with the style you created in the last exercises named Headline. From this list you can pick a style to apply to selected text in your publication. From this task pane, you can also do the following:

■ Import styles from another Publisher file or from a Word file.

■ Create a new style.

■ Show the names of all styles in the publication or just those in use.

■ Right-click and choose to create a new style, modify the selected style, rename the style, and delete the style.

In the next Step-by-Step, you will create a new style using this task pane. When you click Create new style, you will open the dialog box shown in Figure 6-8. Here you may key the name of the style and choose what style the new style is based on. In addition, you can choose what style should be applied to the paragraphs following the one you are formatting. This last option can save you time when you consistently apply the same style to all paragraphs following the one you are formatting.

You can immediately format this style using the choices on the right side of this dialog box that affect the character and paragraph formatting. Clicking each of these buttons will open the specific dialog box for that type of formatting, most of which you have already seen.

If you choose to change this style at a later time, you will open this same dialog box and make the necessary changes to the format. As mentioned earlier, these changes will be reflected throughout the publication.

FIGURE 6-8
Create New Style Dialog Box

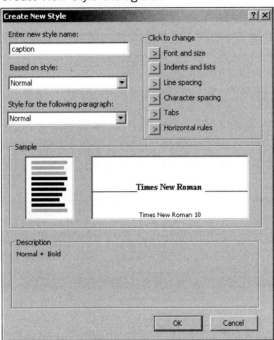

STEP-BY-STEP 6.6

1. With **Parks Newsletter xxx** open in the window, open the **Format** menu and choose **Styles and Formatting**.

2. In the **Styles and Formatting** task pane, click **Create new style**. This will display the Create New Style dialog box, illustrated in Figure 6-8.

3. Key **caption** in the Enter new style name box. Leave the Based on style as **Normal**.

4. Choose **Normal** from the drop-down list in the Style for the following paragraph.

5. Click **Font and size** in the Click to change list. Change the font to Times New Roman, 10 pt., and choose **Bold** in the Font style drop-down list. Click **OK**.

6. Click the **Indents and lists** button. Change the alignment to **Right**. Click **OK**.

STEP-BY-STEP 6.6 Continued

7. Click **OK** again. This saves the style and closes the dialog box.

8. From the **Format** menu, choose **Styles and Formatting** again. Right-click on the caption style name and choose **Modify**. The Change Style dialog box appears.

9. Click the **Font and size** button and change the Font style to **Italic** instead of bold. Click **OK** twice. (Now when you use the caption style, it will be italics instead of bold.)

10. Create another style for the text formatting for the inserted text files. The name of the style is **body text** and the formatting should be Times New Roman, 10 pt., and regular. Click **OK** twice.

11. Save your file again as **Parks Newsletter *xxx***. Keep it open as you read on.

Connecting Text Box Frames

Up to this point in your publications you have worked with text box frames that contain an entire story. In a newsletter, it is common for a story to fill a text box frame on one page and continue to another page. When stories take up more than one text box frame, the story is *threaded* by connecting the frames.

When a text file is inserted into a text box frame and it contains more text than can fit into the selected frame, the message shown in Figure 6-9 appears

FIGURE 6-9
Autoflow Message

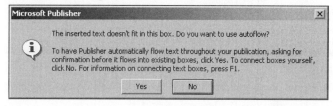

If you choose Yes, Publisher will flow the story into the next unfilled text box frame, or it will create a frame in the next available space into which the story will be poured. This is risky. It is better to click No, and do your own connecting. However, if you have the frames created and are confident they are in the right order for the text to flow, you can click Yes. In the exercises in this lesson, you will choose No.

When No is chosen, the text only appears in the current frame, and a button appears at the bottom of the frame. You have seen the Overflow button, illustrated in Figure 6-10, before. It indicates that there is text in the *Overflow memory* of this file. This is a special memory containing the part of the story that is not showing that remains with the file even when the file is closed. Getting the text out of the memory and into the publication requires creating a text box frame into which the overflow text can be poured.

FIGURE 6-10
Text in Overflow Button

Before trying to connect frames, look for the Connect Frames toolbar (Figure 6-11) at the top of your window. If it is NOT showing, you may display it from the Toolbar portion of the View menu. Create the frame where you wish to continue the story. Click to select the frame containing the first part of the story, and click the Create Text Box Link button on the Connect Frame toolbar. Your mouse pointer will become a cup with an arrow and drops. Use it to click in the new frame. This action will pour text from the Overflow memory into the new text box frame. The two frames are then connected. (You may find that the second frame is too small and that you'll need additional text box frames to complete the story.)

FIGURE 6-11
Connect Frames Toolbar

Once two frames or more are connected, buttons appear at the top and/or bottom of the text box frames. (See the circled buttons in Figure 6-12.) If you click the button pointing to the left (Go to Previous Frame), the previous frame will be selected. If you click the button pointing to the right (Go to Next Frame), the next connect frame will be selected. These buttons help you see the flow of the story. When you delete or add text to a connected frame, the amount of text in the connected frame will be adjusted.

FIGURE 6-12
Go to Next Frame and Go to Previous Frame Buttons

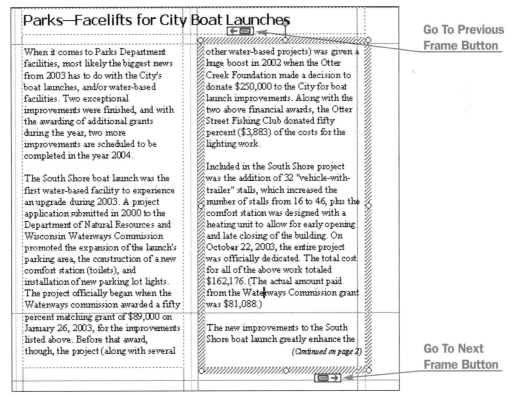

Continuation Statements

When stories start on one page and continue on another page, readers need to know where the story is continued. You can provide this information using *continuation statements*. This option is chosen from the Text Box tab of the Format Text Box dialog box. When the choice has been made, Publisher automatically includes a continuation statement in the bottom of the first text frame and at the top of the continuing text frame. The option has to be turned on individually for each frame involved.

In Step-by-Step 6.7, you will create two text box frames on page 1 and two more text frames on page 2 to hold a text file. Then you'll add continuation statements.

STEP-BY-STEP 6.7

1. With page 1 of **Parks Newsletter *xxx*** showing in your publication, bring down a horizontal ruler guide to **3** inches on the vertical ruler.

2. Create a text box frame beginning in the middle column at the 3-inch ruler guide and the left margin guide and extending to the right margin guide of the middle column and down to approximately **7.5** inches on the vertical ruler. The box should measure **4.5** inches tall.

3. Copy the text box frame you just created and paste it in the right column so that it starts at the 3-inch ruler guide.

4. Turn to page 2 of the publication. Paste the text box frame again in the middle column and right column so that they start at the top margin guide. Resize both frames on page 2 to be **3.5** inches tall.

5. Return to page 1 and select the text box frame in the middle column.

6. Insert the text file named **facelifts.rtf** from the student data files. When the message appears asking if you want to use autoflow, click **No**.

7. With the first frame still selected, open the **View** menu, point to **Toolbars**, and choose to display the **Connect Frames** toolbar. (The Connect Frames toolbar may already be displayed.)

8. Click the **Connect Text Box Link** button on the Connect Frame toolbar and point in the right column. When you see the pour indicator appear, click the left mouse button. The text should pour into the second frame.

9. With the second frame selected, click the **Connect Text Box Link** button again and click the page 2 navigator button. Click the text box frame in the middle column.

10. If you have text remaining in the overflow memory, connect the middle column of page 2 to the right column on page 2.

With the text in the frames, let's tie them together with continuation statements so the reader knows where to go to finish the story.

STEP-BY-STEP 6.8

1. With page 2 of **Parks Newsletter *xxx*** open in the window, point to the text box frame in the middle column of page 2 and right-click. Choose **Format Text Box**.

2. Click the **Text Box** tab (see Figure 6-13). At the bottom, click to choose **Include "Continued from page..."** option. Click **OK**.

FIGURE 6-13
Continuation Statements

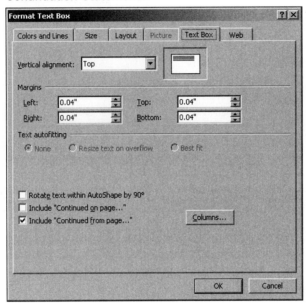

3. On page 1, right-click in the text box frame in the right column and choose **Format Text Box**.

4. Click the Text Box page and turn on the **Include "Continued on page..."** option. Click **OK**.

5. Save your file again as **Parks Newsletter *xxx*** and keep it open.

Add a Picture and Caption

You have inserted pictures in your publications before, but you have not added a caption. In a newsletter, newspaper, or magazine it is common to see a short description under or above a picture. That caption is usually a different format than the body text of the publication so that it stands out. Unlike some word processing or desktop publishing programs that provide an option for attaching a caption to a picture, Publisher requires a separate text box frame for the caption. Since it is not unusual to move a picture around as you edit the stories, it is a good idea to group the picture and the caption.

FIGURE 6-14
Inserted Picture and Caption

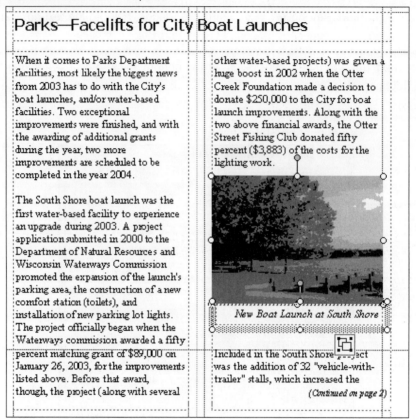

STEP-BY-STEP 6.9

1. With page 1 of **Parks Newsletter *xxx*** displayed, select the **Picture Frame** button on the Object toolbar and draw a frame in the right column at the beginning of the paragraph that starts with "Included in the South Shore…" and extend the frame to the right margin. (See Figure 6-14.)

2. Insert the picture **boat launch.jpg** from the data files.

3. Create a text box frame below the picture that is **0.25** inch tall and key the following text:
New Boat Launch at South Shore

4. Select the text you just keyed and select the **caption** style from the drop-down list on the Style box on the Formatting toolbar.

5. Select the text box frame containing the caption and hold the **Shift** key while you select the picture. Click the **Group Objects** button.

STEP-BY-STEP 6.9 Continued

6. Go to page 2 and look at the text in the two frames there. The text should have shifted down to accommodate the inserted picture and caption.

7. Click in the first frame of the story and choose **Select All** from the **Edit** menu. All the text should be selected in the four connected frames.

8. Turn on the **body text** style from the Style box.

9. Save the file. You can take a break whenever you need one! You can always close the file and continue working on it at a later time!

Setting Tabs

Y ou are now going to add two more objects to page 1. Notice in Figure 6-15 that the frame in the lower right contains public information. It gives the names and phone numbers of people to contact within the Department of Parks. The frame in the lower left is an object from the Design Gallery. The table of contents will be added at the end exercise when all the stories have been inserted.

FIGURE 6-15
Added Objects on Page 1

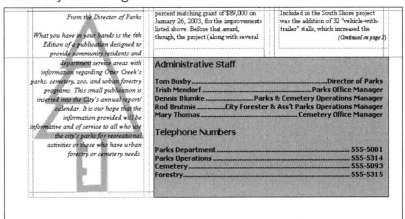

Before you can create the publication information text box frame, you need to learn how to set tabs. *Tabs* are settings on the horizontal ruler that align the text. You probably have set tabs in word processing programs. Publisher tabs are similar.

The different types of tabs include the left (aligns text at the left), center (aligns text at a center point), right (aligns text at the right), and decimal (aligns decimals within numbers at a set point). Tabs may be set on the ruler or in the Tabs dialog box. Figure 6-16 shows you what the different tabs look like on the ruler. They are set by first selecting the type of tab from the tab box at the far left of the horizontal ruler. Each time you click on the tab box, a different tab type appears. When the desired tab type appears, click at the location on the horizontal ruler where you want the tab set.

FIGURE 6-16
Tab Setting Using the Ruler

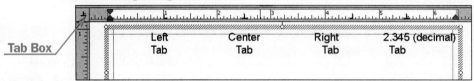

If you need to set a leader tab, which is one that has some character preceding the tab position, you must use the Tabs dialog box. In this dialog box you can set the type of tab, the position of the tab, and a leader character. The Tabs dialog box is chosen from the Format menu and looks like Figure 6-17.

FIGURE 6-17
Tabs Dialog Box

STEP-BY-STEP 6.10

1. With page 1 of **Parks Newsletter xxx** open, bring down ruler guides to **6.75** inches and **7.75** inches on the vertical ruler.

2. Create a text box frame that extends across both the middle and right columns and begins at the **7.75**-inch horizontal ruler guide. Extend it to the bottom margin.

3. Before you start keying the text, change the text format to Tahoma, 10 pt. bold.

4. From the **Format** menu, choose **Tabs**.

STEP-BY-STEP 6.10 Continued

5. Key **4.75** inches in the Tab stop position box, click **Right** for the Alignment, and click **Dot** for the Leader character. Click **OK**.

6. Key the following text. Press **Enter** twice after *Administrative Staff* and before and after *Telephone Numbers*. Press the **Tab** key after the name text at the left to move the insertion point to the right tab for the text at the right.

Administrative Staff
Tom Busby . . . . **Director of Parks**
Trish Mendorf . . . . **Parks Office Manager**
Dennis Blumke . . . . **Parks & Cemetery Operations Manager**
Rod Brutmis . . . . **City Forester & Ass't Parks Operations Manager**
Mary Thomas . . . . **Cemetery Office Manager**
Telephone Numbers
Parks Department **555-5081**
Parks Operations **555-5314**
Cemetery **555-5093**
Forestry **555-5315**

7. Change the font size of the two titles (*Administrative Staff* and *Telephone Numbers*) to 12 pt.

8. Save the file again as **Parks Newsletter *xxx*** and keep it open.

Now let's format the text box and add the object in the left column.

STEP-BY-STEP 6.11

1. With the text box frame selected, change the fill color to gray and turn on a ½-pt. border.

2. To create the second object, click the **Design Gallery**, choose **Pull Quotes,** and then choose the **Straight Edge Pull Quote**.

3. Move the object to the left column beginning at the 6.75-inch vertical ruler guide and extend it to the right margin of the left column and down to the bottom of the column.

4. Select the text in the object and change the format to Times New Roman, 10 pt. bold and italics and key the following text:
From the Director of Parks
What you have in your hands is the 6th Edition of a publication designed to provide community residents and department service area users with information regarding Otter Creek's parks, cemetery, zoo, and urban forestry programs. This small publication is inserted into the city's annual report/calendar. It is our hope that the information provided will be informative and of service to all who use the city's parks for recreational activities or those who have urban forestry or cemetery needs.

STEP-BY-STEP 6.11 Continued

5. Using the Clip Organizer, insert a tree on top of the pull quote frame. Format the tree using washout or grayscale. Send the object to the back as shown in Figure 6-15. Change the pull quote frame to **No Fill**.

6. Save the file again as **Parks Newsletter xxx**. (Newsletters take a lot of time setting up and fine-tuning!)

Adding Objects to the Inner Pages

Your next job is to add objects to pages 2 and 3 (see Figure 6-18). This will include using the outer columns for a special story or pull quote and using the two other columns on each page for full stories. You will also add some pictures to help keep it from being too *gray*.

FIGURE 6-18
Pages 2 and 3

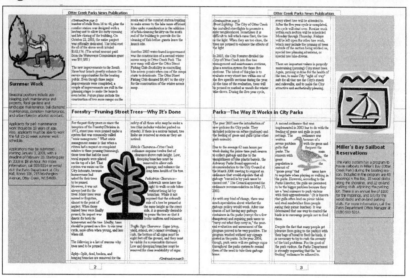

STEP-BY-STEP 6.12

1. With **Parks Newsletter xxx** showing in the window, turn to page 2.

2. In the left column, create a rectangle that fills the whole column. Fill it with a gray color.

3. Create a text box frame in the middle of the rectangle that measures approximately 4.250 inches tall and the width of the column.

STEP-BY-STEP 6.12 Continued

4. Key in the following text and format it using Tahoma, 10 pt.

Summer Work

Seasonal positions include zoo keeping, park maintenance and projects, floral gardens and landscape maintenance, ball diamond maintenance, cemetery maintenance, and urban forestry arborist assistant. Applicants for park maintenance work shall be 18 years of age. Also, applicants must be able to work the full 15-16 week summer work schedule.

Applications may be submitted starting January 3, 2003, with a deadline of February 28. Starting pay in 2003 is $8 an hour. For more information, call 555-5314 or write/visit the Parks Department at City Hall, Room 106, 215 Washington Avenue, Otter Creek, WI 54999.

5. Format the title using 14 pt. bold.

6. Insert an appropriate clip art above the text box frame using **tree** or **foresters** to search.

7. Save your work and keep it open.

Now let's add another story beginning on page 2.

STEP-BY-STEP 6.13

1. With **Parks Newsletter** *xxx* open in the window, bring down ruler guides to **4.25** inches and **4.75** inches on the vertical ruler.

2. Create a text box frame on page 2 that starts at the 4.25-inch ruler guide and extends from the left margin of the middle column to the right margin of the right column and extends down **0.40** inch in height.

3. Key the following text and apply the **Headline** style:

Forestry—Pruning Street Trees—Why It's Done

4. Create two text box frames, one in the middle column and one in the right column starting at the 4.75-inch ruler guide and extending to the bottom of each column.

5. Insert the text file named **Forestry.rtf** in the middle column text box frame you just created. When you get the autoflow message, click **No**. Connect the story from the middle column to the right column.

6. Add a **Continued on page...** statement to the right column frame. (The continuation statement won't show until you complete the story.)

7. Add a clip art of a **tree** or **foresters** that measures approximately **2.0** inches wide and **2.75** inches tall. Drag it to the middle of the two columns containing the story. Set the text wrap to **Tight**.

8. Scroll over so that you can see page 3. Create a text box frame in the left column that starts at the top left corner and extends to the right margin and down to approximately **3.75** inches on the vertical ruler.

STEP-BY-STEP 6.13 Continued

9. Copy the text box frame you created in Step 8 and paste it in the middle column starting at the top margin. (You'll have to adjust the width slightly to make it fit.)

10. Connect the story from the bottom of page 2 to the top of page 3. It will take both frames you just created to complete the story. Add the **Continued from page...** statement to the upper-left column text box frame on page 3.

11. With your insertion point in any of the four frames that contain the Forestry story, press **Ctrl+A** to select the entire story and turn on the **body text** style.

12. Italicize all the words that precede the dash in the reasons why pruning trees needs to be done.

13. Save your publication again. With **Parks Newsletter *xxx*** still open in the window, we'll add a new story to page 3.

STEP-BY-STEP 6.14

1. Create a text box frame across the left and middle columns of page 3 that starts at the 4.25-inch ruler guide and extends down **0.40** inch in height.

2. Key the following text and apply the **Headline** style:
Parks—The Way it Works in City Parks

3. Create two text box frames, one in the left column and one in the middle column starting at the 4.75-inch ruler guide and extending down to the bottom of each column.

4. Insert the text file named **Parks.rtf** in the left column text box frame you just created. When you get the autoflow message, click **No**. Connect the story from the left column to the middle column.

5. Format the text in the new story using the **body text** style.

6. Insert a clip art of a goose in the middle column since the story relates to geese, and make it approximately **1.4** inches wide by **1.4** inches tall. (You may have to play with the size of this in order to get the story to fit in the two columns.) Set the text wrap for the clip art to **Tight**.

7. In the right column of page 3, create a rectangle that fills the column and fill it with a gray color.

8. Create a text box frame in the middle of the right column that measures **2.4** inches wide and **3.0** inches tall. Key the following text and format it using Tahoma, 10 pt.
Miller's Bay Sailboat Reservations
The Parks system has a program to house sailboats in Miller's Bay (Otter Creek Park) during the boating season. Included in the program are 48 moorings on the Bay, 15 wood docks along the shoreline, and 22 on-land parking stalls adjoining the parking lot. The Parks system is charging an annual fee of $100 for the moorings and $70 for the wood docks and on-land parking stalls. For more information, call the Parks Department Office Manager at (920) 555-5314.

9. Format the title using 14 pt. bold.

STEP-BY-STEP 6.14 Continued

10. Add a clip art of a sailboat that measures approximately **2.4** inches wide and **2.5** inches tall above the text box frame you just created.

11. Save the file again as **Parks Newsletter** *xxx* and keep it open.

Finishing the Newsletter

You are almost done with the newsletter! You have just one page to go. On the last page of a newsletter, it is common to save half the page for the mailing information, which would include a return address and room for the label and postage. In this newsletter, however, you will not do that. Page 4 of the newsletter will look like Figure 6-19.

FIGURE 6-19
Page 4

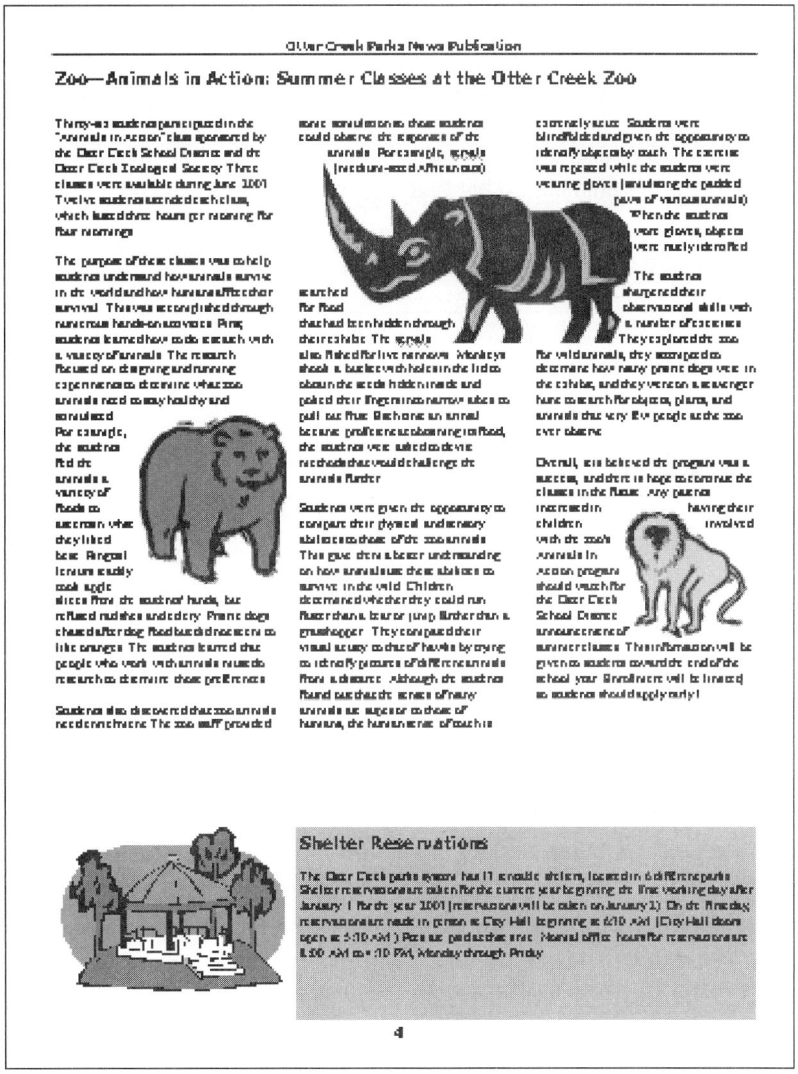

STEP-BY-STEP 6.15

1. Create a text box frame that starts at the top of the page and extends from the left margin guide in the left column to the right margin guide of the right column and measures **0.40** inch tall.

2. Key the following text and apply the **Headline** style:
   Zoo—Animals in Action: Summer Classes at the Otter Creek Zoo

3. Bring down a ruler guide to **1.125** inches on the vertical ruler.

4. Create a text box frame the width of the left column that starts at the 1.125-inch ruler guide. Make it approximately **6.625** inches tall.

5. Copy the text box frame and paste it in the middle and right columns both starting at the ruler guide at **1.125** inches.

6. Insert the text file from the data disk named **animals in action.rtf** in the left column. In this case, you may click **Yes** on the autoflow message, since the story should fit easily in the three frames you created. If you prefer, you may click **No** and connect the other two frames yourself.

7. Select the text in the three frames and turn on the **body text** style.

8. Insert three animals of your choice anywhere within the three columns. You will have to be careful that you do not make the animals so big that all the text doesn't fit. Turn the text wrap to **Tight** for all three clip-art frames.

9. Save your file and read on.

Now let's add the final story and another graphic image.

STEP-BY-STEP 6.16

1. Bring down a ruler guide to **8.5** inches on the vertical ruler.

2. Create a text box frame across the middle and right columns that starts at the 8.5-inch ruler guide and extends to the bottom margin of both columns.

3. Key the following text and format it using Tahoma, 10 pt.
   Shelter Reservations
   The Otter Creek parks system has 13 rentable shelters, located in 6 different parks. Shelter reservations are taken for the current year beginning the first working day after January 1 for the year 2003 (reservations will be taken on January 2). On the first day, reservations are made in person at City Hall beginning at 6:30 AM. (City Hall doors open at 5:30 AM.) Fees are paid at that time. Normal office hours for reservations are 8:00 AM to 4:30 PM, Monday through Friday.

4. Format the title using 14 pt. bold. Change the fill color of the text box to gray.

<u>STEP-BY-STEP 6.16 Continued</u>

5. Insert a clip-art object in the left column to the left of the text box frame using **parks** or **shelter** for the search. Resize the object to fit the width of the column. Don't make it taller than the text box frame in the middle and right columns.

6. Save the file.

Create the Table of Contents

One more object that needs to be created is the table of contents. Now that all the stories have been inserted, you have the story titles and page numbers to include. You will use a Design Gallery object for the table of contents, which will make the process very easy!

STEP-BY-STEP 6.17

1. Turn to page 1 of **Parks Newsletter *xxx***.

2. Using the **Design Gallery** tool, choose **Table of Contents** and then **Crossed Lines Table of Contents**. Click **Insert**.

3. Move the object to the left column starting at **2.5** inches on the vertical ruler.

4. Enlarge the object to fit within the column and measure approximately **3.25** inches tall.

5. Change the text labeled *Inside Story* to the text shown in Figure 6-20. Change the page numbers to match those in Figure 6-20.

FIGURE 6-20
Table of Contents

INSIDE THIS ISSUE:	
Parks—Facelifts for City Boat Launches	1
Forestry—Pruning Street Trees—Why It's Done	2
Summer Work	2
Parks—The Way it Works in City Parks	3
Miller's Bay Sailboat	3
Zoo—Animals in Action: Summer Classes at the Otter Street Zoo	4
Shelter Reservations	4

6. Increase the size of the font of the story titles and page numbers to 10 pt. The title (INSIDE THIS ISSUE:) is ok the way it is.

7. Using the mouse, adjust the lines separating the names of the stories so the entire title shows for each story. For those that take only one line, make the space smaller accordingly. (If you move the line separating the page numbers from the story titles, hold the Shift key so you can move that line only.)

8. Save the **Parks Newsletter *xxx*** file again.

Using the Design Checker

Wow! That was quite the project, wasn't it? It takes a long time to gather (or write) the stories to include in a newsletter, play with the layout to fit all the text in the most appealing design, proof it, edit it, and print it. One tool that Publisher has that makes your job a little easier is the Design Checker. This tool will check an individual story or the entire publication for the following formatting concerns:

- Text in overflow area
- Disproportional pictures
- Empty frames
- Covered objects
- Objects partially off page
- Objects in nonprinting region
- Blank space at top of page
- Spacing between sentences
- Pages unreachable by hyperlinks

When you run the Design Checker, a dialog box appears asking what you'd like checked. You can click the Options button and choose whether you want to check a selected story or all the stories, as well as what formatting you want checked. As you run the Design Checker a dialog box will pop up telling you about a potential problem (see Figure 6-21). You may click in your publication and make the changes without closing the Design Checker. You can choose to ignore the problem by clicking Ignore or Ignore All. You can also click Explain to find out more about the design error. You will use the Design Checker in the next Step-by-Step. (You may get different formatting prompts than those in the exercise depending on variations in your design.)

FIGURE 6-21
Design Checker Choices

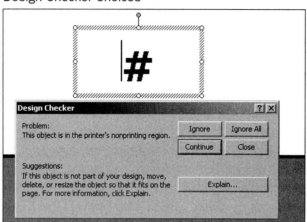

STEP-BY-STEP 6.18

1. With **Parks Newsletter xxx** open in the window, open the **Tools** menu and choose **Design Checker**.

2. Choose **All** for the pages to check. Click **Options** and turn on **Check all problems**. Click **OK** twice.

3. Your first design problem may be the one showing in Figure 6-21. This one is showing because you put an object on the master page outside of the margin guide. You should have enough room for it to print—depending on your printer. Click **Ignore**.

4. Continue to click **Ignore** on the prompts regarding the objects being in nonprinting regions.

5. Continue to look at the messages that appear. If you feel you need to fix the problem, click in the publication and correct the problem. Then click **Continue** in the Design Checker dialog box. (You will get messages regarding the pages not being accessible from the home page. Those are relevant only if you are doing Web pages. Click **Ignore**.)

6. The last message you should see is **The Design check is complete**. Click **OK**.

7. You can go back and make any necessary changes when you are finished running the Design Checker, if necessary.

8. Finally, save the **Parks Newsletter xxx** publication and print all four pages. Look over your copy and make any additional editing changes needed and print it again. Close the file.

Good job! You have successfully created your first newsletter from scratch! Don't hesitate to try out the newsletter wizard in the future and see if you like any of the design features. You might find it easier to use a wizard and modify it. You can also use the newsletter you created from scratch as a template and modify it each time you use it.

SUMMARY

In this lesson, you learned:

■ To set up columns and pages for a newsletter.

■ To use master pages for objects appearing on all pages.

■ To create styles for consistent formatting of text objects.

■ To create styles by example and from scratch.

■ How to modify styles, and that doing so affects all occurrences of where the style has been applied throughout a publication.

■ How to connect text box frames when a text file is longer than one text box frame so that the frames are threaded.

■ How to add continuation statements in frames in which a story continues on another page as well as on the page where the story is being continued.

■ To add a caption to a picture and group the two objects.

■ To set up tabs either using the ruler or the Tabs dialog box.

■ To create a table of contents using the Design Gallery.

■ How to check the publication for formatting problems using the Design Checker.

VOCABULARY *Review*

Define the following terms:

Continuation statements	Master page	Overflow memory
Footer	Mirrored guides	Style
Gray	Newsletter	Threaded
Header		

REVIEW *Questions*

FILL IN THE BLANK

Complete the following sentences by writing the correct word or words in the blanks provided.

1. The area on the front cover of a newsletter that contains the name of the newsletter is known as the _____ .

2. The article or paragraphs in the text box frame is called the _____ .

3. A special memory holding text that remains with the file even when it is closed is called _____ .

4. Text pulled out from a story to catch the reader's attention is called a _____ .

5. A line that tells the reader where to turn for the rest of the story is called a _____ .

6. The _____ is information that appears at the bottom of every page.

7. The _____ explains a picture in a short sentence or paragraph.

8. The _____ lists the articles and features and page numbers.

9. The _____ is information that appears at the top of every page.

10. The return address and space for a mailing label is called the _____ .

11. A short phrase that describes the purpose and audience and lists the date of the issue is called the _____ .

12. The _____ area identifies contact information for the newsletters and organization.

13. The _____ is the layer of the newsletter that contains headers and footers.

WRITTEN QUESTIONS

Write a brief answer to the following questions.

1. What is the importance of *white space* when designing a newsletter?

2. What is the importance of *consistency* when designing a newsletter?

3. What is the main purpose of the master page(s)?

4. What are the advantages of using styles?

5. What does it mean when text box frames are *threaded*?

6. What Publisher feature did you use to insert an already-formatted pull quote?

7. List at least five design problems that the design checker could find.

PROJECTS

PROJECT 6-1

In this exercise, you create a newsletter from scratch, starting with page one. Set up the publication using the following steps:

1. Create a new publication using the standard 8½ × 11-inch page size. Refer to Figure 6-22 for guidance.

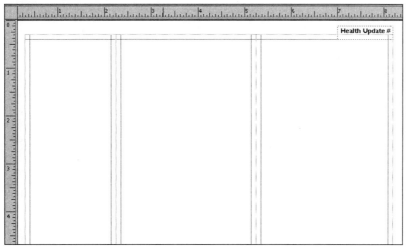

FIGURE 6-22
Master Page Setup

2. Change all four margins to 0.3 inch and set up three columns in the Layout Guides dialog box. DO NOT turn on Create Two Master Pages With Mirrored Guides.

3. On the Master Page, hold down the Shift key and adjust the first column guide to line up at 2.25 inches on the horizontal ruler. HINT: Set the Zoom to 100% so you can see the ruler increments better.

4. Adjust the second column guide to line up at 5.25 inches on the horizontal ruler.

5. Add a text box frame in the upper-right corner sitting on top of the top margin guide. Right align **Health Update**, space once, and insert a Page Number code.

6. Select the words and page number code and change the font to Gill Sans MT, 10 pt. bold.

7. Turn off the Master Page and insert three additional pages after the first page.

8. On the first page, choose Ignore Master Page from the View menu.

9. Save the publication as **Health Update** *xxx*. Keep it open.

FIGURE 6-23
Banner and Tagline

CREATE THE BANNER AND TAGLINE

1. Study the parts of the banner and tagline area of the newsletter in Figure 6-23. Bring down a ruler guide to 0.50 inch on the vertical ruler.

2. Create a WordArt frame with the following text: **Health Update**. Change the font to Gill Sans Ultra Bold.

3. Drag the frame to begin the frame at the left margin guide and the horizontal ruler guide. Make it 6.0 inches wide and 1.0 inch tall.

4. Format the WordArt box as follows: Change the fill color to Accent 1 (if necessary), change the line color to Black, and change the weight of the line to 0.25 pt.

5. Create a text box frame below the WordArt object that starts at approximately 1.625 inches vertically and is 6.0 inches wide and 0.25 inch tall.

6. Key the following text: **Quarterly Newsletter Published for Otter Creek Health Services Division Patrons**

7. Format the text using Gill Sans MT, 10 pt. bold, and small caps.

8. Bring a ruler guide from the vertical ruler to 6.5 inches on the horizontal ruler.

9. Create a text box frame that starts at the vertical and horizontal ruler guides and extends to the right margin. Make it approximately 0.20 inch tall.

10. Right align the text, **July 2003**, and format it using Gill Sans MT, 10 pt.

11. Copy the frame containing the date and paste it into the document. Move it down so it begins at 0.825 inch on the vertical ruler.

12. Change the text to **Volume 1, Issue 2**.

13. Draw a horizontal line between the two text box frames that starts at the vertical ruler guide and extends to the right margin guide.

14. Format the line using the Accent 1 color in the Line Color dialog box. Choose 6 pt for the Line/Border Style.

15. At 2.0 inches on the vertical ruler, draw a horizontal line across the first column. Make it 6 pt thick and change the color to Accent 1.

16. Create another horizontal line at 2.0 inches on the vertical ruler that starts where the line created in the step above leaves off. Extend it all the way to the right margin. Make it 1.5 pt thick and change the color to Accent 1.

17. Group these two lines together because you will use this group throughout the publication as a separator between stories.

18. Check your publication with Figure 6-23. Is it close?

19. Save your file again as **Health Update *xxx*** and keep it open for the next part of the project.

INSERT STORIES ON PAGE 1

1. Bring down three ruler guides to 2.25 inches and 6.5 inches, and 6.875 inches on the vertical ruler.

2. In column two, create a text box frame that starts at the ruler guide at 2.25 inches and the left margin of the column and extends to the right of the column and down to the ruler guide at 6.5 inches.

3. Copy that text box frame and paste the copy in the third column starting at the 2.25-inch ruler guide and the left margin of the column.

4. In the first text box frame, insert the text file named **Swimming Pool Safety Tips.doc**.

5. When you get the Autoflow message, click **No**.

6. Click the link button on the Connect Frames toolbar to connect the frames, and pour the story into the second frame. (The rest of the story will be continued on the second page.)

7. Select the first letter in the first paragraph and format the letter to be a drop cap. Create a custom drop cap using Gill Sans MT for the font. Make it three lines high.

8. Insert a clip-art object that helps to convey the message of the story. Size the clip-art object so it is approximately 2 inches square, and turn on the Tight text wrap option. Position the picture attractively within the two columns.

9. Create a text box frame in the first column that starts at the 2.25-inch ruler guide and measures approximately 1.0 inch tall. Key **Swimming Pool Safety Tips**.

10. Format the text using Gill Sans MT, 18 pt., bold, and Accent 1 color.

11. Select the text and click in the Style name box. Key **Title** as the name of the style. Press **Enter**. Click **OK** in the **Create Style By Example** dialog box. (You will use this style for other story titles.)

12. Create two text box frames in the lower half of columns 2 and 3 starting at the 6.875-inch ruler guide. Insert the text file named **Dog Bites.doc**.

13. Format the first letter in the first paragraph using the same drop cap style as in the first story.

14. Add an appropriate clip-art object and turn on **Tight** text wrap. You may choose where to position the clip-art object.

15. Add a text box frame for the title in the first column and key **Dog Bites**. Apply the Title style.

16. Copy the grouped horizontal lines created earlier and paste the object above the second story. Refer to Figure 6-24 for the placement of these lines.

FIGURE 6-24
Inserted Stories on Page 1

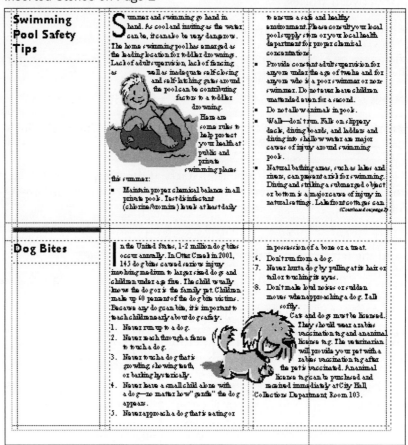

17. Save the file again as **Health Update *xxx***. Keep it open in the window.

ADD A DESIGN GALLERY OBJECT TO PAGE 1

1. Create a Design Gallery object for the table of contents. Choose the Top Notches Table of Contents design.

2. Position it in the first column below the Swimming Pool Safety Tips title. Resize the object to be the width of the column and about 3 inches tall.

3. Key the following story titles and page numbers. Adjust the space for the titles of the stories so the entire title shows.

Swimming Pool Safety Tips	1
Dog Bites	1
Sun Sense	2
Heat Stress	2
Summer Food Safety Tips	3
Fireworks Safety Tips	3
Volunteers Needed	4

4. In the first column below the Dog Bites title, create a Design Gallery object for a pull quote.

5. Choose the Crossed Lines Pull Quote from the Pull Quotes category and key the following text using the 20 pt. font size:

Children make up 60 percent of dog bite victims

6. Resize the object to be the width of column 1 and about 2.75 inches tall.

7. The two objects should resemble those in Figure 6-25. Save the file.

FIGURE 6-25
Table of Contents and Pull Quote on Page 1

PROJECT 6-2

You are now finished with page 1 except for the continuation statement, which will be added later. Take a good look at page 1. Except for the banner, the same format will be used for the other three pages. The title of the story goes in the first column; the text frames are in the other two columns. The grouped lines will go above each section of the newsletter. Your instructions will be brief. Now let's go to page 2.

1. Bring down ruler guides from the horizontal ruler to 0.625 inch, 6.125 inches, and 6.75 inches.

2. Create a small text box frame in the first column starting at the 0.625-inch ruler guide and extending the width of column 1. Make it approximately 0.375 inch tall.

3. Key the text **Sun Sense,** and apply the **Title** style.

4. Create a text box frame in the second column starting at the 0.625-inch ruler guide and extending the width of the column and down to the 6.125-inch ruler guide.

5. Insert the text file named **Sun Sense.doc.**

6. Make the first letter a drop cap that matches the stories on page 1.

7. Add an appropriate clip-art object of your choice making it about 2 inches square. Move it so part of it is in the blank area of column 1 as shown in Figure 6-26. Change the text wrap to Tight.

FIGURE 6-26
Completed Page 2

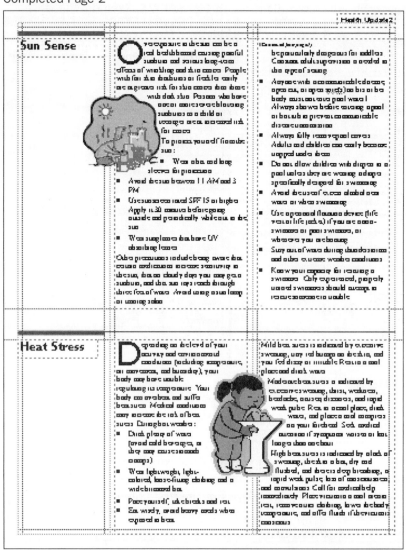

8. Create a text box frame in the third column starting at the 0.625-inch ruler guide and extending it across column 3 and down to the 6.125-inch ruler guide.

9. Link the rest of the **Swimming Pool Safety Tips** story from page 1 into this column.

10. From the Format Text Box dialog box, click the Include "Continued from page…" option.

11. Turn back to page 1 and turn on the Include "Continued on page…" option for the text box frame in column 3.

12. Create a text box in column 1 of the lower half of page 2 for the title. Key **Heat Stress** and apply the **Title** style.

13. Add two text box frames at the bottom half of the page starting each frame at the 6.75-inch ruler guide. Insert **Heat Stress.doc** into the frames.

14. Format the first letter as a drop cap.

15. Add an appropriate clip art and size it so all of the text still fits in the two frames. Change the text wrap to Tight.

16. Turn back to page 1 and copy the grouped horizontal lines. On page 2, paste the lines above each story as shown in Figure 6-24.

17. Save the file again as **Health Update *xxx***.

SCANS PROJECT 6-3

Now that you did so well with page 2, you should have no problem at all with page 3! You will do exactly the same thing you did on page 2. Study Figure 6-27.

FIGURE 6-27
Completed Page 3

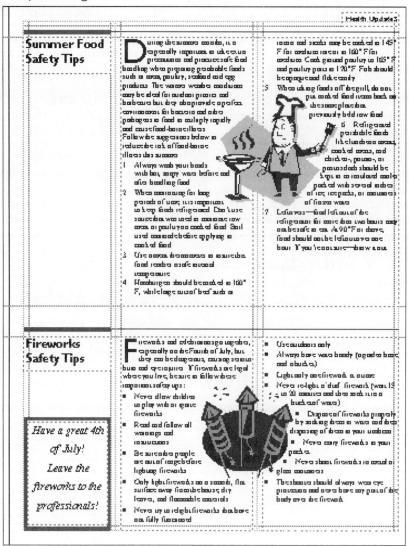

1. Create the title and story frames for the story in the top half of the page.

2. Insert the text file **Summer Food Safety Tips.doc**. Use **Summer Food Safety Tips** as the title.

3. Continue the story from column 2 to column 3.

4. Format the first letter as a drop cap and add an appropriate clip-art object.

5. Repeat the steps for the bottom half of the page.

6. Insert the text file **Fireworks Safety Tips.doc**. Use **Fireworks Safety Tips** as the title.

7. Continue the story from column 2 to column 3.

8. Format the first letter as a drop cap and add an appropriate clip-art object.

9. Add a pull quote in the first column below the story title (Fireworks Safety Tips) using the Crossed Lines Pull Quote design from the Design Gallery. Key and format the text:
Have a great 4th of July!
Leave the fireworks to the professionals!

10. Save the file again.

You have one more page to go! Page 4 will have a story on the top half and the mailing information on the bottom half. This page will be different from the rest.

1. Bring down ruler guides from the horizontal ruler to 2 inches, 5 inches, 5.5 inches, and 5.75 inches.

2. Create a text box frame starting in the second column at the 2-inch ruler guide and extend it across BOTH columns 2 and 3 and down to the 5-inch ruler guide.

3. Insert the text file **Volunteers Needed.doc**. Format the drop cap as in the other stories.

4. Insert an appropriate clip-art object in the story and perhaps a little above the story as shown in Figure 6-28. Change the text wrap to Tight.

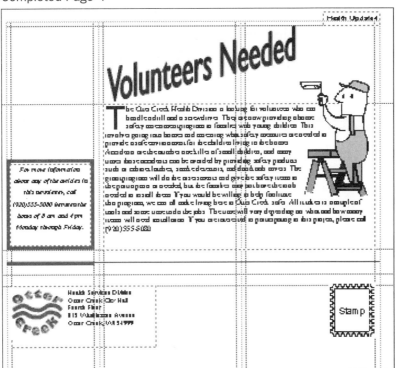

FIGURE 6-28
Completed Page 4

5. Add a WordArt object of your choice above the story that reads Volunteers Needed. Use Gill Sans MT.

6. Add a pull quote in the first column that "sits" on the 5-inch ruler guide. Key the following text, making sure there are no hyphenated lines:

   For more information about any of the articles in this newsletter, call (920) 555-5080 between the hours of 8 am and 4 pm Monday through Friday.

7. Copy the grouped horizontal lines from another page and paste the lines below the story in the top half.

8. Add a text box frame starting in the left column at the 5.75-inch ruler guide and extend it to measure approximately 3 inches wide and 1.25 inches tall.

9. Key the following text and format it with Gill Sans MT, 10 pt.
   Health Services Division
   Otter Creek City Hall
   Fourth Floor
   215 Washington Avenue
   Otter Creek, WI 54999

10. Insert the **Otter Creek Logo.jpg** file to the left of the text and size it to be a little taller than the address and 1.25 inches wide.

11. Draw a rectangle to represent the stamp in the right column. Make sure the top border snaps to the 5.75-inch ruler guide.

12. Key and center the word **Stamp** in the rectangle. You may have to add a space above the word to center it vertically.

13. Save the file and print it. If your printer does not have a lot of memory, you may have to print one page at a time.

CRITICAL *Thinking*

 ACTIVITY 6-1

   You now have some idea of how long it takes to create a four-page newsletter. However, you were given most of the text stories to insert. Identify what you think you would need to do if you were in charge of the entire newsletter from creation to distribution.

BOOKLETS AND CATALOGS

OBJECTIVES

Upon completion of this lesson, you should be able to:

■ Use the booklet page setup to create a folded publication.

■ Add BorderArt to a frame.

■ Create a catalog from a wizard.

■ Edit a catalog created from a wizard.

■ Observe how Microsoft Publisher prints folded publications in the correct page order.

■ Insert an Object.

Estimated time: 3 hours

VOCABULARY

Booklet

BorderArt

Catalog

Embedded object

Folded publication

What Are Booklets and Catalogs?

Booklets and *catalogs* are publications with a front and back cover and two or more inside pages. Table 7-1 explains their differences.

TABLE 7-1
Comparing Booklets and Catalogs

FEATURE	BOOKLET	CATALOG
Purpose	A booklet is usually four or eight pages and is used for some event like a program at a play that lists the characters and actors and the sequence of the acts.	A catalog is usually several pages, and it generally contains information about products for sale.
Paper	Booklets are printed on regular bond paper.	Catalogs differ from a booklet in that their first and last page may be printed on heavier paper than the inside pages.
Cover	Displays title and picture representing the program.	May include one picture or a group of pictures representing the products listed in the catalog. A title is included that reflects the contents.

TABLE 7-1 Continued
Comparing Booklets and Catalogs

FEATURE	BOOKLET	CATALOG
Frequency	Booklets are printed as often as there is a program.	Catalogs are printed periodically on a set schedule.
Color	Usually only black, except, perhaps, for the paper on which it is printed.	Often the color is a high-resolution color if photographs of the products are included.
Inside Pages	Simple layout containing text explaining the activity.	Usually divided into sections for product photos, descriptions, and prices.

While the preceding table describes their differences, Publisher treats booklets and catalogs the same with regard to their layouts. They both are considered to be a folded publication, and both are folded at the center as shown in Figure 7-1. Each half of the fold is considered a page so that one sheet of paper actually contains two pages.

FIGURE 7-1
Page Setup Dialog Box

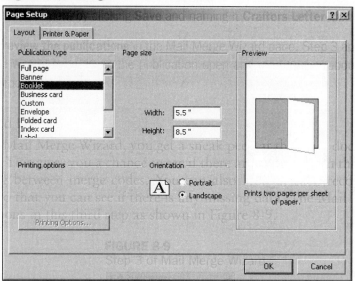

In Publisher, a booklet is created from scratch using the Page Setup dialog box to get started. A catalog is created from a wizard. Both of them, however, are always created as four pages or two pieces of 8½ × 11-inch paper in landscape orientation. One sheet of paper contains the first and last pages, which are referred to as covers. The other sheet of paper contains the inside two pages. When you want to add more pages to a booklet or a catalog, four more inside pages are always added.

Fortunately, you do not have to worry about what page is the cover, or the back, or the inside pages because Publisher takes care of that for you. The Page Navigator indicates the page numbers. Publisher ensures that the publication will appear in correct order and orientation when printed. Once the page setup is complete, each page is just like any other publication.

Create a Booklet

The booklet you will create is for a Veterans Day activity. You will use the Page Setup feature described above to create four pages (two sheets of paper). This Step-by-Step will give you a chance to review many of the skills you learned in previous lessons. Figure 7-2 shows you the front cover, or page 1, of the booklet.

FIGURE 7-2
Front Cover of the Veterans Booklet

STEP-BY-STEP 7.1

1. Start a new publication using the Blank Publication option.

2. From the **File** menu, choose **Page Setup**.

3. On the **Layout** page, choose **Booklet** in the Publication type list. Make sure Landscape orientation is selected. Click **OK**.

4. Publisher will ask if you would like to automatically insert pages. Click **Yes** since you want four pages.

5. From the **Arrange** menu, choose **Layout Guides** and change the four margins to **0.5** inch each. Click **OK**.

6. On page one (cover) at approximately **5.6** inches on the vertical ruler, create a text box frame that extends from the left to the right margin and down to the bottom margin.

STEP-BY-STEP 7.1 Continued

7. Change to the Arial font. Center the following text, and format it as shown in parentheses.
   11 November 2003 (18 pt.)
   Otter Creek, Wisconsin (18 pt.)
   5:00 PM (18 pt.)
   (Leave a blank line)
   Veterans Home on the Lake (14 pt.)
   567 Lakeshore Drive (14 pt.)
   (Leave a blank line)
   Recognizing the Veterans (20 pt. bold)

8. To insert the picture in the center, choose **Picture** from the **Insert** menu. Click **From File**.

9. Select the **veterans.gif** file from your student data files and click **Insert**.

10. Center the picture on the page starting at approximately **2.25** inches vertically. (Do not enlarge the picture. It is a *.gif* file and may become too grainy.)

11. Because the picture has a white background, change the background to transparency using the **Set Transparent Color** button on the Picture toolbar, as shown in Figure 7-3.

FIGURE 7-3
Set Transparent Color Button

Now let's finish the cover by adding the title.

STEP-BY-STEP 7.2

1. Create a WordArt frame using the second style on the top row from the WordArt Gallery dialog box.

2. Key **Veterans Day**. Use your WordArt formatting skills to change the color of the WordArt text to a gradient color of your choice. (The one in Figure 7-2 is Diagonal Up.)

3. Size the frame so it starts at the top margin and extends across the page from the left to the right margins.

4. Create a line under the WordArt frame as shown in Figure 7-2, making it **2.25 pt.** thick.

5. Add the arrows at each end by right-clicking on the line and choosing **Format AutoShape**. Choose the second style in the top row for both the **Begin Style** and the **End Style**.

6. Nudge the line using the up or down arrows to be parallel to the WordArt text and close to the base of the "y" in the word Day.

7. Save the file as **Veterans Booklet *xxx***, where xxx are your initials. Keep the file open to continue with the next pages.

When you click on the Page Navigator buttons for Page 2, you will see Page 2 and Page 3 in a two-page spread as shown in Figure 7-4. You can turn off the two-page spread view from the View menu.

FIGURE 7-4
Pages 2 and 3 of the Veterans Booklet

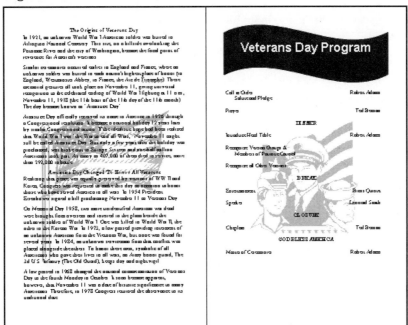

STEP-BY-STEP 7.3

1. On Page 2, insert a clip-art object that is a flag of your choice.

2. Move it to the center of the page and size it to approximately **3.5** inches wide and **4** inches tall. Take care not to make it disproportionate when you resize it.

3. Change the color to **Washout** using the Washout button on the Picture toolbar, as shown in Figure 7-5. (This choice makes it look like a watermark.)

FIGURE 7-5
The Washout Button

4. Create a text box frame that fits the entire page from left to right margins and from top to bottom margins.

5. Insert the text file named **The Origins of Veterans Day.doc** from your data files. (If the entire story does not fit in the frame, you may have to enlarge the frame slightly.)

6. Make sure you can see the picture behind the text like a watermark. (If you need to edit the picture in any way, you will have to send the text box frame to the back first. Then, when you are done editing the picture, send the picture back. Do you remember how to do that?) Save the file and keep it open.

For page 3, you'll copy the clip art from page 1 to be used as a watermark. Follow along carefully.

STEP-BY-STEP 7.4

1. Turn back to Page 1 and right-click on the clip-art object. Choose **Copy**.

2. Turn to Page 3, right-click, and choose **Paste**.

3. Move the clip-art object to **3** inches on the vertical ruler and center it between the left and right margins. Change the color to **Washout** from the Picture toolbar.

4. Create a text box frame starting at **2** inches vertically and extending from the left to the right margin and down to the bottom of the frame.

5. With the frame selected, set a left tab at **0.25** inch and a right leader tab using dots as leaders at **4.25** inch on the horizontal ruler. (You may need to look back to Lesson 6 to review how to do this.)

6. Key the following text single-spaced. You will change the spacing after it is keyed. For the two items with the indented second line (Call to Order and Recognize Veteran Groups), press **Shift+Enter** at the end of the first line and **Tab** to indent the second line.

Call to Order	**Robert Adams**
Salute and Pledge	
Prayer	**Ted Benson**
DINNER	
Introduce Head Table	**Robert Adams**
Recognize Veteran Groups &	
Members of Patriotic Council	
Recognize all Other Veterans	
BREAK	
Entertainment	**Brass Quintet**
Speaker	**Leonard Smith**
CLOSURE	
Chaplain	**Ted Benson**
GOD BLESS AMERICA	
Master of Ceremonies	**Robert Adams**

STEP-BY-STEP 7.4 Continued

7. Select all the text and from the **Format** menu, choose **Line Spacing**. Set the space in the **Before paragraphs** text box to **12 pt**.

8. Bold and center the words keyed in all caps.

9. Create a Banner AutoShape object starting at the top margin of the page that measures approximately **1.25** inches tall and extends from the left to the right margin.

10. Center the text, **Veterans Day Program**.

11. Format the text as Arial, 24 pt., bold, and **white** color.

12. Fill the banner WordArt shape with **black**.

13. Do your Pages 2 and 3 look like Figure 7-4? If not, get help from your instructor. Save the file again as **Veterans Day *xxx*** and keep it open.

Adding BorderArt

On the last page, you will try a new feature called *BorderArt*. BorderArt is a collection of creative borders for use as frames and/or rectangles to call attention to text boxes. This feature provides 165 different designs for picture borders, plus the ability to create a custom design. You will add a black star BorderArt to the text box illustrated in Figure 7-6. Like any formatting feature, be sure it will help enhance your message.

FIGURE 7-6
Page 4 of the Veterans Booklet

S TEP-BY-STEP 7.5

1. With **Veterans Day** *xxx* open in the window, turn to page 4. Create a text box frame starting at **5** inches on the vertical ruler. Extend it from the left margin to the right margin and down to the bottom margin.

2. Center the following text using Times New Roman, 12 pt, bold. (You may have problems trying to key a lowercase letter at the beginning of a line. Key the entire text. Then go back and delete the unwanted uppercase letters and replace them with lowercase letters.)
   GOD BLESS AMERICA
   (Leave a blank line)
   God bless America,
   land that I love.
   Stand beside her and guide her,
   through the night with a light from above.
   From the mountains
   to the prairies
   to the oceans white with foam.
   God bless America,
   my home sweet home.
   God bless America,
   my home sweet home.

3. Right-click on the text box frame and choose **Format Text Box**. In the **Fill** section, choose a medium-to light-gray color from the **Color** option.

4. From the **Line** option, click the **BorderArt** button near the bottom. You will see a list of border designs illustrated in Figure 7-7. Study the different designs.

FIGURE 7-7
BorderArt Dialog Box

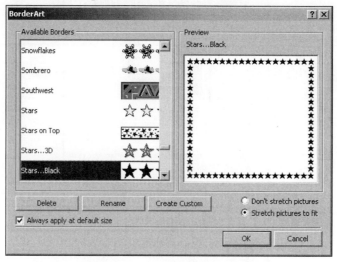

5. Choose the **Stars...Black** design and click **OK** twice.

STEP-BY-STEP 7.5 Continued

6. Insert the same flag you inserted on page 2 (or a different flag graphic) at **2** inches on the vertical ruler. Center it between the left and right margins.

7. Create a WordArt object using a design of your choice containing the words **Veterans Day 2003**. Choose a gradient-fill pattern.

8. Size the object to begin at the top margin and stretch between the left and right margins. Make it approximately **1.5** inches tall.

9. Save the file, proofread it, and print it. Notice how it prints in the right order. Fold and arrange the pages and look it over. If it is acceptable, close the file.

> **Hot Tip**
>
> If you edit a booklet and wish to print only the current page, choose Print from the File menu and click Current Page. A dialog box will ask if you'd like the page printed as a separate booklet. Choose No so your pages will be properly arranged.

Create a Catalog

Now that you know how easy it is to create a folded publication, we'll create a catalog using a wizard. This publication will advertise various one-day trips for members of the Otter Creek Seniors Center. You will keep some parts of the Wizard-created publication and delete others. This exercise will be a good review of the Master Page feature, styles, and ruler guides as well as basic formatting functions you have used before.

STEP-BY-STEP 7.6

1. Start a new publication. Choose **Catalogs** from the **New Publication** task pane.

2. Choose the **Tilt Catalog** design. Cancel the dialog box that asks for personal information.

3. From the **View** menu, choose **Master Page**.

4. Drag down ruler guides to **1.25** inches and **2** inches on the vertical ruler.

STEP-BY-STEP 7.6 Continued

5. Drag over ruler guides to **1.5** inches and **9.5** inches on the horizontal ruler. The top portion of your Master Pages should resemble Figure 7-8.

FIGURE 7-8
Master Pages

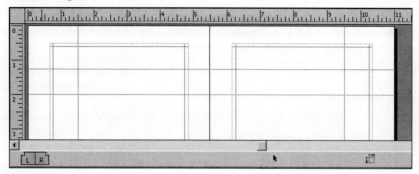

6. Close the Master Page view. Save your format as **Seniors Trips Catalog *xxx***. Keep it open.

Let's begin by placing objects on page 1.

STEP-BY-STEP 7.7

1. Delete the following text box frames: Catalog Title, Catalog Subtitle, and Date.

2. In the Business Name text box frame, key **Otter Creek Seniors Tours**

3. In the Sidebar Heading, select the title and center the following two lines:
   One-Day Trips
   June–August 2003

4. Delete the bulleted lines.

5. Select the two lines you just keyed, turn on bold, and enlarge the text to approximately 28 pt.

6. Select the picture and click the **Clip Organizer Frame** button. Key the word **city** in the Search For box. Choose a picture of a city that could be used to advertise tours.

7. Resize the picture to be approximately **2.25** inches wide and **2.25** inches tall. If the picture looks disproportionate, resize it to look proportionate.

8. Above the picture, create a WordArt object. Select the first style in the first row and key **Otter Creek Seniors**.

9. Format the WordArt object to have a gradient fill of one color (default gray) and choose the horizontal shading style. Select the second design on the top row with the darker blend at the top.

10. Resize the WordArt object to be **3** inches wide and **0.75** inch tall.

STEP-BY-STEP 7.7 Continued

11. Turn on the first shadow style in the first row from the Formatting toolbar for the WordArt object.

12. Select the WordArt object and hold down your **Shift** key as you select the picture and the text box frame. With all three selected, choose **Align or Distribute** from the **Arrange** menu. Choose **Align Center**.

13. Your Page 1 should resemble Figure 7-9. Save your file again as **Seniors Trips Catalog** *xxx*.

FIGURE 7-9
Completed Page 1 of the Seniors Trips Catalog

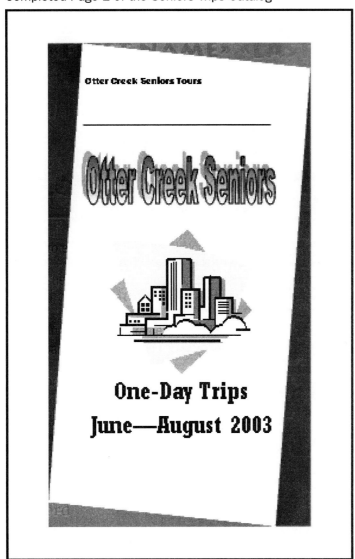

The remaining pages are going to be similar in appearance. Each will include one large text box frame in which you will insert a text file describing a trip as well as a rotated WordArt object showing the name of the trip. After you create and format the WordArt object on Page 2, you will copy and paste the object on the remaining six pages. Then you'll change the text and rotate it on some of the pages. On some of the existing pages, you may have to delete frames before you add your own frames. You will also create two styles to make your formatting consistent. Your Pages 2 and 3 will resemble Figure 7-10.

FIGURE 7-10

Completed Pages 2 and 3 of the Seniors Trip Catalog

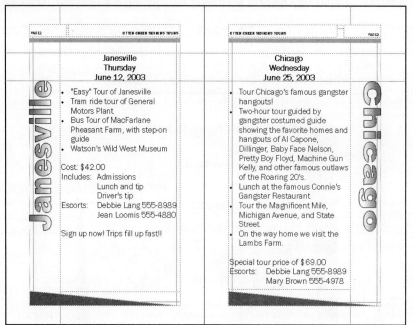

STEP-BY-STEP 7.8

1. Turn to Page 2 of **Seniors Trips Catalog** *xxx*.

2. In the text box frame in the upper-right corner containing a phone number, key **Otter Creek Seniors Tours**.

3. Create a text box frame that starts at the 1.25-inch vertical ruler guide and the 1.5-inch horizontal ruler guide. Extend it to the right margin and down to just above the AutoShape.

4. Insert the file named **Janesville.txt** from the student data files.

5. Select the text from "Easy" Tour ... to the end. Format it using Franklin Gothic Book, 16 pt.

6. With the text still selected, click in the **Style Name** box on the Formatting toolbar. With the current style name selected, key **triptext** and press **Enter**. Click **OK** in the **Create Style By Example** dialog box.

7. Select the top three lines and format the text using Franklin Gothic Book, 16 pt. bold, and center alignment.

8. With the text still selected, click in the **Style Name** box on the Formatting toolbar. With the current style name selected, key **triptitle** and press **Enter**. Click **OK** in the **Create Style By Example** dialog box.

STEP-BY-STEP 7.8 Continued

9. Select the first six lines formatted with **triptext** style and click the **bullet** button on the Formatting Toolbar. If any of the lines hyphenate, turn off automatic hyphenation in the Hyphenation dialog box (Tools, Language).

10. Create a WordArt object using the first style in the first row in the first row of styles. Key **Janesville** and click **OK**.

11. Format the object with a gradient fill of one color (default gray) and choose the horizontal shading style. Select the second design on the top row with the darker blend at the top.

12. Rotate the object **90 degrees** to the left and align it at the 2-inch horizontal ruler guide and the left margin guide.

13. Size the object to be **4** inches wide and **0.6** inch tall.

14. Save the file again as **Seniors Trips Catalog** *xxx*. Compare your Page 2 with Figure 7-10. Keep the file open for the next Step-by-Step.

> **Hot Tip**
>
> To delete a text box frame containing text or a table frame that contains text, right-click on the frame and choose **Delete Object**.

The remaining pages will be formatted much like Page 2. The only difference will be that additional frames on the page will need to be deleted. The directions will be given for Page 3. You will do the rest on your own—except for Page 7—which has special instructions.

S TEP-BY-STEP 7.9

1. Turn to page 3. Study page 3 of Figure 7-10. Delete any frames except the two at the very top.

2. Create a text box frame that starts at the 1.25-inch vertical ruler guide and the left margin guide. Extend the frame to the 9.5-inch vertical ruler guide and down to just above the AutoShape.

3. Insert the **Chicago.txt** text file from your student data files.

4. Select the top three lines and turn on the **triptitle** style. Select the remaining lines and turn on the **triptext** style.

5. Select the lines formatted with triptext style down to *Lambs Farm* and turn on bullets. Again, make sure no lines hyphenate.

6. Turn back to Page 2 and right-click the WordArt frame. Choose **Copy**.

7. Right-click on Page 3 and choose **Paste**.

8. Move the WordArt frame to the right margin guide aligning it at the 2-inch vertical ruler guide.

9. Rotate the WordArt object **180 degrees**.

STEP-BY-STEP 7.9 Continued

10. Choose **Edit Text** from the WordArt toolbar or double-click the WordArt object and key **Chicago** as the new text. Compare your Page 3 with Figure 7-10. Is it similar?

11. Save the file again as **Seniors Trips Catalog xxx**. Keep the publication open.

STEP-BY-STEP 7.10

1. Look at Table 7-2. It contains the names of the text files to be inserted from the data files as well as the text for the WordArt frames.

TABLE 7-2
Files for Pages 4 through 8

PAGE	TEXT FILE	WORDART TEXT
4	Central Wisconsin	Central Wisconsin
5	Lake Winnebago	Lake Winnebago
6	Edelweiss Riverboat	Edelweiss Riverboat
7	Leave blank	Leave blank
8	Trip Rules	Trip Rules

2. For pages 4, 5, 6, and 8, you will be on your own as you insert the text file, turn on the two styles, paste the WordArt object, and edit it.

3. On Page 6, format the lines under the bulleted item **Featuring:** as follows. Select the lines and turn off the bullets.

4. Set a left tab on the ruler at **0.25** inch. From the **Indents and Spacing** dialog box, select **Hanging Indent** under **Preset**.

5. On page 8 you will notice that there are no text boxes at the very top or an AutoShape at the bottom. This is the default for the last page, or back cover.

6. Save the catalog again as **Seniors Trips Catalog xxx**. Keep it open for one more Step-by-Step.

Insert an Object

Up until now, you have inserted text files from word processing programs and picture files. You can insert files from other types of programs such as spreadsheets. This works very well when you want to include the spreadsheet data or a chart. The Insert Object dialog box is used to insert an existing file as well as create a new file from programs on your computer. You will insert an Excel chart at the bottom of Page 7 of the catalog. The chart is illustrated on the portion of the finished page in Figure 7-11. You need to have Excel installed on your computer for this process to work. This is because the object will be *embedded* on the page. When an ***embedded object*** is double-clicked, the tools for the program in which the object was created will appear, providing editing options.

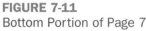

FIGURE 7-11
Bottom Portion of Page 7

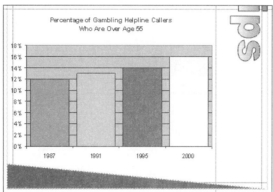

STEP-BY-STEP 7.11

1. Turn to Page 7 of **Seniors Trips Catalog *xxx***.

2. Paste a WordArt object from another page to the right side of the page, similar to Page 5, and change the text to read **Casino Trips**.

3. Create a text box frame at the 1.25-inch horizontal ruler guide at the left margin. Extend it to the 4-inch horizontal ruler guide and to the bottom margin.

4. Insert the story named **gambling.txt** from your student data files. Apply the **triptitle** style to the top four lines.

5. Apply the **triptext** style to the rest of the story. Select the text you just formatted and change the font to 11 pt. Resize the bottom of the frame to just below the last line of text.

6. Bring down a ruler guide to **5.2** inches on the vertical ruler.

7. From the **Insert** menu, choose **Object**.

8. Click **Create from File**. Click **Browse**. Go to your data files and select the file named **Gambling.xls**. Click **OK**.

9. Move the object so that it starts at the 5.2-inch ruler guide.

10. Resize it so that it fits between the left margin and the 4-inch ruler guide and ends above the AutoShape that appears at the bottom of the page. Check the object on your page with Figure 7-11.

STEP-BY-STEP 7.11 Continued

11. Save your file and print all eight pages. If your printer will print double-sided pages, print it that way, which will be four sheets of paper. If you cannot print double-sided pages, fold your pages as follows and arrange your booklet.
Pages 1 and 8, 3 and 6—fold so that the text is on the outside.
Pages 2 and 7, 4 and 5—fold so that the text is on the inside.

12. Save and close the file.

SUMMARY

In this lesson, you learned:

■ The booklet page setup will produce a four-page folded publication.

■ BorderArt is a special formatting feature that adds a design to the outside of a frame.

■ The catalog wizard will produce an eight-page folded publication with many frames set up for you.

■ Sometimes it is necessary to do extensive editing to a document created by a wizard.

■ Folded publications are automatically printed in the correct order for folding purposes.

■ Objects created in programs compatible with Publisher, other than word processing, can be inserted in a publication.

VOCABULARY*Review*

Define the following terms:		
Booklet	Catalog	Folded publication
BorderArt	Embedded object	

REVIEW*Questions*

TRUE/FALSE

Circle T if the statement is true or F if the statement is false.

T   F   1. Booklets are usually printed in high-resolution color.

T   F   2. Catalogs generally advertise products.

T   F   3. Booklets generally are printed on high-gloss, heavy paper.

T F 4. BorderArt should be used only when it enhances a design or message.

T F 5. It is possible to print selected pages of a booklet as a separate booklet.

T F 6. Catalogs created using the Wizard begin with four pages.

T F 7. The printed pages of a booklet or catalog are printed in the same order as shown on the screen—1, 2, 3, 4, etc.—before being folded.

T F 8. Each page of a booklet or catalog prints on a separate piece of paper.

T F 9. Booklets and catalogs created in Publisher are printed on 8½ × 11-inch paper in portrait orientation.

T F 10. Objects from other programs can be inserted into Microsoft Publisher files.

WRITTEN QUESTIONS

Write a brief answer to the following questions.

1. What is a *folded* publication?

2. What is the difference between a *booklet* and a *catalog* with regard to their *purpose*?

3. What is the difference between a booklet and a catalog with regard to the *design* of their inside pages?

4. What are the first and last pages in a booklet and a catalog?

5. What is the purpose of the *Set Transparent Color* button?

6. In what dialog boxes are margins changed in a publication?

7. What color do you choose from the Picture toolbar for pictures that are sent behind text frames?

8. How do you add *BorderArt* to a frame?

9. What was the advantage of using the *triptext* and *triptitle* styles in the Seniors Trips Catalog?

10. How can you quickly delete a text box frame or a table frame that contains text?

PROJECTS

 PROJECT 7-1

You have been asked to design a booklet that describes the history of the Otter Creek Seniors Center for its 25th anniversary. You will use the booklet page setup, but will extend it to eight pages. The first project directs you to set up the publication, format the Master Pages, and format the first page.

1. Start a new publication using the Blank Publication option.

2. From the **File** menu, choose **Page Setup**.

3. On the Layout page, choose **Booklet** in the Publication type list. Make sure Landscape orientation is selected. Click **OK**.

4. When Publisher asks if you'd like to insert pages, click **Yes**.

5. From the **Arrange** menu, choose **Layout Guides**. Change the four margins to 0.5 inch each and click **OK**.

6. From the **Insert** menu, choose **Page**. Click **OK** to insert 4 more pages.

7. On the Master Page, bring down a ruler guide to 1.125 inches and another to 1.375 inches on the vertical ruler.

8. On the left Master Page, insert a picture from the data files named **Silver Images Left Header.jpg**. Size the object to fit the space between the margins above the 1.125-inch ruler guide.

9. On the right Master Page, insert a picture from the data files named **Silver Images Right Header.jpg** and resize it, if necessary.

10. Create a small text box frame at the bottom center of the left page in which the top of the text box frame touches the bottom pink margin guide. Make the frame approximately 0.625 inch wide and 0.250 inch tall.

11. Insert a page number code in this text box frame and center the code using Tahoma, 12 pt.

12. Select the text box frame and choose **Copy** on the Standard toolbar. Paste it at the bottom center of the right Master Page so that the top of the frame is touching the bottom pink margin guide. Compare your Master Pages with Figure 7-12. Save the publication as **Silver Images** *xxx*.

FIGURE 7-12
Master Pages for Silver Images

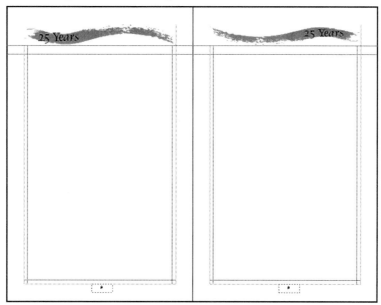

13. Turn off the Master Page view and turn to Page 1 of your publication.

14. On Page 1, turn on Ignore Master Page.

15. Insert the picture file from the data files named **Silver Images title.jpg** in the top half of the page.

16. At 4.5 inches on the vertical ruler, create a text box frame that is 2 inches tall and extends across the page between the left and right margins. Center the following text and format it using Tahoma, 24 pt. bold.
    Celebrating the
    25th Anniversary
    of the Otter Creek
    Seniors Center

17. At approximately 7 inches on the vertical ruler, insert the picture from the data files named **Silver Images Years Span.jpg**.

18. Your first page should look like Figure 7-13. Save the file.

FIGURE 7-13
Page 1 of Silver Images

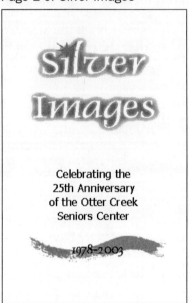

SCANS PROJECT 7-2

The second project takes you through the formatting of the inside pages and back cover of the Silver Images Booklet.

1. On the remaining pages, you will insert text files and some graphics as shown in Table 7-3. Start the frames at the 1.375-inch ruler guide unless they are designated as being in the bottom half of the page. Use your best judgment as to where to place the frames in the bottom half. The stories will not each exactly fit in one-half of the page. In a later step, you'll format the text. After formatting, adjust the size of the frames so the text fits comfortably.

TABLE 7-3
Inserting Text Files, Pictures, and Objects

PAGE	TEXT FILE	GRAPHICS
2	**Foreword.txt**	None
3	**Committee on Aging and Friends.txt** (in the top half) **Center Financing.txt** (in the bottom half)	**sign.jpg** to the left of the first paragraph of Center Financing. Turn the text wrap to square. It will look much like a drop cap.
4	**Historical Panorama.txt** (this will need to be continued on Page 5 with continuation statements on Pages 4 and 5.)	
5	Historical Panorama is continued from Page 4	Insert **center.jpg** on the bottom half of Page 5 starting at 4.5 inches vertically. Resize it to 4 inches wide and 2.5 inches tall. Add a text box frame below the picture that reads **Otter Creek Seniors Center 2003** and center it using Tahoma 12 pt. bold. Center the text box frame under the picture.
6	**Staff Evolution.txt** in the top half **Senior Volunteers.txt** in the bottom half.	Insert a clip-art image representing volunteers at the left of the first paragraph of the Senior Volunteers story. Size it to approximately 1.5 inches square.
7	No story	Use the Insert Object feature to insert an Excel chart named **Senior Center Attendance.xls** at 2.5 inches on the vertical ruler. Resize the chart to fit between the left and right margins.
8	**Mission Statement and Future Directions.txt**	

2. Save the file again as **Silver Images** *xxx* and continue working as instructed.

3. To format each of the stories in a consistent manner, create two styles as shown in Table 7-4. Apply these styles to the story titles and the paragraphs containing the body text.

TABLE 7-4
Styles

STYLE NAME	FORMATTING
StoryTitle	Tahoma 18 pt. bold, center alignment
BodyText	Times New Roman 11 pt. regular

4. Apply a drop cap to all of the text stories EXCEPT Center Financing (Page 3) and Senior Volunteers (Page 6). You may choose any drop cap style, but make it 3 lines tall. Use the same drop cap style on all pages for consistency.

5. Your pages should resemble Figure 7-14, which shows Pages 2 and 3.

FIGURE 7-14
Completed Pages 2 and 3

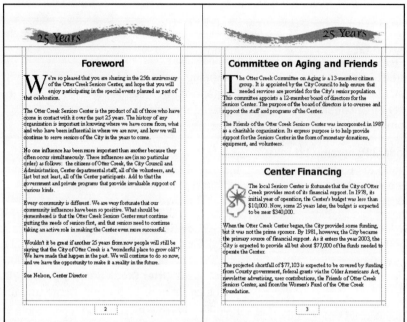

6. On Page 8, insert a Horizontal Scroll Banner AutoShape at 6 inches on the vertical ruler and size it to be 4 inches wide and 2 inches tall. Fill the shape with a light-gray color. Center the following text and format it as shown in parentheses. It should resemble Figure 7-15 when you are done.
Otter Creek (Tahoma, 20 pt. bold)
Seniors Center (same as above)
220 North Campbell Road (same as above but use 16 pt.)
Otter Creek, WI 54999 (same as above)

FIGURE 7-15
Horizontal Scroll Banner on Page 8

7. Save the file again and print it as a booklet. Fold it in the same manner as you did the Seniors Trips Catalog. Close the file.

PROJECT 7-3

Create a certificate for a friend or a relative using the Award Certificate wizard. Save it as **certificate xxx**. Print it and show your instructor.

CRITICAL*Thinking*

 ACTIVITY 7-1

In Step-by-Step 7.11 you inserted a chart from Excel. This object is embedded in Publisher. If you double-click on the object, you will be able to use Excel tools to fix the object, but it only affects the copy of the chart embedded in your Publisher file. Using the Paste Special feature in the Edit menu, it is possible to copy an object from the original program in which the chart was created, and paste it into Publisher so that it is linked. When a linked object is double-clicked, you actually affect the original file when changes are made. A linked file is connected to the original file. Describe the advantages and disadvantages of embedded files and of linked files.

FORM LETTERS, LABELS, AND TENT CARDS

What Are Form Letters?

Form letters are documents that contain the same text for several or hundreds of people. The documents contain codes that bring in variable information, such as names and addresses from some other source. In Microsoft Publisher, the letter (or any publication) containing the text and codes is referred to as the ***main document***. The database file containing the variable information is referred to as the ***data source***. When the two files are combined, you are using the ***mail merge*** feature of Publisher. Normally mail merge is completed in word processing software, but the procedure in Publisher is very much the same as in word processing. Following are some additional terms related to the mail merge process:

- ***Merge codes*** A merge code is a code in the main document that represents a field in a data source file. It tells Publisher what data to bring in during a mail merge. For example, a field named Last Name would tell Publisher to bring in the last name of one of the individuals in the data source.

- ***Record*** A record is one complete entry in the data source. In a list of names and addresses, all of the information about one person is a record.

- *Field* A field is one piece of data in a record. Each of the following could be a field: Last Name, First Name, Street, City, State, Zip Code, Telephone, or Fax. There is no limit to the number of lines in a field. Dividing records into more fields with smaller chunks of information makes data files more versatile.

In some situations, the variable information may be keyed in for each individual letter rather than combining the form document with a data source.

Form Letter Design Considerations

A form letter should be formatted as a typical business letter. This includes a letterhead or return address, current date, inside address, salutation, body of the letter, closing, signature block, and the preparer's reference initials. Other possible parts may be a subject line, an enclosure notation, or a notation for copies.

Margins may vary depending on the length of the letter. The following table shows some margin guidelines, based on a letter to be prepared using letterhead paper.

TABLE 8-1
Margin Guidelines for Letters

NUMBER OF WORDS	DATE LINE	LEFT AND RIGHT MARGINS
Short (under 100 words)	2.5 inches	1.5 inches
Medium (100-200 words)	2 inches	1.25 inches
Long	2 inches	1 inch

Two basic styles of letter formats include the block style where all the paragraphs begin at the left margin, and modified block style where the date and closing and signature blocks begin at the center of the page.

If a letter is longer than one page, the second and succeeding pages should have a 1-inch top margin with a header at the top of each succeeding page at the left margin. The header should contain the following text on three separate lines:

Recipient's full name

Page #

Current date in long format (November 11, 2003)

The Mail Merge Wizard

To assist you with the mail merge process, you will use the Mail Merge Wizard. This is selected from the Mail Merge feature in the Tools menu. A submenu appears, and from that you choose Mail Merge Wizard to display the Mail Merge task pane as illustrated in Figure 8-1. As you can see from the bottom of the task pane, this is a four-step process. The first step is to create a data source.

FIGURE 8-1
Mail Merge Task Pane

Creating the Data Source

You have been asked to create form letters to be sent to the people participating in the annual art and craft fair at the Otter Creek Seniors Annex, informing them of the cost and various other arrangements. The program coordinator, Judy Baker, gives you a list of the names and addresses of last year's participants to enter into the data source file. Since this is a new data source, you will choose Type a new list from the Select recipients choices. A form will appear listing several fields. You will use some of the fields listed and add an additional field by customizing the data source. The data source file is saved as an Access table in an Access database by default. You choose the name for the Access file. Inside this database file is a table named (by default) **Office_Address_List**. This table will contain the records you will create in the steps that follow. If you do not have Access on your computer system, you will have to choose a different file format for the data source file, as instructed by your instructor. Other file formats that are compatible with Publisher for data sources include the following:

Microsoft Excel (versions 3.0 and later)

Microsoft FoxPro (version 2.0 and later)

Microsoft Outlook (all versions)

Microsoft Word tables or merge data documents

Microsoft Works for MS-DOS 3.0 (if database contains no formulas)

Microsoft Works for Windows 3.x, and 4.x (if database contains no formulas), dBase III, IV, and V

ASCII text files (except for fixed-field width files)

STEP-BY-STEP 8.1

1. Start a blank publication.

2. From the **Tools** menu, choose **Mail Merge**. Choose **Mail Merge Wizard**.

3. The Mail Merge task pane appears at the left side of your screen.

4. Click **Type a new list** from **Select recipients**.

5. Click **Create** from the **Type a new list** section. You will see the New Address List dialog box as shown in Figure 8-2.

FIGURE 8-2
New Address List Dialog Box

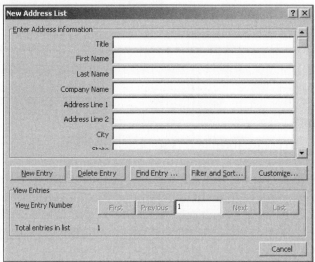

6. The fields that are listed when this dialog box first opens include Title, First Name, Last Name, Company Name, Address Line 1, Address Line 2, City, State, ZIP Code, Country, Home Phone, Work Phone, and E-mail Address. You are going to modify the fields by deleting the Address Line 2, Work Phone, Country, and E-mail Address fields; rename Home Phone; and add a Craft field.

STEP-BY-STEP 8.1 Continued

7. Click **Customize**. To delete fields, select **Address Line 2** and click **Delete**. Confirm the deletion. Follow the same procedure for **Country**, **Work Phone**, and **E-mail Address**. Select **Home Phone** and click **Rename**. Key **Phone** and click **OK**. Click **Add**, key **Craft,** and click **OK**. Your dialog box should resemble Figure 8-3. Click **OK** to close the Customize Address List.

FIGURE 8-3
Customize Address List Dialog Box

8. Key the data in Table 8-2. In each record, you will tab from field to field. Notice that not all fields will be filled in. Tab over each empty field to the next one. The City, State, and Zip Code are the same for all the records: **Otter Creek, WI 54999** (Unfortunately, there is no duplicate feature that would allow you to copy the data from the previous record for each field.)

9. As you finish a record, click **New Entry** to start another record.

TABLE 8-2
Records for Data Source

TITLE	FIRST NAME	LAST NAME	COMPANY NAME	ADDRESS LINE 1	PHONE	CRAFT
Mr.	Fritz	Kraker	Chain Saw Wonders	443 South Main Street	(920) 555-1344	chain saw carvings
Mr.	Adam	Hart	Hart Wood Carving Studio	6219 Hunter Way	(920) 555-3022	wood carvings
Ms.	Barbara Jean	Nelson	Otter Creek Studios	555 River Drive	(920) 555-9021	watercolors
Mr.	Lucas	Jacobs		800 Packer Ridge Road	(920) 555-3225	doll houses
Ms.	Megan	O'Malley		3490 Irish Road	(920) 555-1888	oil paintings
Ms.	Sara	Anderson	Up North Crafts	349 Kohler Road	(920) 555-3020	cabin decorations
Ms.	Kathy	Carlson		8893 North Main Street	(920) 555-3025	quilting

STEP-BY-STEP 8.1 Continued

TABLE 8-2 (Continued)
Records for Data Source

TITLE	FIRST NAME	LAST NAME	COMPANY NAME	ADDRESS LINE 1	PHONE	CRAFT
Mr.	John	Kruller	Kruller's Wood Carvings	1298 Kohler Road	(920) 555-2087	wood carving
Mr.	Norris	Christensen		4215 Main Street	(920) 555-3115	wooden toys
Ms.	Gina	Petra		8720 North Lake Road	(920) 555-2133	rug making
Ms.	Chi	Liang		923 Washington Avenue	(920) 555-3004	embroidery
Ms.	Kay	Katterman		873 Ohio Avenue	(920) 555-3007	stamping
Mr.	Charles	Wales		7811 Parkway	(920) 555-2076	frames
Ms.	Violet	Greene	Plant Buddies	3410 Ninth Avenue	(920) 555-3121	plants
Ms.	Gloria	Keebler		78-C Illinois Street	(920) 555-2008	crocheting
Mr.	Paul	George		7812 John Street	(920) 555-2133	oil paintings
Mr.	Charlie	Hart	Charlie's Fly Tying	98 River Run	(920) 555-3015	fly tying
Ms.	Ilena	Mendez	Mendez Photography	798 North Main Street	(920) 555-3024	photography
Ms.	Carla	Copper		7822 River Run	(920) 555-3018	stenciling
Mr.	Ole	Johnson		9833 Fisherman Way	(920) 555-2199	metal sculpting

10. When you have keyed in all 20 records, click **Close**. You are prompted to save the data source file. Make sure it is directed to the location of your other saved files. Key **Crafters** *xxx* (where *xxx* are your initials). Click **Save**. Your data source is saved as an Access database named **Crafters** *xxx*.**mdb**.

11. The Mail Merge Recipients window will remain open, showing the data you entered. Proofread your work carefully. If you find an error, click to highlight the record containing the error and click **Edit**. Fix the error and click **Close** to return to the Mail Merge Recipients window.

12. Click **OK** to close the Mail Merge Recipients window. Keep the publication open.

Customizing the Data Source File

In the previous exercise, you used the Customize Address List dialog box (Figure 8-3) to edit the fields in the data source file. This is a very powerful tool. This tool lets you set up your data source file to fit your specific data needs. Here are some tips to keep in mind when designing your data source file.

■ Field names should clearly represent the data. Use simple field names.

■ Break down the fields into the smallest fields that are logically possible. One example of this is to use Title, First Name and Last Name instead of putting all the data into one field called Name. Another example is to use Address, City, State, and Zip code instead of putting all the data into one field called Address.

■ Try to arrange the order of the fields as you see the data arranged on a printed source document such as an application form. The Move Up and Move Down buttons in the Customize Address List dialog box can be used to rearrange the order of the fields by selecting a field name and clicking either Move Up or Move Down.

■ Try to think of all the types of main documents in which you might want to use merge field codes as you create the original data source file. This will eliminate having to add a field later.

Creating the Publication (Main Document)

Still using the Wizard, you will proceed to step 2 of the Mail Merge Wizard. It prompts you to create your publication and insert the merge codes where needed. At this point, you treat the publication like any other publication in that you first add text box frames where needed. You then have to add codes representing the fields in your data source into the appropriate text box frames. These codes pull in the data when the two documents are merged. Since the main document is a letter, you will start with the Address block, then add the Greeting line (salutation), and then add more items as needed. These codes are shown in Figure 8-4.

FIGURE 8-4
Step 2 of Mail Merge Wizard

STEP-BY-STEP 8.2

1. Click **Next: Create the publication** at the bottom of the Mail Merge Wizard pane. Step 2 appears as shown in Figure 8-4.

2. From the Insert menu, choose **Picture**. Choose **From File**. Select the **Otter Creek Seniors Logo.gif** from the data files. Center the image horizontally at the top margin guide.

STEP-BY-STEP 8.2 Continued

3. Create a text box frame that begins at 3 inches on the vertical ruler and fills the page from the left to right margins and down to the bottom margin.

4. At the top of the text box frame, insert the date by clicking the **Insert** menu and choosing **Date and Time**. Select the month day, year format (December 10, 2003). Click **OK**. Press **Enter** 5 times.

5. Click **Address block** in the Mail Merge Wizard pane. The Insert Address Block dialog box in Figure 8-5 allows you to choose a format for the inside address. Study the choices.

FIGURE 8-5
Address Block Dialog Box

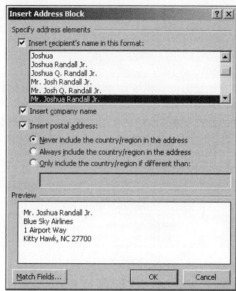

6. Unless instructed otherwise by your instructor, leave the default settings selected as shown in Figure 8-5. (The Match Fields button opens a dialog box that gives options for matching specific field names from the data source that is required by the Mail Merge feature.)

7. Click **OK**. At this time, you will see an <<AddressBlock>> code. Press **Enter** 2 times.

8. Click **Greeting line** in the Mail Merge Wizard pane to display the dialog box in Figure 8-6. It provides options for formatting the greeting (or salutation). Look at each drop-down list to preview the choices. (Note that the last one gives you a choice of greetings for records missing the first and last names.)

STEP-BY-STEP 8.2 Continued

9. In the punctuation drop down list, which shows a comma by default, choose the **colon (:)**. The preview should match the one showing in Figure 8-6.

FIGURE 8-6
Greeting Line Dialog Box

10. Click **OK** and press **ENTER** twice.

11. Beginning with the first paragraph, key the letter as shown in Figure 8-7. When you get to the second paragraph that shows <<Craft>>, click **More items** in the Mail Merge Wizard pane and choose **Craft** from the Insert Merge Field dialog box as shown in Figure 8-8. Click **Insert** and **Close**. Be sure to space with the space bar before and after each field code within a sentence.

12. Select all the text in the text box frame, including the merge codes, and change the font size to 12.

FIGURE 8-7
Completed Letter

The Otter Creek Seniors Center is again sponsoring an Art & Craft Fair on Saturday, October 11, 2003 at the Center.

Last year we were fortunate to have you display your «Craft» items and are hoping that you will join us again this year. The cost per table/space is $10 to display and sell your «Craft» items. Tables are 8 feet long.

Call the Otter Creek Seniors Center at 555-0023 to reserve your table/space. Reservations are required by October 1, 2003. Space is limited. The FRIENDS of the Otter Creek Seniors Center will have lunch available.

We will have posters around the community including at various housing complexes, city hall, and local businesses. We will also advertise in the seniors newsletter and the local newspapers.

We look forward to your participation in this year's craft and art fair. Please call with additional questions and/or concerns.

Sincerely,

Judy Burton
Otter Creek Seniors Center Volunteer Coordinator

STEP-BY-STEP 8.2 Continued

FIGURE 8-8
Insert Merge Field Dialog Box

13. Save your main document by clicking **Save** and naming it **Crafters Letter *xxx***.

14. Click **Next: Preview the publications** in the Mail Merge Wizard pane. Step 3 appears as shown at the bottom of the Wizard pane. Keep the publication open and read further about the third step of the mail merge process.

Preview the Merged Documents

In Step 3 of the Mail Merge Wizard, you get a sneak peek at the main document merged with the data source file. This gives you a chance to see if there are any errors in the documents. A typical error is spacing between merge codes. You can also look at each record as shown in the merged document so that you can see if there is any missing data. The Mail Merge Wizard pane gives you some options in this third step as shown in Figure 8-9.

FIGURE 8-9
Step 3 of Mail Merge Wizard

■ The << and >> buttons are used to preview one record at a time.

■ Find a recipient is used to search for a particular record. Key unique information about a record in the Find box, click Find Next and then Cancel the Find box. The first document containing the *found* text will appear in the document pane.

■ Edit recipient list opens the Mail Merge Recipients dialog box as shown in Figure 8-10. In this dialog box, you can add or remove a recipient from the current merge task. You can sort the list by clicking on the field name button. Clicking once will sort the records in ascending order by the selected field. Clicking again will sort the list in descending order. You can filter the records by clicking the down arrow on the field name button. You can choose All to show all the records, Blanks to show records that contain no information in that field, Nonblanks to show records that do contain information in that field, or Advanced that brings up a Filter and Sort dialog box from which to enter criteria for filtering as well as sort by multiple fields. You can also click Edit to bring up an individual record in the data source for editing.

■ Exclude this recipient will exclude the current record showing in the document pane from the final merge.

STEP-BY-STEP 8.3

1. Look at the first merged letter. Check for correct spacing between the AddressBlock and GreetingLine.

2. Check the spacing before and after the Craft codes entered in the paragraphs.

3. Click the >> button several times to show the letters containing the next record in the data source file.

4. Click **Find a recipient** and key **quilting** in the Find box. Click **Find Next**. Click **Cancel**. The letter to Kathy Carlson should be showing in the document pane.

5. Click **Edit recipient list**. The Mail Merge Recipients dialog box will appear, similar to Figure 8-10.

FIGURE 8-10
Mail Merge Recipients Dialog Box

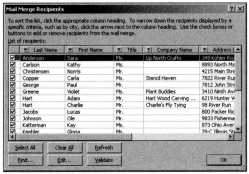

6. Click the **Last Name** column heading (button). The records should be sorted by last name in ascending order. Click again on the Last Name button and it will sort in descending order. Click the button a third time to sort by ascending order.

STEP-BY-STEP 8.3 Continued

7. Click the down arrow on the Company Name button. Select **(Nonblanks)**. Notice that only those records containing a company name are now showing. Your final merge would only contain these filtered records. Click the down arrow again and select **(All)** to show all records again.

8. Click the record for Carla Copper.

9. Click **Edit** at the bottom of the dialog box. This opens the dialog box that shows the individual records one at a time.

10. Key **Stencil Heaven** for Carla's company name.

11. Click **New Entry**.

12. Enter data for yourself including a craft you can do or would like to be able to do. Click **Close** and then **OK** to close the data source. (When you make changes in the individual records, the changes are automatically saved when you click Close.)

13. Click **Next: Complete the merge**. This takes you to the final step, which is printing the merged documents. Keep the publication open and read on.

Complete the Merge

The final step is to print the merged documents. It is important that you are sure you are ready to print and have checked as much as you can on the screen, because reprinting is expensive. Some merge operations contain hundreds of records in the data source. When you click the Print button (Merge to Printer) in the Mail Merge Wizard pane, you will see the Print dialog box. You have the choice of printing all the documents or certain documents based on their sequence in the merged documents. Figure 8-11 shows you the Print Merge dialog box.

> **Note** ☑
>
> You cannot save the merged documents like you can in word processing applications. You will have to remerge the main document and data source files if you need to print them again.

FIGURE 8-11
Print Merge Dialog Box

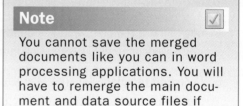

STEP-BY-STEP 8.4

1. Click **Print** in the Mail Merge Wizard pane.

2. Click **Entries** from: and key **1** in the first text box. **Tab** to the second text box and key **1**. This will print only the first merged letter.

3. Click **OK**.

4. Did your first letter print ok?

5. Close the Mail Merge Wizard task pane and close the **Crafters Letter *xxx*** file. Click **Yes** if you are prompted to save.

Printing Filtered Records

In the previous Step-by-Step, you printed only one record selected with the Print Merge dialog box. Another way to limit the number of documents printed is to first filter the data source file. Only the filtered records will print. To filter out records that meet specific criteria, you need to use the Filter and Sort dialog box illustrated in Figure 8-12.

FIGURE 8-12
Filter and Sort Dialog Box

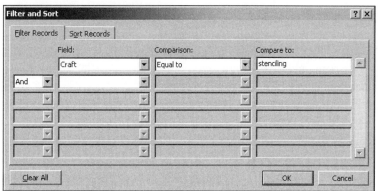

STEP-BY-STEP 8.5

1. Open Crafters Letter *xxx*. Open the **Tools** menu, choose **Mail Merge**, and choose **Mail Merge Wizard**.

2. Click **Edit Recipient List**. (Browse to find **Crafters *xxx*.mdb**, if necessary.)

3. Click the down arrow on the **Craft** button and choose **Advanced**.

4. In the Filter Records tab, click the down arrow in the **Field** column and choose **Craft**.

5. In the Comparison column, leave the setting at **Equal to**.

6. In the Compare to column, key **stenciling**. Click **OK**.

STEP-BY-STEP 8.5 Continued

7. Note that only one record is filtered—the record for Carla Copper. Click **OK**.

8. From the **File** menu, choose **Print Merge**. Note that the Entries from: box shows 1 to 1. Either choose **All entries** or **b**. Click **OK**. Only the letter to Carla Copper should print.

9. Close **Crafters Letter *xxx***. Do not save the changes.

Computer Concepts

When preparing a merge, the data file is linked to the main document. If the main document is opened from a different computer, a dialog box will try to send you to the original location. You must choose to "Work without merged information." Later, you'll have to browse for the data file.

Editing a Mail Merge Publication

You are done with your first mail merge project. That may have been a little complicated for you if it was the first merge activity you have ever done. What would you do if you needed to edit the main document? Let's find out in the next Step-by-Step.

STEP-BY-STEP 8.6

1. Open the **Crafters Letter *xxx*** publication.

2. From the **Tools** menu, choose **Mail Merge**. Choose **Mail Merge Wizard**.

3. You should see your main document, containing the merge codes in the document pane and the Mail Merge Wizard showing in the task pane. From here you may edit either the main document or open the data source for editing.

4. Save and close the main document.

Create Labels

Labels are addresses that print on self-stick label paper that can be adhered to an envelope or postcard. Some businesses prefer to print addresses directly on envelopes for a more personal and professional look. In this lesson, we will print addresses on labels.

Labels come in various sizes. Usually you will choose a size based on label manufacturer specifications. You can also create a custom label size if you are using a label brand not in Publisher's list of labels. These different label sizes are found in the Page Setup dialog box as shown in Figure 8-13. In the next Step-by-Step, you will create labels for the letters you created in the previous exercises. You will be able to use the Crafters.mdb file you created earlier in this lesson.

FIGURE 8-13
Page Setup Dialog Box

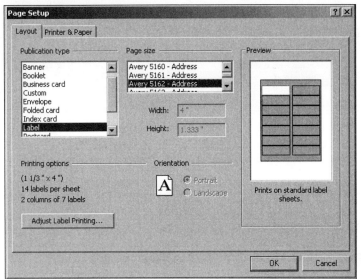

STEP-BY-STEP 8.7

1. Create a blank publication.

2. From the **Tools** menu, choose **Mail Merge**. Then click **Mail Merge Wizard**.

3. In Step 1 of the Mail Merge Wizard, choose **Browse** in the **Use an existing list** section.

4. Locate and open the **Crafters *xxx*.mdb** file.

5. Click **OK** when the Mail Merge Recipients dialog box appears.

6. Click **Next: Create the publication** at the bottom of the pane.

7. From the **File** menu, choose **Page Setup**. In the **Publication type** list, choose **Label**.

8. Choose **Avery 5162-Address** from the **Page size** list. Click **OK**.

9. Using the text box frame tool, draw a text box frame that starts at 0.2 inch on the horizontal ruler and fills the rest of the frame snapping to the top, right, and bottom margins.

10. Click the **Address block** choice in the Mail Merge Wizard pane. Stay with the default settings. Click **OK**.

STEP-BY-STEP 8.7 Continued

11. Select the **<<AddressBlock>>** code showing the label, and change the font size to 12. Your main document label should resemble Figure 8-14.

FIGURE 8-14
Label Main Document

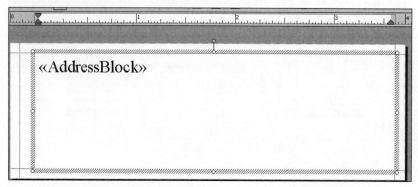

12. Save the main document as **Crafters Labels** *xxx*.

13. Click Next: Preview the publications at the bottom of the pane.

14. Click Edit recipient list and sort the data source file alphabetically by the **Last Name** field. Click **OK**.

15. Click **Next: Complete the merge**. Click **Print**. In the Print dialog box, make sure **All entries** is selected in the Print range and click **OK**.

16. Your labels should print out on two sheets of paper. Circle the label containing your name.

17. Close the main document file. Read on to find out how to create tent cards containing the crafter's name to display at each crafter's table.

Create Tent Cards

Tent cards are folded publications that measure 5½ × 8½ when folded. They stand up like a tent and are ideal for displaying information—such as a name—on a table. Because you want it to stand up like a tent, you will need to print each card on a heavier-stock paper.

Since tent cards are used to display information, you should not include too much on a card. The text can be formatted in a display font design that matches the occasion. The font size should be large enough to be seen from a distance of up to six feet, and yet it needs to fit inside the dimensions of the page. Graphics can be added to decorate the tent card.

In the next Step-by-Step, you will first change the page setup before starting the mail merge wizard. Then you will add merge codes to the tent cards so that you can make one for each crafter displaying his or her crafts at the craft and art fair.

> **Note**
>
> It doesn't matter if you do the page setup before or during the mail merge wizard.

STEP-BY-STEP 8.8

1. Create a blank publication.

2. From the **File** menu, choose **Page Setup**.

3. In the Publication type list, choose **Folded card**.

4. Choose **Tent card** in the Page size.

5. Choose **Portrait** as the orientation. When you click **OK**, you will see the message appearing in Figure 8-15. Click **Yes**. This means that each 8½ × 5½ half-sheet of paper is considered a *page*. By choosing **Yes**, you will end up with two pages that print per one sheet of 8½ × 11 paper. You can put the same, or different, information on both pages.

FIGURE 8-15
Formatting Message for Tent Cards

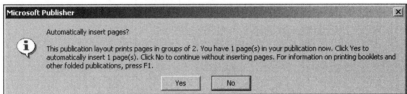

6. From the **Tools** menu, choose **Mail Merge** and then **Mail Merge Wizard**.

7. In Step 1, select the **Crafters *xxx*.mdb** file as the data source.

8. In Step 2, create the publication as follows:

9. Draw a text box frame around the margins of the page and change to center alignment.

10. Press **Enter** 6 times and change the font to Lithograph 36 pt (or something similar).

11. Click **More items** in the Mail Merge Wizard pane.

12. Select **First Name** and click **Insert**. Select **Last Name** and press **Insert**. Close the Insert Merge Field dialog box. Position the cursor between the two codes and press the space bar once to space between the first and last names.

13. Move the cursor so it is after the Last Name code. Press **Enter** to start a new line.

14. Change the font to size **48** pt.

15. Click **More items** again and select **Craft**. Click **Insert** and close the Insert Merge Field dialog box.

16. Save the publication as **Crafters Tent Cards *xxx***. Keep the file open and read on for more information about formatting your tent cards.

Adding Custom BorderArt

You added BorderArt in Lesson 7 to a text box frame by choosing one of the 165 designs that come with Publisher. Now you are going to learn how to create custom BorderArt. Custom BorderArt is turned on using the Text Box Properties dialog box as shown in Figure 8-16.

FIGURE 8-16
Creating Custom BorderArt

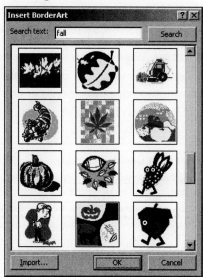

STEP-BY-STEP 8.9

1. Click anywhere in the text box frame containing the mail merge codes.

2. From the **Format** menu, choose **Text Box**.

3. On the **Colors and Lines** page, click the **BorderArt** button.

4. Click **Create Custom** and then **Select Picture**.

5. In the Insert BorderArt dialog box, key **fall** and click **Search**. Move the slider down until the images in Figure 8-16 are showing.

6. Choose a picture that you feel best represents fall and will look good as a border object that is repeated all around the edges of the text box frame. It can't be too busy, because it will be small. (The completed text card in Figure 8-17 contains the pumpkin clip-art object.)

7. Click **OK**.

STEP-BY-STEP 8.9 Continued

8. In the Name Custom Border dialog box, key a name for your border that best describes the picture. For the border showing in Figure 8-17, the custom border is named **Orange Pumpkin**.

FIGURE 8-17
Applied Custom BorderArt

9. Click **OK** three times to exit out of all of the dialog boxes.

10. You should see your custom BorderArt outlining the margins on your publication. Save your publication again.

11. With your cursor still in the text box frame, but NOT having any text selected, click the **Copy** button on the Standard toolbar.

12. Click the page 2 button on the page navigator.

13. Click **Paste** on the toolbar. You should see the exact same text box frame with the mail merge codes and the BorderArt.

14. Save the publication and keep it open for one more Step-by-Step.

Printing a Select Record

Up to this point you have printed the first record of a data source file (form letters), and you have printed all the records (labels). In the next Step-by-Step, you will learn how to print a selected record.

STEP-BY-STEP 8.10

1. You should still have the Mail Merge Wizard pane showing on your screen. If you do not, select **Mail Merge** from the **Tools** menu. Choose **Mail Merge Wizard**.

2. Click **Next: Preview the publications** to proceed to Step 3 of the wizard.

3. Click **Edit recipient list**.

4. Click in the record containing your own information.

5. Click **Edit** and make a note as to the record number appearing in the View Entry Number box toward the bottom of the dialog box.

6. Click **Cancel** and then **OK** to return to the main document.

7. Click **Next: Complete the merge** to proceed to Step 4. Then click the **Print** button in the wizard pane.

8. In the Print Merge dialog box, key your record number in both text boxes in the **Entries from**: boxes. Click OK.

9. Your name and craft should appear on both the top and bottom halves of the printed sheet.

Congratulations, you are now officially ready to display your crafts! Mail merge wasn't so bad, was it?

SUMMARY

In this lesson, you learned:

- The mail merge function merges a data source file and a main document.

- A data source file contains records for individuals, such as a mailing list.

- Each record in a data source file is composed of fields or pieces of information about one person.

- Merge codes that represent the fields from a data source file are added to a main document.

- Main documents can be set up like any publication.

- Merged documents can be printed for all or selected records in a data source file.

- Custom BorderArt can be created using clip-art pictures.

- Folding tents display eye-catching information.

- Mail Merge can be used to create mailing labels.

VOCABULARY *Review*

> **Define the following terms:**
>
> | Data source | Labels | Merge codes |
> |---|---|---|
> | Field | Mail merge | Record |
> | Form letters | Main document | Tent cards |

REVIEW *Questions*

MATCHING

Match the correct term in Column 2 to its description in Column 1.

Column 1	Column 2
___1. Form letters	**A.** One piece of data in a record. Examples are a person's first name, last name, and address.
___2. Main document	**B.** Decorative border for a frame.
___3. Data source	**C.** The process of merging a main document and data source file together.
___4. Mail merge	**D.** Addresses that print on self-stick label paper that can be adhered to an envelope or postcard.
___5. Merge codes	**E.** Documents set up in a letter format containing text and codes that may be sent to a number of people.
___6. Record	**F.** Codes representing fields in a data source file that tell Publisher what data to bring in during a mail merge.
___7. Field	**G.** Folded publications that measure 5½ × 8½ inches folded.
___8. Labels	**H.** The database file containing the variable information.
___9. Tent cards	**I.** One complete entry in the data source. In a list of names and addresses, all of the information about one person.
___10. BorderArt	**J.** Any publication that contains mail merge codes.

WRITTEN QUESTIONS

Write a brief answer to the following questions.

1. What is one advantage of using mail merge when the same letter is going to several people?

2. What are the four steps in the Mail Merge Wizard?

3. What is the file extension on the data source file you prepared?

4. Describe the appearance of the merge codes in a main document. Why is spacing around the code so important?

5. In what dialog box can you delete, rename, and add new fields to the data source file in Publisher?

6. What option in Step 2 of the Mail Merge Wizard will bring up a list of all the fields available in the data source file when inserting the merge codes in the main document?

7. Describe how you can sort records in the Mail Merge Recipients dialog box.

8. Describe how you can filter records in the Mail Merge Recipients dialog box.

9. In what dialog box will you find all the preformatted label sizes when setting up a main document for labels?

10. When adding BorderArt to a text box frame, in what dialog box do you find the BorderArt button?

PROJECTS

SCANS PROJECT 8-1

A very important reason why the Otter Creek Humane Society succeeds in the community is the volunteers who help with the care of the animals in the shelter and various other administrative duties. Each year a picnic is given to honor those volunteers. A data source needs to be created from the applications on file for the volunteers.

1. Start a blank publication using the default letter publication.

2. Start the Mail Merge Wizard and create a new data source file and customize the fields to contain the following fields: Title, First Name, Last Name, Address Line 1, City, State, Zip Code, Home Phone, and Duties (this is a new field you have to add).

3. Key the following records as shown in Table 8-3. Again the City, State, and Zip Code will all be the same and will be as follows:
   Otter Creek   WI   54999

TABLE 8-3
Records for Volunteers Data Source File

TITLE	FIRST NAME	LAST NAME	ADDRESS LINE 1	HOME PHONE	DUTIES
Ms.	May	Day	73 Spring Street	(920) 555-2154	animal exercising
Mr.	Andreas	Graf	12-C2 Frankfurt Court	(920) 555-3002	kennel cleaning
Mr.	Vin	Robinson	8971 Kohl Avenue	(920) 555-2067	animal exercising

TABLE 8-3 (Continued)
Records for Volunteers Data Source File

TITLE	FIRST NAME	LAST NAME	ADDRESS LINE 1	HOME PHONE	DUTIES
Ms.	Barb	Nelson	9832 Oak Street	(920) 555-3014	clerical duties
Ms.	Ramona	Feliz	8933 Regan Road	(920) 555-2012	clerical duties
Mr.	Thi	Thompson	544 Feline Avenue	(920) 555-1554	kennel cleaning
Ms.	Luisa	Moreno	8731 Maple Street	(920) 555-3005	animal exercising
Mr.	Frances	Leske	8872 Henry Street	(920) 555-3027	animal exercising
Mr.	George	Amez	492 Hollywood Boulevard	(920) 555-1666	kennel cleaning
Mr.	Ole	Johnson	9833 Fisherman Way	(920) 555-2199	repair work
Mr.	Keenen	Brooklyn	7811 Manhattan Blvd.	(920) 555-1777	kennel cleaning
Mr.	Wally	Wiesel	3512 Mulberry Street	(920) 555-1444	animal exercising
Mr.	Rollie	Brewer	7832 Fingers Avenue	(920) 555-3012	repair work
Mr.	Fritz	Becker	8722 Oak Street	(920) 555-3102	repair work
Ms.	Phyllis	Linkletter	125 River Run	(920) 555-3106	clerical duties
Ms.	Kris	Reynolds	983 Maple Street	(920) 555-3006	animal exercising
Ms.	June	Summers	8721 August Avenue	(920) 555-2231	clerical duties
Ms.	Candace	Cardigan	112 Afghan Alley	(920) 555-2033	animal exercising
Mr.	Curly	Stuge	8712 Larry Street	(920) 555-2167	kennel cleaning
Ms.	Theresa	Van Handel	983 John Street	(920) 555-3029	clerical duties

4. Name the file **OCHS Volunteers xxx.mdb.** Continue on with the next project to create the main document.

 **PROJECT 8-2**

In this project you will create the main document, which will be a letter inviting all the volunteers to attend a picnic in their honor.

1. Still using the Mail Merge Wizard, create the letter.

2. Create a letterhead of your own design that contains the name of the shelter, address, and phone number in a text box frame (as shown in the text that follows). You may add any graphic you desire. Keep the size of the letterhead to 1 inch.
Otter Creek Humane Society
2345 Alpine Road
Otter Creek, WI 54999
(920) 555-7833

3. Add a text box frame that starts at 2.5 inches from the top margin.

4. Add the date at the top of the new text box frame.

5. Insert the Address Block six lines below the date.

6. Insert the Greeting Line a double space below the Address Block. Use only the first name in the Greeting Line followed by a comma. The preview should show **Dear Joshua,**

7. Key the letter in Figure 8-18. Insert the <<Duties>> field in the first paragraph.

FIGURE 8-18
Completed Letter to Volunteers

Thank you for your support of the Otter Creek Humane Society by volunteering your time to help with «Duties» at the shelter. Without your help, we would not be able to serve our community by providing temporary homes for the many homeless animals.

To show our extreme gratitude for your time and efforts, we are having our annual picnic in honor of you and the other volunteers at the Otter Creek Park on Sunday, August 3, at 2:00 p.m. Food and fun will be provided for you! Your family is invited to attend as well. Please let Mary Jones know by July 25 how many will attend from your family.

Once again, thank you for all your volunteer efforts, time, and dedication. We enjoy working with you and hope you continue to volunteer at the shelter.

Sincerely,

Jim Johnson, Director
Otter Creek Humane Society

8. Save the main document as **OCHS Volunteer Picnic Letter xxx.**

9. Preview the merged letters and correct any errors in either the main document or the data source file.

10. Filter the records so that only those volunteers that do clerical work show in the recipient list. There should be five in the list.

11. Print the letters to the five people who volunteer to do clerical work.

12. Turn off the filter so that all the volunteer records show. Close the file.

PROJECT 8-3

Create nametags for the 20 volunteers at the Otter Creek Humane Society. Use the **OCHS Volunteers xxx** file for the recipient list. Use the Avery 5095 nametag label for the main document. On the label, center on three separate lines the volunteer's first name, last name, and Volunteer OCHS. Use your own design for the text and add a graphic if you desire. Save the main document as **OCHS Volunteer Name Tags xxx**. Merge and print the nametags.

CRITICAL*Thinking*

 ACTIVITY 8-1

Collect a copy of a letterhead from at least three different sources—local offices, manufacturing establishments, educational institutions, etc. Evaluate each of the letterheads. What information is included? Do you like the design? Why or why not?

WEB SITES

OBJECTIVES

Upon completion of this lesson, you should be able to:

- Set up a blank document as a Web page.
- Choose the page size for a Web site.
- Add a background.
- Insert and format additional Web pages.
- Add alternative text to a Web page graphic.
- Create a thumbnail graphic.
- Add a hotspot to a thumbnail graphic.
- Add form control objects to a Web page.
- Change the properties of a form control object.
- Insert hyperlinks to other places in the same Web site.
- Insert an e-mail hyperlink.
- Use the Web Page Preview to check the format and hyperlinks in a Web site.
- Add keywords and a description to a Web site.
- Save a Microsoft Publisher file as a Web page.

Estimated time: 3 hours

VOCABULARY

Background

Browser

Form

Home page

Hot spot

Hyperlinks

Image map

Keywords

Masthead

Modem

Navigation bar

Search engines

Thumbnail picture

Web pages

Web sites

What Are Web Sites?

The Internet is an immense network of smaller networks that connect computers all around the world. A service provided on the Internet is the World Wide Web (WWW), which is a collection of pages containing text, graphics, animation, and various other multimedia objects. A collection of pages for one company or organization or individual is referred to as a ***Web site***. The individual pages that make up a Web site are referred to as ***Web pages***. The first page that a viewer sees when opening a Web site is the ***home page***. Creating a Web site is very popular today and will continue to be important with the increasing number of businesses and people connecting to the Internet for marketing purposes.

Many software programs on the market today (such as word processing, presentation graphics, and desktop publishing) provide the features necessary for creating a Web site. There are also many software programs that specialize in Web site creation. Some people prefer to create their web sites by keying a special code called Hypertext Markup Language (HTML) that describes the design and content of a Web page to a *browser*. A browser is a program for viewing sites on the WWW. The two most popular browsers today are Microsoft Internet Explorer and Netscape Navigator.

Programs such as Microsoft Publisher contain tools to help you create your Web site. A Web site can be created in Publisher using the Custom Web Page option on the Blank Publication tab in the Catalog dialogue box. In this document setup, formatting choices are only appropriate for Web publishing. You can also use a Web Site Wizard, which provides extensive formatting already completed for you. When you are finished, Publisher will automatically convert your publication to HTML code.

Creating and publishing a Web site is a four-step process. You will be able to do the first three steps in this lesson. Ask your instructor if it is possible to publish this web site to a Web server to complete the process.

- Create the Web site using the Custom Web Page option or using the Web Site Wizard.

- Preview the Web page as it would appear on the World Wide Web.

- Check the design of the Web page using the Design Checker.

- Publish your Web site to a folder on your system or network or to the World Wide Web.

Web Site Design Considerations

There are many considerations when designing a Web site. Table 9-1 describes some of these design features.

TABLE 9-1
Web Site Design

FEATURE	CONSIDERATIONS
Audience	Identify your target viewers by considering their age, sex, interests, culture, and needs.
Overall Design	Make sure your Web site is simple, but also attractive. Use a tone or style that is compatible with your message and your intended audience. Keep the design consistent from page to page so the viewer is not confused.
Download Time	Keep each Web page to between 40 and 60 KB in size for fast downloading.
Color	Choose a color scheme that will enhance your message and fit the mood of the viewers. Use the same color scheme throughout the Web site. Avoid bright colors that are hard to look at for long periods of time. Also avoid color combinations that hinder readability such as off-white text on a white background.
Background	Keep the background subtle. It should not overwhelm the content.
Text	Choose a typeface that conveys the purpose of the Web site. Choose a text color that contrasts with the background. It is ok to use more than one typeface on a Web page as long as the different typefaces don't clash.

TABLE 9-1 Continued
Web Site Design

FEATURE	CONSIDERATIONS
Hyperlinks	*Hyperlinks* are buttons or text to click to jump to another location in the same Web site or a different site completely. Hyperlinks can be comprised of graphics or text. Make sure hyperlinks are easy to see and use. Choose a color for hyperlink text that stands out. Don't use that color for any other text.
Used Hyperlinks	Choose a color that contrasts with unused hyperlinks. Don't use that color for any other text.
Graphics	There are many tips for choosing graphics: 1. Choose graphics that help to convey the purpose of the Web site. 2. Use graphics that are compatible with Web browsers. These formats include *.gif*, *.jpg*, animated *.gif*, and *.png*. 3. Choose graphics with color schemes that visually enhance the look of the Web site without being overwhelming. 4. Choose graphics that download quickly. The larger the size of the graphic, the longer it will take to download. Keep the size of your graphics to fewer than 40 KB per page. 5. Use a thumbnail graphic for viewers to click to look at a larger graphic on a separate page if you want to include larger graphics. 6. Use images more than once in a Web site. After the graphic is downloaded the first time, it will remain in the viewer's computer memory for additional pages containing the graphic.
Home Page	1. It should convey the kind of information that the site contains. 2. It answers such questions as who, what, when, where, and why. 3. It contains links to the topic pages contained in the Web site primarily through the use of navigation bars, buttons, and hypertext links.

There are many books available that describe Web site design. You can also spend time looking at Web sites already published and get ideas for designing your own Web site. You can save objects you see on other's Web sites by right-clicking on an object, such as a picture, and choosing Save Picture As in the shortcut menu that appears. You have to be careful, however, of copyright laws. Look for copyright information on the Web site and contact the Web designer for permission to use objects from that Web site.

Create a Web Site

You have created publications using the blank publication option in previous lessons. The only difference you will encounter when creating a Web site will be the insertion of some new objects you have not used before. These objects include a background, form controls, hyperlinks, and an animated graphic. The Web site you are going to create is for the city of Otter Creek. You will create a home page, a page for the Parks & Recreation Department, and a page showing a full-sized graphic. At the end of the lesson, you will create two additional pages.

The size of the Web page is different from the letter-size you are accustomed to using. When you choose Web page in the Page Setup dialog box, you have a choice of three page sizes as shown in Figure 9-1.

FIGURE 9-1
Web Page Size

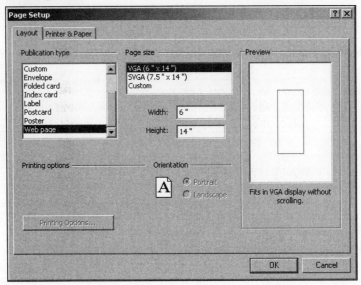

- VGA is the size recommended for viewing on monitors that only support low-resolution objects. As it shows at the bottom of the Preview window, viewers will not need to scroll (horizontally) if viewing this size on a low-resolution monitor.

- SVGA is recommended for high-resolution monitors.

- Custom allows you to set up a special size of your choosing.

STEP-BY-STEP 9.1

1. Start Publisher, if necessary, and go to a Blank Publication.

2. Display the **File** menu and click **Page Setup**. The **Layout** tab should be displayed.

3. Under **Publication type**, click **Web page**.

4. From the **Page size** list, choose **SVGA (7.5" × 14")**. Click **OK**.

5. From the **Arrange** menu, choose **Layout Guides** and change all four margins to **0 inches**. Click **OK**.

6. Keep your publication open and read about changing the background.

Add the Background

Many Web sites are formatted with a color or texture or picture showing behind the text, table, and picture objects. This is called the *background*. The background can enhance the look of each page, but you have to be careful not to choose a color that will clash with objects in the foreground. It should be subtle. When you apply a Background to a Web site, you need to decide whether you want that background for the current page or for all the pages in your Web site. It is advisable to choose Apply to All Pages. Being consistent in your Web design makes the site more user-friendly. The Background Pane is illustrated in Figure 9-2.

FIGURE 9-2
Background Pane

STEP-BY-STEP 9.2

1. From the **Format** menu, choose **Background**.

2. As shown in Figure 9-2, choose **No Color** from the strip at the top of the pane.

3. Choose the seventh box in the left column. When you point to it, the words *Picture fill (custom)* should appear.

4. Click the down arrow at the right of the picture and choose **Apply to All Pages**.

5. Click the **X** to close the Background pane. Keep the file open.

Add Text Objects to the Home Page

Now you are ready to add some objects to your home page. You will start with the text objects. One text box frame will contain the *navigation bar*. The navigation bar is a group of buttons or words that link the current page to additional pages in a Web site. In this case, the navigation bar consists of a bulleted list representing the linked pages.

The other text box that you will add will contain the welcome information for your Web site. Before beginning, study the finished home page in Figure 9-3.

FIGURE 9-3
Finished Home Page

STEP-BY-STEP 9.3

1. Bring a ruler guide down from the horizontal ruler to **0.25** inch.

2. Create a text box frame that starts at the ruler guide and at **0.5** inch on the horizontal ruler. Make the frame **2.5** inches wide and **0.625** inch tall.

3. Key the text **Welcome to** and format it using Forte, 28 pt.

4. Bring a horizontal ruler guide down to **2.250** inches.

5. Create a text box frame that starts at the 2.25-inch ruler guide and **2.5** inches on the horizontal ruler. Extend it to the right margin and make it **5** inches tall.

STEP-BY-STEP 9.3 Continued

6. Insert the text file named **Home Page Welcome.doc** from your data files. If the text file does not fit into your text box frame, make the frame taller to accommodate all of the text.

7. Create another text box frame starting at the left margin and the **2.250**-inch ruler guide. Make it **2.15** inches wide and **2.5** inches tall.

8. Key the bulleted items showing in Figure 9-3. If necessary, change the font to Times New Roman, 12 pt. (You may also press F9 to zoom in on the text if you have trouble reading it. Press F9 a second time to zoom back out.)

9. Select the items you just entered and click the **Bullet** button.

10. Change the line spacing for the bulleted items to **1.5** sp (Format, Line spacing).

11. With the text box frame still selected, open the **Fill Color** drop-down menu and choose **More Fill Colors**. Choose the second blue from the right in the third row on the Standard tab (or a medium-blue).

12. Change the font color to **white** and turn on **bold**.

13. Bring down a ruler guide from the horizontal ruler to **5** inches on the vertical ruler.

14. Create a small text box frame that starts at the 5-inch ruler guide and approximately **0.375** inch from the left edge of the page. Make it **1.25** inches wide and **0.3** inch tall. Center the text **Contact us:** and change the font to 12 pt. Times New Roman.

15. Save the file as **City of Otter Creek Web Site** *xxx*. Keep the file open for more objects.

Adding Graphics

Inserting pictures and other graphics is nothing new to you. You are an expert at this by now! The same design principles apply to Web pages when it comes to adding graphics as it does to any publication. Only add graphics if they enhance the message! The graphics you insert need to be *.gif*, *.jpg*, or *.png* file format to be compatible with the Internet browsers. If you are using the clip-art files in Publisher, you can tell what format the graphic is by pointing at the picture in the Clip Organizer pane. A tool tip will appear showing the size and file format.

In addition, you have to be concerned about the size of the graphics. If they are too big they will make the download time from the Web server very slow, especially if the viewer has a slow *modem*. A modem is a device that sends and receives data over the phone line so the computers can understand the message.

If you have a large picture that you want to include in a Web site, a common technique that is used is the *thumbnail picture*. This is a small-size version of a larger picture that is linked to the full-size graphic on a separate Web page. You will experiment with thumbnail pictures on a different Web page in this site in a later exercise.

Another factor in download time is the layering of a text object on top of a graphic. Publisher treats these two objects as one big graphic. At the top of the page you will insert a photograph from Clips Online and then add a WordArt object. Together, these two objects will make up the *masthead*, or banner, that identifies the site.

STEP-BY-STEP 9.4

1. With the **City of Otter Creek Web Site *xxx*** publication showing in the window, open the **Clip Organizer**. At the bottom of the Clip Organizer pane, choose **Clips Online**.

2. Use **river** as the search text, and find a photograph showing a river that you think may be in a Midwest location. In other words, don't choose a picture of a river with big mountains in the background. Add this photograph to the Clip Organizer.

3. Insert the picture at the **0.25**-inch ruler guide and at **3** inches on the horizontal ruler. Make the picture approximately **3** inches wide and **1.75** inches tall.

4. Add a WordArt frame in front of the picture. Choose the first style in the WordArt Gallery and change the font design to Arial instead of Arial Black. Key the text **Otter Creek, Wisconsin**.

5. Size the WordArt object to **5** inches wide and **1** inch tall.

6. Edit the fill effects of the WordArt shape to match what is showing in Figure 9-4. Choose the same blue color used to fill the text box frame with the bullet list as Color 1 and choose white for Color 2. Choose the lower-left variant in the vertical shading style.

FIGURE 9-4
Fill Effects for WordArt

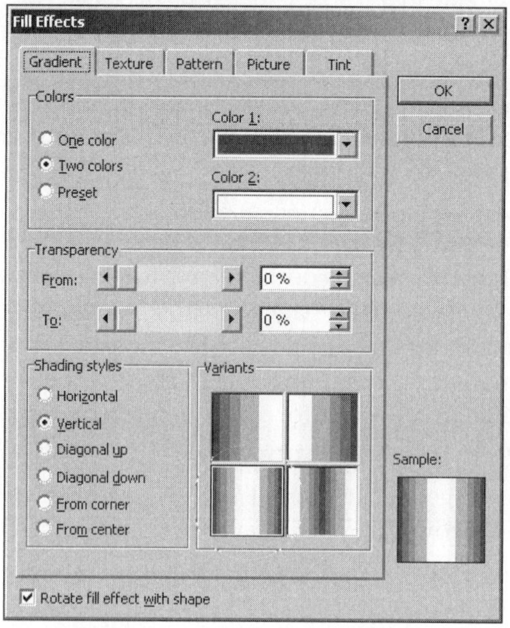

7. Change the color of the WordArt line to the same blue color used in the previous step.

8. Using the Shadow button on the Formatting toolbar, choose the second shadow style in the second row. Change the shadow color to a light blue.

9. Save the file again with the same name.

Preview a Web Page on a Browser

At any time during the creation of a Web page in Publisher, you can click the Web Page Preview button on your toolbar to see what your page will look like in a browser. (You can also select Web Page Preview from the File menu.) Publisher actually generates your page for the Web and then opens it in your browser. Your page is not published on the Web yet, so you do not have to actually be "online" to preview your page. You do have to have a browser available on your computer or the preview will not work. It is important to note that a Web page can look different in one browser than in another.

When you preview a Web page, you will see an address in the URL (Uniform Resource Locator) box at the top of your browser screen that gives the file location of your Web page file. You will not see the http:// address. The address you see is just a temporary location on your hard drive for the purpose of previewing the design of the page and for testing the hyperlinks. When you are finished previewing your site, you need to close the browser.

You will add an animated graphic on the home page. (You can tell it will be animated because there is a little star in the lower-right corner of the graphic in the Clip Organizer task pane.) The animation will not show in the normal Publisher view, but it will show when you preview the page.

STEP-BY-STEP 9.5

1. Choose the Clip Organizer tool and key **email** in the *Search text* text box.

2. Find a suitable animated graphic (look for the yellow star in the lower-right corner) that is a *.gif* file format and place it to the right of the *Contact us:* text box frame. Align it vertically at the 5-inch ruler guide.

3. Size it to approximately **0.6** inch wide and **0.4** inch tall.

4. Save your file and click the **Web Page Preview** button. Look at the graphic you just inserted. Is it animated? Close the Web page Preview window.

5. Save the file again with the same name.

Add Alternative Text to a Web Page Graphic

Also related to graphics is the ability to add alternative text to a Web page graphic. Some viewers whose computers are connected to slower modems choose to have their graphics displays turned off. In this case, no picture appears. By adding alternative text to a graphic, a description of what should be showing will appear instead of the graphic. This is done in the Format Picture dialog box.

STEP-BY-STEP 9.6

1. With **City of Otter Creek Web Site** *xxx* showing, select the picture of the river at the top of the home page.

2. Open the **Format** menu and click **Picture**. Click the **Web** tab.

3. Under **Alternative text**, key **Otter Creek River** and click **OK**.

4. Save the file and read on.

Add a Second Web Page

You have completed the home page for your Web site with the exception of the hyperlinks on the navigation bar. Now you are going to add a page about the Otter Creek Parks & Recreation Department. This will include many of the same items as the home page along with a thumbnail picture and a form. To make the process go faster, you are going to insert a new page that will duplicate all the objects on the home page so that you don't have to spend time recreating the same objects. This will also provide consistency within your Web site. You will then edit the duplicated objects to include the information pertinent to your new Web page.

STEP-BY-STEP 9.7

1. Open the City of Otter Creek Web Site publication, if necessary.

2. From the **Insert** menu, choose **Page**.

3. In the Insert Page dialog box, key **1** in the Number of new pages text box. Choose **After current page** and **Duplicate all objects on page: 1**. Do not turn on Add hyperlink to Web navigation bar. Click **OK**.

Note

Add the company name or logo to every Web page in your Web site to reassure viewers that they are still in the company-related site.

4. On your new Web page, delete the following objects: the text box frame containing *Welcome to*, the picture of the river, and the text box and graphic for e-mail.

5. Edit the WordArt frame to replace the text with: **Parks & Recreation**. Enlarge the object to approximately **5** inches wide and **1** inch tall.

6. To the left of the WordArt frame, insert the **Otter Creek Logo.jpg** picture from the data files. With the logo selected, use the **Set Transparency Color** tool on the **Picture** toolbar to show the background color of the Web site behind the picture instead of the white background.

7. Move both the WordArt frame and the logo up to the **0.25**-inch ruler guide.

STEP-BY-STEP 9.7 Continued

8. Delete the text in the text box frame in the middle of the page but do not delete the frame. Insert the text file named **Parks Page.doc** from the data files. Resize the text box frame to be **3** inches tall and **3** inches wide. Do not move the text box frame to the right. Check Figure 9-5 for the placement of this text box. If some of the text is not showing, make the text box frame taller.

Partially Completed Page 2

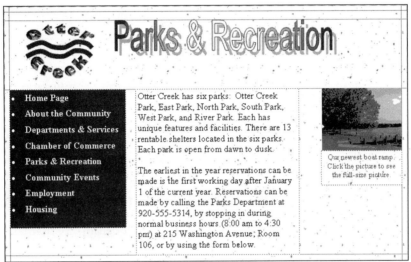

9. Move the ruler guide at **2.25** inches up to **1.5** inches. Move both text box frames up to the **1.5**-inch ruler guide.

10. Move the ruler guide below the text box frames up to the bottom of the taller text box frame, which should be at approximately **4.5** inches. Keep the file open to add a new graphic.

Add a thumbnail

Your next step is to add a small picture that will link to a full-size picture on a separate Web page. Below the picture will be a caption or small text box frame that will contain instructions for the viewer to click on the picture to open the Web page containing the full-size picture.

STEP-BY-STEP 9.8

1. With page 2 of the **City of Otter Creek Web Site** *xxx* showing in the window, draw a Picture frame to the right of the middle text box frame that measures approximately **1.5** inches square. As soon as you release your mouse button, the **Insert Picture** dialog box appears.

2. Locate the **boat launch.jpg** picture from your data files. Click **Insert**. The picture frame will be resized to be proportionate to the original size of the picture. Resize the picture to be **1.5** inches wide and **1.125** inches tall.

STEP-BY-STEP 9.8 Continued

3. Move the picture up to the 1.5 inch ruler guide, if necessary, and over to the right-margin guide.

4. Below the picture frame, create a small text box frame that is as wide as the picture.

5. Center the following text: **Our newest boat ramp. Click the picture to see the full-size picture.**

6. Change the color of the text to a medium green.

7. Save the file. Your Web page should resemble Figure 9-5 at this time.

Add a Form

It is common to add a form to a Web site for viewers. A *form* provides a tool through which a viewer can submit information, request information, or purchase goods and services. The data the viewer keys and submits is sent to a designated computer in the format of a database. In order for the data to be sent back from the Web site to the designated computer, certain form processing features have to be available on the computer on which the Web site is stored. Processing forms is something to check out when looking for an Internet Service Provider.

Publisher has predesigned order, response, and sign-up forms available through the Design Gallery. Unfortunately none of these will fit our current situation. Therefore, you will create a form using the Form Control feature on the Objects toolbar. The objects that can be included on a form are shown in Figure 9-6. The following list explains the purpose of each object.

FIGURE 9-6
Forms Control Objects

- Text box—This control provides a one-line text box for viewers to enter text.

- Text Area—This control provides several lines for viewers to enter text. A scroll bar appears for viewing the multiple lines.

- Check box—A check box provides a yes or no choice. When "yes" is chosen, a checkmark appears in the box.

- Option Button—This control provides a choice among two or more options in a group. Viewers can only select one option button (choice) within the group.

- List Box—This provides a group of items in a list. Viewers can select one choice in the list box.

- Submit—This control provides a submit button and a reset button. A submit command button allows viewers to send their form data. A reset button allows viewers to clear old data showing in the form. You should have both buttons on a form.

On the second Web page of your Web site, you will create a table and add the form objects as directed. Your form should resemble Figure 9-7 when you are done.

FIGURE 9-7
Completed Form

Open Shelters: Otter Creek Park #1, #2; East Park; North Park #1, #2; South Park #2, #3; West Park; River Park				
Date (MM/DD/YY)	Park (Number of shelter if applicable)	Hours of Rental	Residents	Non-Residents
[_____]	Otter Creek Park #1 ▼	0-4	$20.00	$25.00
[_____]	Otter Creek Park #1 ▼	4-8	$25.00	$35.00
[_____]	Otter Creek Park #1 ▼	8-12	$30.00	$40.00
Enclosed Shelters: Otter Creek Park, East Park, South Park, River Park				
Date (MM/DD/YY)	Park (Number of shelter if applicable)	Hours of Rental	Residents	Non-Residents
[_____]	Otter Creek Park ▼	0-4	$30.00	$40.00
[_____]	Otter Creek Park ▼	4-8	$35.00	$45.00
[_____]	Otter Creek Park ▼	8-12	$40.00	$50.00
Name: [_____]				
Address: [_____]				
City: [_____] State: WI Zip: [_____]				
Day Phone: [_____] [Submit] [Reset]				

S TEP-BY-STEP 9.9

1. With page 2 of **City of Otter Creek Web Site *xxx*** showing, bring over a vertical ruler guide to **0.5** inch on the horizontal ruler.

2. At the intersection of the new ruler guide and the horizontal ruler guide below the text box frames at **4.5** inches, create a table frame extending the table frame to the right margin and down to approximately **11** inches on the vertical ruler.

3. Define the table as **14** rows and **5** columns.

4. Resize the five columns to match the widths showing in rows 2-5 and 7-10 of Figure 9-7, remembering to hold the Shift key down as you adjust the widths. (NOTE: You will merge the cells in the other rows after resizing the columns. It is easier to adjust column widths first.)

5. Select the table and change the font to size 12.

6. Key the text as shown in Rows 2-5 and 7-10. If necessary, further adjust the widths of your columns to fit the text.

7. Merge the cells in Rows 1 and 6 and key the data as shown in Figure 9-7. Format the text in bold.

8. Merge the cells in Rows 11-14 and key the text, pressing the space bar twice after the words in Row 13 to make room for text box objects.

9. Save the file and proceed to the next step to insert the form objects.

Adding Form Control Objects and their Properties

In the next Step-by-Step, you will insert several form control objects. Each form control object added to a form is considered a field in the database in which it is collected, and therefore should be given a field name or label. This is done through the use of a form field property dialog box such as the Single-Line Text Box Properties dialog box shown in Figure 9-8. In this dialog box, you can insert default text that would show up automatically. Even though the default text will appear in the field, the viewer can key different text when filling in the form. You can limit the number of characters that can be entered into the box, which helps keep the size of the database small. You can hide sensitive text such as a password, and you can add a label that will be returned with the actual data to your database. You may use any character or number for the label, but you cannot use spaces in the form field's label. An underline character may be used to represent the space.

FIGURE 9-8
Single-Line Text Box Properties Dialog Box

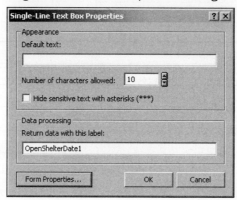

Another form field control you will add to the form will be the List Box. In this control, you will add all of the park names from which the viewer can choose. In the dialog box that is shown in Figure 9-9, you will either modify the default values listed or add new values to make the choices of parks complete. You will add a label to identify the form field control so that the data returned will be identifiable in the database.

FIGURE 9-9
List Box Form Properties

It is very important that you add each form control object individually to the designated selected cell. DO NOT copy and paste objects. If you copy and paste objects, those objects are not embedded in the cells. Consequently, the only way you can move the table and all of its objects is to group them. It is important to follow the directions in the following Step-by-Step and work with a cell at a time. This may well be one of the most challenging activities of this lesson.

STEP-BY-STEP 9.10

1. Click in the first cell in Row 3 in the date column. Click the **Form Control** button on the Object toolbar. Choose **Text box**. Resize the object to be almost as wide as the cell.

2. It is necessary to assign the new form field a name so that when the data is returned to the computer collecting the data, the data will be identifiable. Right-click on the text box and choose **Format Form Properties**. In the **Number of characters allowed** text box, key **10**. In the **Return data with this label** box, key **OpenShelterDate1** as shown in Figure 9-8. Click **OK**.

3. Repeat this step for the first cells in Rows 4, 5 and 8-10. For each new label, right-click and choose Format Form Properties and limit the number of characters allowed to 10 each and name each label respectively: **OpenShelterDate2, OpenShelterDate3, EnclosedShelterDate1, EnclosedShelterDate2, EnclosedShelterDate3**.

4. Following Figure 9-7, repeat the process of inserting text boxes in Rows 11-14. In Row 13, click to the right of each word before inserting each text box and press the space bar twice. Resize the text boxes to be close to the sizes shown in Figure 9-7. Right-click on each label and choose **Format Form Properties, limiting** the number of characters and naming each label respectively, as shown here:
   Name (50)
   Address (50)
   City (25)
   State (15) Key **WI** as the default text.
   ZIP (10)
   Phone (15)

5. Save the form, but keep it open.

Your text box objects are all inserted. Now you'll add list boxes that list the park choices for each of the dates. Please work carefully.

STEP-BY-STEP 9.11

1. Click the cell in Row 3, in the park column. Insert a **List Box** form control. Don't worry about the width of the control at this time, but **do** resize the height of the form control to show only one name.

2. Right-click on the new form field and choose **Format Form Properties**. The dialog box shown in Figure 9-9 should appear.

STEP-BY-STEP 9.11 Continued

3. Key **OpenShelterList1** in the label text box at the top of the List Box Properties.

4. Select the first item in the list and click **Modify**.

5. Key **Otter Creek Park #1** in the Item text box in the Add/Modify List Box Item dialog box.

6. Leave the **Selected** option turned on in the *Show item as:* section of the dialog box. The dialog box should look like Figure 9-10. Click **OK**.

7. Modify the next two items to read **Otter Creek Park #2** and **East Park**. These items should be **Not selected** in the *Show item as*: section of the Add/Modify List Box Item dialog box.

FIGURE 9-10
Add/Modify List Box Item

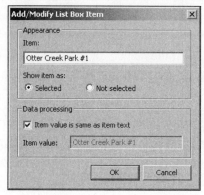

8. Add the following items and also leave them as not selected. When you finish the list, click **OK**.
   North Park #1
   North Park #2
   South Park #2
   South Park #3
   West Park
   River Park

9. Repeat Steps 1 through 8 for the next two cells in the parks column. Name the list box control in Row 4 **OpenShelterList2** and in Row 5 **OpenShelterList3**. Modify or add the same park names as you did in Steps 5 through 8.

10. Click the cell in Row 8 of the park column and insert a List Box form control. Resize the height of the object to one item.

11. Right-click on the new form control and choose **Format Form Properties**. Name the form control **EnclosedShelterList1**.

12. Modify or add items so that your list includes the following items: **Otter Creek Park** (selected), **East Park** (not selected), **South Park** (not selected), and **River Park** (not selected).

STEP-BY-STEP 9.11 Continued

13. Repeat Steps 10 through 12 for the next two cells in the parks column. Name the list box control in Row 9 **EnclosedShelterList2** and in Row 10 **EnclosedShelterList3**.

14. Save the form again as **City of Otter Creek Web Site *xxx***. Keep it open.

As you can see, lists are tedious to insert. However, they make it easy to collect the needed data. Your form is almost complete. Let's add a few finishing touches.

STEP-BY-STEP 9.12

1. With the form of page 2 of the Web site displayed, click in the last row to the right of the phone text box. Choose **Submit** from the Form Control list to display the Command Button Properties dialog box as illustrated in Figure 9-11. Click **OK** to accept the default settings.

FIGURE 9-11
Command Button Properties

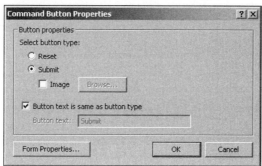

2. Press the space bar two times to the right of the Submit button and choose **Submit** from the Form Control list.

3. Choose **Reset**. Click **OK**.

4. Resize the height of all rows except 1, 2, and 7 to make each row less tall.

5. Select the entire table. Turn on all grid lines and format them using the medium-blue color for the lines that you have used throughout the Web site. Set the weight of the lines at **1** pt.

6. Check your form with the one showing in Figure 9-7.

7. Save your file again with the same name. Keep it open to finish up with the hyperlinks.

Add a Page for the Thumbnail Link

You will insert a new page for the full-size picture of the boat launch as instructed in the next Step-by-Step and add a Web button to link back to Parks & Recreation. Study Figure 9-12 to see how the page will look when you finish.

FIGURE 9-12
Newly Created Page for Thumbnail Link

STEP-BY-STEP 9.13

1. With Page 2 still showing, insert one new page after the current page, but do not duplicate any objects.

2. On the new blank page, add the background you used on the first two pages.

3. Add a new WordArt frame at the top of the page that contains the following text: **Otter Creek Park's Newest Boat Launch**. Resize it to be **4.75** inches wide and **0.55** inch tall. Change the color to a solid medium-blue.

4. Bring down a ruler guide from the Horizontal ruler to **0.375** inch and one to **1.25** inches. Align the WordArt object so it's at the **0.375**-inch ruler guide and even with the right margin.

5. Insert the picture named **boat launch.jpg** from your data files. Do not create a picture frame first because this will restrict the size of the picture. Instead, use the Picture command from the **Insert** menu. Then choose **From File**. Select the file and click **Insert**.

6. The picture will be huge! Zoom to 33% so you can see it, and size the picture to about **6.6** inches wide and **5** inches tall. Center it horizontally at the **1.25**-inch ruler guide.

7. To the left of the WordArt object (see Figure 9-12), insert a Web button from the Design Gallery. Choose the **Link Open Center** button.

8. Select the word **Link** in the inserted button and replace it with **Return to Parks & Recreation**.

9. Resize the Design Gallery object using the Measurement Toolbar to be approximately **2.5** inches wide and **0.75** inch tall.

10. Save the Web site again. Keep it open.

Adding Hyperlinks

As you learned earlier, hyperlinks are buttons or text that a Web user clicks to jump to another position in the same Web site or a different site completely. The navigation bar contains buttons that would link the Otter Creek home page to seven other pages. You have only created the Parks & Recreation page. You can create hyperlinks to link this page, as well as links to take the viewer to and from the full-page picture of the boat launch.

You can also create a hyperlink that will connect to an e-mail address from your Web site. Viewers may use this link to contact someone at the Web site's organization (in this case, the Chamber of Commerce) to ask a question or submit a comment regarding the information on your Web site. When the e-mail link is clicked in a Web site, an e-mail program will open in which you can create a message to send to the address in the To: box. Usually the default e-mail program on your computer will be the one that will open with a new message window.

To create hyperlinks, you will use the Insert Hyperlink dialog box. You can choose to link to a different file, to a page in the current file, or to an e-mail address, or you can create a new file. You will begin by creating links to pages in the current file. In doing so, you will need to change the titles of the pages being linked. This is done in the Insert Hyperlink dialog box. These page titles will appear in the title bar when previewed in the Web browser.

STEP-BY-STEP 9.14

1. With the full-page picture of the boat launch in the Otter Creek Web site open, in the window, select the words **Return to Parks & Recreation** in the Web button at the top of the large picture page and click the **Insert Hyperlink** button on the Standard toolbar.

2. Choose **Place in This Document** in the *Link to:* pane.

3. Select the **Page 2 title** in the list in the center of the dialog box and click **Change Title**. Key **Parks & Recreation** as the new page title. Click **OK**.

4. Select the **Page 3 title** in the list in the center and click **Change Title**. Key **Boat Launch** as the new title. Click **OK**.

5. Select the **Page 1 title** in the list and click **Change Title**. Key **City of Otter Creek Home Page** as the new title.

STEP-BY-STEP 9.14 Continued

6. When your dialog box looks like Figure 9-13, select **Page 2. Parks & Recreation** as the link for the Web button on Page 3. Click **OK**. The text should have changed to a different color in the Web button and will be underlined.

FIGURE 9-13
Insert Hyperlink Dialog Box

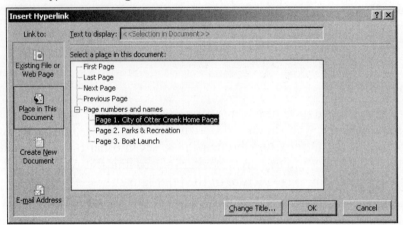

7. Instead of using the default color for hyperlinks in the color scheme being used for this publication, you are going to change the color scheme.

8. From the **Format** menu, choose **Color Schemes**. Choose **Bluebird**, which is the current or default color scheme.

9. Click **Custom color scheme** at the bottom of the task bar. Edit the **hyperlink** and **viewed hyperlink** colors to **red** and **orange**, respectively. Click **OK**. You have now created a custom color scheme, which will appear at the top of the color task pane, and your Page 3 should now look like Figure 9-12.

10. On page 2, select the words **Home Page** in the navigation text frame. Click the **Insert Hyperlink** button.

11. Create a link to the **Home Page** in the **Insert Hyperlink** dialog box by selecting **Page 1** and clicking **OK**.

12. On page 1, select the words **Parks & Recreation** in the navigation text frame and create a link to **Parks & Recreation** in the **Insert Hyperlink** dialog box.

13. On page 1, select the words **Contact us:**. Click the **Insert Hyperlink** button and choose **E-mail Address**.

STEP-BY-STEP 9.14 Continued

14. In the E-mail address text box, key **chamber@ottercreek.net**, as in Figure 9-14.

FIGURE 9-14
E-mail Address Hyperlink

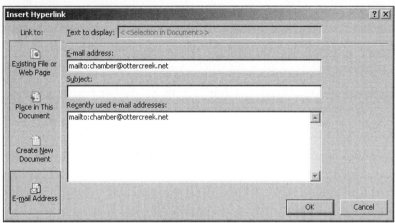

15. Save the file and continue to learn how to add a hot spot.

Add a Hot Spot

On Page 2, you will add a hot spot to the thumbnail picture. A *hot spot* is an area—usually on a picture—that will link the viewer to a different part of the Web site. When the viewer moves the mouse over the hot spot area, a hand appears in place of the insertion point indicating the viewer can click on the picture. If a picture is large, it may contain more than one hot spot. This larger picture with multiple hot spots is referred to as an *image map*.

In this case, the hot spot will link the viewer to the page containing the larger picture of the new boat launch. It is a good idea to add text near the hot spot to instruct viewers to point to the picture containing the hot spot so they know that there is an area on the picture containing a hyperlink.

STEP-BY-STEP 9.15

1. Turn to Page 2 of the Otter Creek Web site.

2. Click the Hot Spot button on the Objects toolbar.

3. When you click the button, the Insert Hyperlink dialog box appears. Choose the **Place in This Document** button at the left.

4. Choose **Boat Launch**. Click **OK**.

STEP-BY-STEP 9.15 Continued

5. A dotted-line square appears on the page. This is the hot spot object.

6. Move it to the center of the small picture of the boat launch. The dotted line will not show when the page is being previewed using the Web Page Preview tool, or when it is published to a Web server.

7. Save the file and click **Web Page Preview** to try all of your links. Select the Web site option. Did the hot spot work? If you have any problems, be sure to check with your instructor.

Add Keywords and a Description for your Web Site and Check the Design

You did a great job creating this Web site. Now you need to add the Web site description and keywords as well as run the design checker. Finally, you need to save it as a Web page.

As you probably know, people search the Internet frequently to find sites that contain certain information. This is done most often by the use of *search engines*. Search engines are special programs that create an index of keywords that are saved when Web sites are created. *Keywords* are words that describe the information contained in a Web site. When you use a keyword to search the Web, that search engine checks its index for that keyword or keywords and quickly locates the sites that it has in its index that contain those keywords. The more keywords you use, the more likely your site will appear in a search engine's results. These keywords may also include various spellings used by viewers. You can include words that are not in your Web site, but that describe the site in general as well. A description can also be added when a Web site is saved. This description describes the purpose of your site. It shows within the results brought back by the search engine. There is a limit of approximately 256 characters in both the keyword and description boxes. You will add keywords and a description in the Web Options dialog box.

STEP-BY-STEP 9.16

1. Turn to page 1 of the Web site. Open the **Tools** menu and click **Options**. Click the **Web Options** button on the General page.

2. In the *Description* text box, key the following description:
Otter Creek is a quiet but forward-moving community in the heart of Wisconsin. Explore our Web site to find out more about our community and why it is a great place to live and work.

3. In the *Keywords* text box, add the following keywords: **Otter Creek, Wisconsin, fishing, boating, industrial center, paper industries, family-oriented, snowmobiling**.

STEP-BY-STEP 9.16 Continued

4. Scroll through the material you keyed and proofread carefully. When you finish, the Web Options dialog box will look much like Figure 9-15.

FIGURE 9-15
Web Options Dialog Box

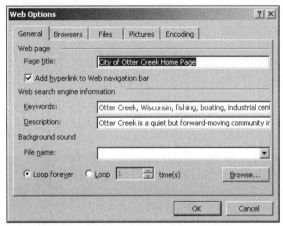

5. Open the **Tools** menu and choose **Design Checker**. Check the entire Web site. Discuss any problems that are indicated with your instructor.

6. View the Web site in the Web Page Browser one more time and show your instructor your completed site.

7. Close the browser.

Converting the Web Site to HTML Format

You are finished creating the City of Otter Creek Web Site. The next step is to save your file as an HTML file. Check with your instructor regarding the possibility of publishing your files. As mentioned earlier in the chapter, the HTML file format is the format the Internet browsers can read and display for the viewers. In Publisher, the HTML file format is referred to as a *Web page* file format. A file saved in this format can be saved to a drive on your computer similar to the standard Publisher file format by using the Save As Web Page dialog box. However, other viewers cannot view the file on the Internet.

In order to have a file viewed on the Internet, it needs to be saved or transferred to a Web server. This is done either through the My Network Places option or the File Transfer Protocol (FTP) option. You will have to check with your instructor regarding these options. In this lesson you will save your Web page file to the designated drive on your computer in which you have been saving your files throughout the course. During this process, a folder is created automatically in which all multimedia objects, such as graphics, and individual pages other than Page 1 (home page) of your Web site are saved.

STEP-BY-STEP 9.17

1. With the **City of Otter Creek Web Site xxx** showing in the window, open the **File** menu and choose **Save as Web Page**.

2. Insert a 3.5 inch floppy disk into your floppy disk drive. If necessary, select the **3½ Floppy** from the Save in: drop-down list.

3. Leave the name showing in the File name. (It should still be **City of Otter Creek Web Site *xxx*.**)

4. If necessary, select **Web Page** from the Save as type: drop-down list at the bottom.

5. Click **Save**. You will see a message box about processing the form on Page 2. Click **No** and close the file.

6. Minimize the Publisher window and double-click **My Computer** on the desktop.

7. Select and double-click the **3½-inch floppy drive** (or select wherever you are saving your files).

8. Double-click the Otter Creek Seniors Center Web Page file that contains the Web browser icon.

9. The Web site should open in your Web browser where you have another opportunity to test your hyperlinks.

10. Show the completed Web site to your instructor. Then close your Web browser. You are finished with this Web site activity.

How did you like creating a Web site? Not too difficult, was it?

SUMMARY

In this lesson, you learned:

- A new Web site can be created from a blank publication and formatted as a Web page.

- The background is easy to add and should be a subtle design.

- Alternative text can be added to a Web page graphic so people who have their graphics turned off will see what the picture represents.

- A small picture is referred to as a thumbnail if it is linked to a larger version of the same picture on a different page.

- There are several different form control objects that can be added to a form for the viewer's feedback.

- Hyperlinks can be added that link to other places in the Web site as well as to contact a representative of the Web site.

- Adding a hotspot to a thumbnail graphic provides one way to link to the larger picture on a separate page.

- Adding keywords and a description to a Web site will help viewers find your site when using a search engine.

- The properties for form control objects relate to the database in which the data is stored when submitted by the viewer.

- The Web Page Preview is a great tool to use through the building of a Web site to check the format and hyperlinks.

- When a Publisher file is saved as a Web page, the Publisher file is converted to HTML format.

VOCABULARY *Review*

Define the following terms:

Background	Hyperlinks	Search engines
Browser	Image map	Thumbnail picture
Form	Keywords	Web navigation bar
Home page	Masthead	Web pages
Hot spot	Modem	Web sites

REVIEW *Questions*

MULTIPLE CHOICE

Select the best response for the following statements.

1. Which of the following graphic formats is NOT compatible with a Web page?
   A. bmp
   B. png
   C. gif
   D. jpg

2. Which of the following objects will NOT take the viewer to another place in the Web site or to another Web site on the Internet when clicked?
   A. hyperlink
   B. navigation bar
   C. hot spot
   D. text box

3. Which of the following hyperlink options in the Insert Hyperlink dialog box provides a link to communicate with a person who is responsible for the Web site or works at the company for which the Web site is developed?
   A. Create new document
   B. E-mail address
   C. Place in this document
   D. Existing file or Web page

4. The file format recognized by Web browsers is which of the following?
   A. doc
   B. txt
   C. HTML
   D. pub

5. The object that contains a list of links to other pages is referred to as which of the following?
   A. Bullet list
   B. Numbered list
   C. Navigation bar
   D. List box

6. The page that first appears when a viewer opens a Web site is called the:
   A. Home page
   B. Default page
   C. Form page
   D. First page

7. Which of the following form control objects displays a scroll bar?
   A. Text box
   B. Check box
   C. List box
   D. Text area

8. A small picture that represents a larger picture on another Web page in the same Web site is referred to as which of the following?
   A. Hot spot
   B. Thumbnail
   C. Miniature picture
   D. Snapshot

9. In what menu/dialog box do you find the Web Options button?
   A. File/Page Setup
   B. File/Properties
   C. Tools/Tools on the Web
   D. Tools/Options

10. What is the name of a large object that contains multiple hotspots?
    A. Image map
    B. Navigation bar
    C. Masthead
    D. Table

WRITTEN QUESTIONS

Write a brief answer to the following questions.

1. What are the four steps involved in creating and publishing a Web site?

2. Why is it important to have consistency in design in a Web site?

3. What is the purpose of *keywords*?

4. What is the purpose of *alternative text* for graphics?

5. What is the purpose of a *form*?

6. What is the main consideration to keep in mind when choosing a background for a Web page?

7. What effect does the size of a graphic inserted into a Web page have on the time it takes a Web page to download to your computer?

8. Why is it a good idea to assign a label to each form control object you use in a Web page?

9. What feature can you use to insert already-designed Web buttons, Web navigation bars, and Web mastheads?

10. What is the name of the graphic type that moves on the screen when you preview your Web site in Web Page Preview?

PROJECTS

 PROJECT 9-1

You are going to add another page to the City of Otter Creek Web site you created earlier in this lesson. It is a page containing information about the Chamber of Commerce. You will keep the format consistent with the Home Page as well as the Parks & Recreation page. Part of the formatting will be the need to create the hyperlinks between the new page and the other two pages, excluding the page showing the new boat launch. The instructions will be rather brief because you have had so much practice already, that this should be easy for you! Study Figure 9-16 before you begin.

FIGURE 9-16
Completed Chamber of Commerce Page

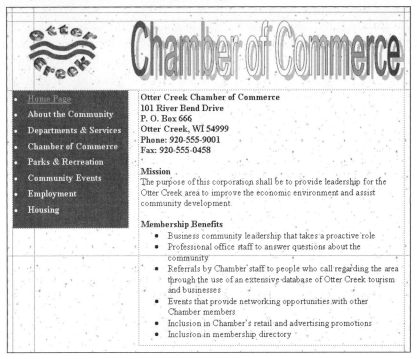

1. Open the City of Otter Creek Web Site (HTML version) using Publisher.

2. Turn to Page 2 (Parks & Recreation) and insert one new page duplicating all the objects.

3. Delete the form, the thumbnail picture containing the hot spot, the hot spot, and the caption of the thumbnail picture.

4. Change the words in the WordArt object to **Chamber of Commerce**.

5. Delete the current text in the text box frame relating to the parks and make the frame wider and longer (approximately 5 inches wide and 5 inches tall).

6. Insert the text file from the data files named **Chamber Page.doc**. Size the text box frame to fit the file.

7. Select **Parks & Recreation** in the Navigation box and open the **Insert Hyperlink** dialog box. You will see two Parks & Recreation pages listed. Change the title of the Page 3 title to **Chamber of Commerce**.

8. Select **Parks & Recreation** for the hyperlink. Click **OK**. Your completed page should resemble Figure 9-16.

9. On Page 1 and Page 2, add the hyperlink to the Chamber of Commerce.

10. Test the links on the Web Page Browser and show your instructor your completed Web site.

11. Save your file and close it.

PROJECT 9-2

You are going to add yet another page to the City of Otter Creek Web site. This page will be titled "About the Community." Keep the format consistent with the Home Page as well as the Parks & Recreation page. Create the necessary hyperlinks between the new page and the existing pages. Two new Design Gallery objects will be added to this page, however. One will be a coupon entitling viewers to a free mug stamped with the Otter Creek logo and the other a Web pull quote containing one sentence that should be highlighted. It is important that you do not layer these objects on top of existing objects, because the browser will not separate them.

1. Open the City of Otter Creek Web Site (HTML version).

2. Turn to Page 3 (Chamber of Commerce) and insert one new page duplicating all the objects.

3. Insert the text file in the data files named **About Otter Creek.doc** in the text box frame, replacing the previous text. Resize the frame as necessary to show all of the text.

4. Change the words in the WordArt object to **About the Community**.

5. Insert a coupon of your choice from the Design Gallery offering a free coffee mug stamped with the Otter Creek logo. Inform the viewer that they can print the Web page and cut out the coupon to be redeemed at the Chamber of Commerce. Move the coupon to a place by itself, such as the bottom or left side of the Web page.

6. Insert a Web pull quote from the Design Gallery that highlights a sentence of your choice that you feel will entice people to visit Otter Creek. Move the pull quote to a place by itself, such as the bottom or left side of the Web page.

7. Insert the necessary hyperlinks between the Home page, Chamber of Commerce page, the Parks & Recreation page, and the new page.

8. Test the links on the Web Page Browser and show your instructor your completed Web site.

9. Save your file and close it.

PROJECT 9-3

As a team, you are going to create a new Web site. It can be about you, or it can be about an organization you belong to or a project assigned to you by your instructor. You and your team members can decide on which method to use, as well as what the format should be. Review the Web site design considerations listed at the beginning of the lesson. You should, however, include the pages and objects from the list that follows. When you are done, show it to your instructor.

Publisher has a wizard to help you with Web sites. Like the wizards you used in previous lessons, the Web site wizard creates the publication and then provides a task pane with options for changing the publication. Be careful when inserting pages into your wizard-created Web site. Publisher will ask you what type of Web page you want, and whether you'd like a hyperlink automatically added to the Web navigation bar. Your Web site should have the following characteristics:

1. A home page with a masthead.

2. At least one additional page with an appropriate title or masthead.

3. A navigation bar on each page with links to each page.

4. At least one text box frame on each page containing relevant text.

5. Graphics are optional.

CRITICAL*Thinking*

CANS ACTIVITY 9-1

You have now created publications that are printed and publications that are viewed on the Internet. These publications have similarities and they have differences. Use the following table to describe these comparisons.

FEATURE	PRINTED	INTERNET
Output media		
Publisher objects typically used		
Page size		
Use of color		
Use of white space		
Layout of objects		
Other		

REVIEW AND PRACTICE

OBJECTIVES

OBJECTIVES

Upon completion of this lesson, you should be able to:

- Fill in the Personal Information.
- Design a logo.
- Design an advertisement.
- Design a letterhead.
- Design a price list using a table.
- Design a business card.
- Design a flyer.
- Design a postcard.
- Create labels.
- Design a brochure.
- Design a newsletter.
- Design a Web site.

Estimated time: 4 hours

The Scenario

Dr. Glen Parker, D.V.M has just graduated from veterinary college and is opening a veterinary clinic in Otter Creek, Wisconsin. The clinic will specialize in companion animal services such as services for dogs, cats, rabbits, ferrets, hamsters, gerbils, birds, and exotics. No large animals such as horses or cows will be serviced.

Lesson 10 is provided in its entirety on the disk containing your data files.

APPENDIX A

Using Color in a Publication

Color can be added to a publication using the Font Color tool for text and the Fill Color tool for objects. You can print one or multiple copies of your publication on a color desktop printer. However, if you want hundreds or thousands of copies, you will need to have your publication printed at a copy shop or service bureau. When you do that, you'll need to incorporate spot color or process color into your publication. Microsoft Publisher 2002 supports both spot- and process-color printing. Publisher 2002 publications may now contain both spot color and process color in one publication.

Spot Color and Process Color

Spot color involves adding one or two more colors to the black and gray in a publication. Because different tints or shades of these one or two colors can also be used, it often appears as though even more colors were used. Examples of objects that may be formatted with a different color are draw objects that do not contain texture or gradients, a WordArt object, draw-type clip art, publication titles, header/footer text, shading behind a small text box, or any element that can provide accent to the publication and take away the gray of the text. Typically, newsletters, letterheads, envelopes, business cards, forms, brochures, price sheets, and novelty promotions contain spot color.

Process color is known as four-color printing because it uses percentages of four inks to print full-color documents. These colors are cyan, magenta, yellow, and black, or CMYK. Examples of objects that use process color are photographs or artwork. Some possible full-color publications are newsletters, textbooks, children's books, and flyers. Generally, process-color printing is more expensive than spot-color printing.

Choosing Colors for Spot- and Process-Color Printing

Before choosing colors for your publication, find out from the printing service you'll use what colors they support. Beginning with Publisher 2000 was support for the use of three color models and the Pantone Matching System which can be used for either spot- or process-color printing. The color models include RGB (red, green, blue) and HSL (hue, saturation, luminosity), and CMYK. The Pantone Matching System is a universal color set of ink which all commercial printers use. It resembles looking at paint chips in a paint store where each ink color has a unique number.

For spot-color publications, choose one or two colors (and tints of those colors) to use through the publication. Keep in mind that the colors on your screen may not match the actual colors of the ink. Be sure to look at the colors at the printing service before choosing the color in Publisher.

To prepare your publication for spot colors, you have to first set up your publication for spot-color printing and specify a PANTONE spot color. You do this through the Commercial Printing Tools feature found in the Tools menu. In that dialog box, choose Spot Colors and then fill the object the usual way choosing the color from the drop-down list.

The CMYK color model or PANTONE process colors are located by using the Fill Color tool and choosing More Colors. Then select All Colors. Choose either the CMYK color model from the Color Model box and enter the values for each ink or choose the PANTONE process tab and select a color.

Color Separation

For either process, separate plates are prepared for each color. At the printing service, the Publisher document is output to film rather than paper. From file, a printing plate is created for each color. For process color, all colors in text, graphics, and other objects are converted into CMYK values and four separate plates are created for objects colored with one of the four values. For each spot color, the colors are printed on a plate containing objects formatted with that color as well as tints of the selected color. Another plate is printed for the rest of the objects formatted in black ink.

At the printing service, the paper is run through the printing presses separately for each color. Each run adds a different color. This process is best for high-volume printing of 1,000 copies or more. Anything less could be done more economically at a copy shop offering color printing on a high-level color digital printer.

Using an Outside Printer

Consider having your publication copied and/or printed at a copy shop or commercial printing service. A copy shop can provide single- and double-sided copying on a high-resolution copier and perhaps high-resolution color copying. The service also provides such finishing processes as folding, trimming, binding, and laminating. You usually can choose from a wide range of paper stock that can enhance the appearance of your publication.

It is necessary with both types of services that you discuss ahead of time what output you desire and make sure that your publication is created to match that criterion. You need to learn from the printing service what they can do, and they need to understand what you want. Otherwise, you may waste a lot of expense and time.

With either type of service, you may be able to take your disk containing your publication for direct printing. You need to know if they can work with Publisher files and/or convert them to a format that will not change the look of the publication. Publisher 2002 has a "Pack and Go" feature that packs up the file and any linked graphic files and font files through compression to one or more disks. Then it unpacks the file later with an "unpack" feature. It is necessary to know if the printing or copying service has the software on their computers to handle this process.

If you need more information about printing with color and preparing a publication for a commercial printing service, Publisher's on-line Help contains extensive help in these areas. You can also use the Microsoft web site to search for a printing service in your area that supports the Publisher file format. The following link will display a form to help you locate a printer near you:

http://www.microsoft.com/office/publisher/using/printers.asp.

APPENDIX B

Command Summary

Most of the instructions in the lesson exercises have you choose features or actions from Publisher menus. Many of the same features are available from the keyboard. In the following list, some of the keys have the word *(toggle)* following the description of the command. This tells you that the action can be selected or deselected using the same command. Check this list regularly to see if you can find a method of working that is easier for you than opening a menu and choosing a feature.

KEYBOARD SHORTCUTS	
Ctrl+A	Highlight entire story
Ctrl+B	Boldface
Ctrl+C	Copy
Ctrl+E	Center paragraph
Ctrl+F or F3	Find
Ctrl+G or F5	Replace
Ctrl+H	Replace
Ctrl+I	Italic
Ctrl+J	Justify paragraph
Ctrl+K	Insert a hyperlink for the selected object on a Web page
Ctrl+L	Left-align paragraph
Ctrl+M	Background/foreground
Ctrl+N	Create a new publication
Ctrl+O	Open a publication
Ctrl+P	Print
Ctrl+Q	Remove paragraph formatting
Ctrl+R	Right-align paragraph
Ctrl+S	Save
Ctrl+T	Make selected object opaque/transparent

KEYBOARD SHORTCUTS	
Ctrl+U	Underline
Ctrl+V	Paste from Clipboard
Ctrl+W	Snap to guides (toggle)
Ctrl+X	Cut to Clipboard
Ctrl+Y	Redo previous action
Ctrl+Z	Undo previous action
Ctrl+Shift+B	Preview a Web site
Ctrl+Shift+C	Copy formatting
Ctrl+Shift+G	Group objects (toggle)
Ctrl+Shift+H	Hyphenation (toggle)
Ctrl+Shift+K	Small capital letters (toggle)
Ctrl+Shift+L	Full page view
Ctrl+Shift+N	Insert a new page
Ctrl+Shift+O	Hide/show boundaries and guides (toggle)
Ctrl+Shift+V	Paste Formatting
Ctrl+Shift+X	Delete a selected text frame or table frame containing text
Ctrl+Shift+Y	Show/hide special characters

MISCELLANEOUS COMMANDS	
Ctrl+Shift+>	Increase font size by 0.5 pt.
Ctrl+Shift+<	Decrease font size by 0.5 pt.
Ctrl+Shift+[	Decrease space between letters (kerning)
Ctrl+Shift+]	Increase space between letters (kerning)
Ctrl+[/ Ctrl+]	Decrease/increase font size by 1 pt.
F7	Check spelling
F9	Actual Size view/Full page view (toggle)
Ctrl+1/Ctrl+2	Single space/double space paragraph
Ctrl+5	Change line spacing to 1½ lines
Ctrl+Space Bar	Remove character formatting
Ctrl+ -	Add optional hyphen
Ctrl+Shift+Space	Add nonbreaking space
Ctrl+Shift+ -	Add nonbreaking hyphen
Ctrl+Insert	Copy to Clipboard

MISCELLANEOUS COMMANDS	
Ctrl+Delete	Cut to Clipboard
Shift+Insert	Paste from Clipboard
Ctrl+Shift+=	Superscript (toggle)
Ctrl+=	Subscript (toggle)
Alt+Backspace	Undo last action
Alt+←, →, ↑, ↓	Nudges object left, right, up, or down
Ctrl+Alt+→	Rotates object 5 degrees clockwise/counterclockwise
Shift+Enter	New line in same paragraph

INDEX